# EMBRACING
# TRUST

**Book Three of
The Ascending Ladders Series**

## Karen Ann Bulluck

Embracing Trust
Book Three of The Ascending Ladders Series



Inspired Legacy Publishing is a division of (DBA) Inspired Legacy, LLC
PO Box 900816
Sandy UT 84090-0816.



ISBN 979-8-9882276-7-0 (paperback)
ISBN 979-8-9882276-8-7 (hardcover)
ISBN 979-8-9882276-6-3 (ebook)

Printed in the United States of America.

# What People Are Saying

*"Rarely does a novel capture the high stakes of corporate life while keeping such a firm hand on the human heart.* **Embracing Trust** *is a visceral exploration of integrity—how easily it fractures and the immense courage required to rebuild it. I saw my own professional dilemmas reflected in these pages, finding the story equal parts cautionary tale and hopeful roadmap."*
**-Gary Fretwell, #1 International Best Selling Author, Speaker, Consultant**

*"As a woman in leadership, this story by Karen Ann Bulluck, moved me deeply.* **Embracing Trust** *reveals the real life tension leaders face when values, ambition, and integrity collide. This is much more than a corporate novel. It is a rally cry and a call back to courage, self-trust, and heart-led leadership. I highly recommend it."*
**-Karen Gray, President, Texas Business Women, Founder/ CEO Gray Coaching**

*"This poignant business novel is deeply relatable, capturing the loss of trust in colleagues — and ourselves — that many face today. Its powerful women navigate difficult circumstances, offering a moving, courageous roadmap for any woman finding her own way."*
**-Brynn Ammon, President, Credit Union Solutions, Jack Henry**

*"Through three compelling women, Karen masterfully weaves the complexity of trust across business, leadership, and private life, especially in high-stakes, male-dominated environments. This book is a quiet call to integrity, instinct, and humanity; reminding us to lead with conscience, resist premature judgment, and surround ourselves with those who genuinely root for our becoming."*
**-Dr. Brigitte Bojkowszky, Brand Identity Strategist | Success Mindset Coach | Retreat Host |Podcast Host, BridgetBrands**

*"A brilliant look at the human side of leadership roles. Sheryl's approach to management offers a revelatory exploration of trust with herself, and several others. The author is proving that humanity is the true engine of creativity and results. The character development is excellent and pulled me into the story from start to finish. This series is a must-read for aspiring leaders at any level."*
**-Suzanne Catlett,** Founder-CEO-Investor

*"The characters are vibrant. The stories and their experiences are totally relatable to real life personal experiences. I loved how the author wove in the Hero's Journey, and showed so clearly how intricately peoples' lives are woven together through lifetimes. No spoilers here, but in my opinion this is a brilliant piece of writing, and the reader comes away feeling hopeful and empowered."*
**-Sherry Lynn Campbell, #1 International Bestselling novelist of The Storyteller's Quilt: Beginnings Are Boundless**

*"Oh, what an enjoyable read! It's honest, relatable, and speaks to the messiness of work and life in a way that feels very human. It's a reminder that trust - in ourselves and in others - still matters, especially as AI changes everything."*
**-Kendra C. Parker, Director of Talent & Capability**

*"In business and life, we have relationships where we either respect and embrace with trust or fracture when trust is broken. The stories of how these three women each encounter different responses to their choices and how they deal with those reactions are situations many of us have experienced and many others will encounter. Valuable insight can be gained from the events shared in these pages."*
**-Susan K. Younger, Relationship Architect – Engaging Humanity in the Workplace**

# Dedication

To Paulien Meijer, for her invaluable feedback and unstinting support.

# Acknowledgements

This book would not be possible without the support and feedback from the incomparable Bridget Cook-Burch. Her feedback and brainstorming make writing a joy! Getting this book into your hands is due to the amazing efforts of Inspired Legacy Publishing: Rebecca Hall Gruyter, Chisom, and the rest of the team there. Thank you all!

I'd also like to thank my husband for his ongoing support and encouragement. And, last, but not least, big thanks to my accountability partners, friends, and enthusiastic supporters: Susan Younger and Brigitte Bojkowszky. You keep me going.

# Table of Contents

# Dave's Dilemma

"I know my wife still doesn't trust me," I think as I lie next to her in bed, gritting my teeth in frustration.

She sighs and turns her back to me in her sleep. It's just one more example of how she's shutting me out. Not that I don't deserve it. I do. Sort of. It's my fault, yes, but it's mostly Alisha Carson's fault.

It all started last summer, really. Sheryl Simmons, my wife, started becoming increasingly upset by the direction her company, The Diamante, was taking. The firm had taken an infusion of cash from a venture capital group, Alpha VC. Alpha put two of their folks on The Diamante's board, and they were really shaking things up.

I felt bad for Sheryl, but that's just the way business goes, right? After all, one of the Alpha representatives was Hank Turner, a kind of god in the financial services industry. He was a powerful guy. His cohort Anthony Russo was no slouch either.

So, when they pressured The Diamante board into making some deep staffing cuts, I wasn't surprised. Sheryl was, and she was *really* unhappy about how they handled it. I agree that the guards marching people out was a bit over the top, but I understood. Security is so important these days, isn't it?

But when I mentioned all that to Sheryl? Wow. Was she upset. "Dave, it doesn't matter who these people are," she said. "They need to do what's right. And what they did with these layoffs wasn't right."

I tried to explain how these things worked in real life, but she wasn't buying it. I thought she was being naïve and unrealistic. And I made the mistake of telling her that. More than once . . . and, oh yeah, I might have lost my temper more than once too. Not proud of that, I have to admit.

It's also about that time that I started working more closely with Alisha, who by the way is an attractive woman in her thirties. Anyway, Alisha was fun and playful. I enjoyed hanging out with her after hours when I was in California. After all, being based at LSM Consulting's headquarters in New Jersey, what else was I going to do when I was so far from home?

So, while I'm going about my business—and maybe spending more time with Alisha than I should—the pressure on Sheryl continued to ramp up. They fired her boss and mentor, Carl Schmidt, and promoted her to his role. Suddenly, she's the new Chief Information Officer and on the board of directors, reporting directly to Todd Fisher, the president of The Diamante.

I was truly excited for her and tried to support her transition, but, man, all she seemed to want to do was blow things up. She held these crazy meetings to "honor" the people who had been laid off, then she confronted Hank about the new CFO Alpha wanted The Diamante to hire—at a board meeting, no less!

When I told her she was nuts, that she needed to get along and establish herself first, she got really angry . . . and really hurt. But really, I was only trying to help! Alisha agreed with me.

Sheryl got her way though. She wanted the company to hire Blake Jones, which they eventually did. And, she got Hank removed from the board because he totally lost his temper with her and acted all crazy. As it turns out though, that was a really good thing for The Diamante because Hank and his friend Anthony were running some kind of pyramid scheme that Sheryl and her protégé, Keisha Smith, discovered while re-engineering the customer interface portal.

Ah, yes. Keisha. She's a feisty young woman who challenged Sheryl's ethics during the layoffs. The lead programmer on the Portal Project, Keisha is vital to the organization and Sheryl, but, in my view, she's a handful.

That investigation, which is still ongoing, took a lot of Sheryl's time, and that was before the SEC and FBI got involved. I was proud of what she was doing, but she was really pulling away from me by then. Not that I totally blame her. I admit I was being a bit of a jerk, but it was all with good intentions. Truly!

Of course, that's when Alisha pulled her stunt. She moved to New Jersey. Yeah, all the way from sunny California. Stupid me, I thought she was moving for work. Turns out she was moving for me. Not that my buddy Robert didn't warn me, but I thought he was just exaggerating. Ha! When I made it clear to Alisha that I wasn't interested in that way, she accused me of sexual harassment. Officially! To HR.

Thank God for Sheryl. Somehow, she managed to run into Alisha and convinced her to tell the truth. About me. And about Liam Moriarity, Alisha's former boss in California. He was the one who was actually harassing her in the first place. Geez. What a mess, but Sheryl managed to sort it all out so that both Alisha and I kept our jobs.

Not that Alisha's not still in hot water at LSM; she is. But, well, that's not my problem. My problem is that my wife still doesn't trust me.

And I don't know how to fix that.

Trust. It's a funny thing. It's so important and yet so fragile at the same time. And repairing it? Huh.

But enough of my complaining. I'm not the only one who's struggling with trust. Sheryl, Alisha, and Sheryl's friend Gemma Morrison are also. I'll let them tell you the rest of the story . . .

CHAPTER 1

# How Deep Is the Hole?

**Tuesday, January 11**

"You're going to have to dig deeper in this sales territory," Brittany Mollier said, a thread of steel lacing her rich, contralto voice.

Alisha Carson's shoulders tensed. "What do you mean?" she asked her new boss. She used the best of her sales skills to pose the question with curiosity, rather than the growing alarm she was feeling inside.

It didn't alleviate her alarm when Brittany eyed her suspiciously, as if trying to discern what Alisha was thinking. But Alisha was careful to keep her expression open and friendly, just as she would with a potential client.

It was Monday afternoon, and the two women were sitting at a table in one of the many small meeting rooms in the LSM Consulting headquarters. No one actually knew what the initials LSM referenced, but the practice was about fifth in the US in number of employees and had twenty-five locations globally. Neither woman in this conversation had a permanent office or cubicle assignment in the corporate office. They were expected to be out with customers most of the time. When she was checking in, Alisha felt like she was in a bit of a fishbowl. Floor-to-ceiling windows opened onto the interior, giving them virtually no privacy, which only made this conversation more uncomfortable.

"I'm not sure that your predecessor, Mark, was working up to his full potential in the last year or two," Brittany answered diplomatically. "I'm sure you can do better. In fact, I'm counting on it."

"Hmmm. Well, I'll give it my best shot," Alisha promised, raising her blue eyes to meet the older woman's whiskey-colored ones. She wasn't sure, but Alisha guessed that Brittany was at least ten years older than her thirty-six, maybe a little more. Alisha couldn't help remembering the last time she'd faced a woman older than her . . . at the bar of a hotel, stunned to find that appearances weren't quite what she'd presumed.

Brittany's eyes hardened ever so slightly. "You'll have to do more than try, Miss Carson," she said sternly. "The company paid for you to move clear across the country. Expectations are high. Very high."

Feeling her stomach clench, Alisha took a breath. "I know," she replied tightly. "I will make sure that it was worth it." *For me, as well as the company*, she added silently. She resisted the urge to twist a strand of long blonde hair around her finger, knowing that her boss wouldn't miss that telltale sign of nervousness.

"Your sales results last year were exceptional," Brittany reminded her, her tone a little more congenial. With her long, dark hair and a deeply tanned complexion, her boss looked, well, luxurious. It seemed a silly word to describe someone's appearance, but it was the only descriptor that Alisha could come up with. She wondered if her own appearance was too casual in her new work environment.

"Thank you, Brittany," Alisha murmured. "I worked hard to get those results." It had been less than two months since she'd been hitting those impressive sales numbers while at the same time facing the tumult of her former boss's unprofessional harassment and a move across the country, bent on creating a new life . . . with another man entirely, who, in fact, did not feel the same way about her.

"I know you did," Brittany confirmed, her shrewd look indicating that she was not unaware of the trials Alisha had faced, including the ones that Alisha had caused herself. After all, most people at LSM Consulting who were anywhere near the office the day that Alisha falsely filed a claim against her coworker knew the fallout of what happened next. Alisha shuddered. Since then, no one had treated her the same. She expected it but still hated that she saw it in Brittany's gaze now.

*It takes a while to clean up spilled milk*, she thought. It was better than the alternative—her entire personal and professional life imploding, with her holding the detonator.

"I'm looking forward to seeing what you can do with your new territory," Brittany continued. "You'll have far fewer tech companies with large budgets than you did in California, so you'll have to expand your range of industries to meet your goals in the mid-Atlantic region."

Alisha nodded, her blonde ponytail bobbing gently. "I know. I've already started scoping out potential targets. Mark had a number of warm leads that I can follow up on," she responded. Mark had abruptly retired in the middle of October last year, citing health concerns, thus paving the way for Alisha to move from the Silicon Valley area to LSM's headquarters in New Jersey. Things certainly hadn't turned out how she'd expected so far, and now she was having to fight to prove herself worthy of this new space.

"That's a good start," her boss affirmed, leaning back in her chair.

Alisha glanced back at the spreadsheets that were lying on the gray laminate table between them. "When are our bonuses scheduled to be paid out this year?" she asked, diverting the older woman's attention. Alisha had far surpassed her goals for the previous year and was looking forward to a very generous bonus that she desperately needed.

Brittany chuckled. "You know they won't be paid until at least the end of March, probably April."

"Yeah, that's what I thought," Alisha grumbled—but only lightly. "It's just with the move and everything, I was hoping . . ."

"You need a little extra cash," Brittany concluded. "I get that. But you know the drill. These numbers don't even include your bonus calculation."

"Sure. But I can figure that out using the formula," the younger woman said confidently. "If those numbers are correct, my bonus will be a really good one."

A thin, penciled eyebrow rose on Brittany's face. "Yes, but don't forget the bonus cap that was instituted last year. I'd guess you'll hit that, so your payout may not be as much as you think."

Alisha felt her jaw drop. "Cap? What bonus cap?"

"Liam didn't tell you?"

"Tell me what? That's ridiculous! We've never had a cap on our bonuses before," Alisha protested, stunned by this new information.

Brittany leaned forward again, now typing rapidly on her open laptop. "Here it is," she said, pushing the computer toward Alisha. "Only the regional managers got the memo, but we were supposed to communicate it to all the account managers. Liam should have shared this with you a while ago."

Eyes widening as she read, Alisha felt a flash of rage shoot through her. The memo outlined that the company had, indeed, instituted a cap on the bonuses that the salespeople could receive—and it wasn't an insignificant one. It would definitely impact her bonus by tens of thousands of dollars—money she was counting on. "This is crazy," she told her boss indignantly. "Why in the world would they institute a policy like this? I never saw this."

"I'm sorry about that. Liam should have told you. You can see that the memo was dated in September," Brittany replied sympathetically.

"But this means that the deals I closed in November and December—especially the ones that I *rushed* to close in December—were basically worthless, at least to me," Alisha fumed quietly, aware that some of her colleagues were seated just a few feet away on the other side of the glass. She felt enough judgment from them lately, so the last thing she needed to do was make a scene, despite her shock and indignation.

Brittany shrugged in a fatalistic way that showed a bit of her Gallic background. "C'est la vie."

Her casual response sparked further frustration in Alisha's chest. "Are you kidding? I wouldn't have pushed so hard if I had known!"

Her boss's expression turned immediately stony. She leaned forward. "Don't ever let me hear you say something like that again," she reprimanded intensely but quietly. "We're here to close sales and bring in revenue—no matter what. You have a good base salary to cover those things. It's not like you're working on pure commission."

Alisha rocked back in the gray utilitarian chair, startled by Brittany's response. "But doesn't this bother you? Your compensation must have been limited too."

One slender shoulder rose. "Yes, it was. So be it."

Shaking her head, Alisha looked back at the computer screen. She didn't care what Brittany had said. There was no way she would have closed those two sales in December if she had known this, even if it was in the company's best interest. *I would have saved them for this year*, she thought. *That way, I would have been way ahead of the game already!*

She pushed away a niggle of guilt.

*A bonus cap. Ridiculous.* She wondered what her colleague, Dave Simmons, thought about it. *Does he have one too? And will he even talk to me anymore after everything that happened?*

"Do you have any other questions?" Brittany asked as she gathered her own items from the guest cubicle. "I think you have a solid grasp of the new territory, but I'm always available if you need any help."

Alisha dragged her thoughts away from the compensation plan. "The only question I have is, are there any accounts that you need to visit with me? To ease the transition?" She had noticed a couple of large pharmaceutical accounts that she guessed would need more personalized attention.

"Yes, there are," Brittany replied approvingly. "Let's go over the heavy hitters in your territory. It *would* be a good idea for us to visit them together." She pulled her computer back and opened the firm's contact management system. "Let's start here."

Alisha slid her chair over and tried to concentrate on what her boss was saying, but her mind kept slipping back to the memo she had just seen. It was a game-changer. *I wonder how that's going to impact my new territory and my budget living in a new area of the country.*

Brittany's slender hand drew her attention back to the laptop screen. Alisha couldn't help comparing the woman's long, perfectly manicured nails with her own shorter, utilitarian ones. She had never had much patience for manicures, being more interested in sports and other pursuits that invariably ruined them. Her athletic, slightly voluptuous build contrasted sharply with her boss's elegant pencil-thin form.

Holding back a sigh, Alisha carefully noted Brittany's preferences on which accounts they should see together and promised to set up the appropriate appointments. She wondered if she should take a trip to Short Hills mall before the visits to upgrade her California chic wardrobe to the more formal attire that seemed to be favored here on the East Coast. *Ha! Not likely after the bonus cut!* It took everything she had to hold back a grimace.

Twenty minutes later, as she settled back into the cubicle she had chosen for the day, a burst of low male laughter captured her attention. Alisha looked across the floor toward the pod where Dave Simmons and Robert Coleman were sharing a humorous moment. A surge of longing to join them shot through her, but she dared not engage. She had more or less (probably more) promised Dave's wife that she would stay away from him, after Sheryl had rescued her from the terrible situation Alisha had created for herself. Alisha shuddered, hating to think about how close she had come to completely sabotaging her career.

Dave looked up and caught her eye, just as she started to turn away. He gave her a tepid smile, his expression wary, but unbelievably, he beckoned her to join them. *Well, Sheryl can't knock me when it's an open invitation*, Alisha thought. She stood up and nonchalantly crossed the twenty feet to the pod where the two men sat.

"Alisha," Dave greeted her coolly.

Robert merely smiled and nodded, his expression also guarded, Alisha noted with dismay. The easy friendship she'd once enjoyed with these two men was clearly over.

"Hey, guys. It sounds like you are having too good of a time over here," she quipped, disguising her hurt with humor.

The two men exchanged an inscrutable glance.

"Yeah, we're just having a ball," Robert finally responded sarcastically, quirking an eyebrow over his dark eyes.

Dave reached over and pulled a chair from an empty cube. He motioned for her to sit—not too close, she noticed—his brown eyes assessing rather than filled with the warmth she was used to and missed. Once, the older man had made her feel special, but she had learned the hard way that he made almost everyone feel that way.

"How are you settling in?" asked Robert, bending a little toward her, his friendly way of not intimidating people. A former collegiate and professional basketball player, Robert was nearly six-feet-seven. Even sitting, he towered over everyone.

"Good," Alisha answered quietly. "I'm getting the hang of things here. It's not all that different from California, although Brittany is much easier to deal with than Liam—at least in some ways."

Both men nodded sympathetically. They had both witnessed first-hand how badly Liam had treated her months ago with blatant sexual harassment. In fact, they had been instrumental in Liam being fired for his behavior, especially Dave—and his wife.

"I'm sure she is," Dave chimed in, his eyes crinkling with a genuine smile. "I like Brittany. I've always found her good to work with."

"She has high expectations of me," Alisha confessed. "She made me a little nervous when I met with her a bit ago."

"Not surprising," Robert agreed. "You set a high bar with your performance in California."

"Yeah, but I had Silicon Valley there. It's going to be much harder here, I think. Looking at Mark's notes, there are some good prospects in New Jersey and eastern Pennsylvania, but not so much in Delaware, Maryland, and northern Virginia."

Dave nodded, his light brown hair slightly disheveled. "That's about right, although there are more companies moving to Delaware these days. I expect that area to pick up." As technical sales consultants, Dave and Robert were less confined to specific territories than she was as an account manager. That's how she had come to know them, when they helped on some of her projects out West.

"Hey . . ." Alisha began, unable to keep the most worrying thing from her mind as she glanced left and right. "Did you guys know about the bonus cap that was instituted last year? Brittany just told me about it this morning. Liam never said a word."

Robert rolled his eyes and Dave groaned.

"Of course, we did," Dave answered, frustration filling his deep voice. "I can't believe you're just finding out about it."

"Yeah, really," Robert concurred. "Everyone was up in arms about it last fall—including the two of us. Crazy stuff."

"I don't know how I missed that . . . except that Liam may have kept me in the dark on purpose," Alisha muttered. "Liam really was an ass, pardon my French."

"He sure was," Dave agreed. "Clearly in more ways than one."

Alisha tugged on her ponytail, as a brief silence ensured. She guessed that they, like her, were remembering the day on the golf course at Pebble Beach when Liam had been drinking and hit on her relentlessly. It was nothing truly new for Alisha except that finally someone else from the company witnessed it. That day was the start of her friendship with these two men—although she had done a good job of almost wrecking that by assuming that Dave wanted to be more than friends. Her cheeks turned pink just thinking about that. At least today he had been willing to meet her eyes for the first time, and even asked her to come sit with them, to commiserate as coworkers . . . *that meant everything was okay, right?*

"But the bonus cap," Alisha finally insisted "that burns me. I told Brittany I wouldn't have tried so hard to close those deals in December had I known, although she got pissed when I said that. Still, those deals basically didn't count at all."

Robert raised his eyebrows. "Well, that explains it!" He tossed his pen on his desk and leaned back. "I wondered why you pushed so hard for that last deal at Apple that we were working on. You didn't know? Damn, I should have said something!"

Alisha shot him a dark look. "Yeah, you should have. Did that deal count for you?"

"Not much," Robert admitted.

Dave laughed. "Not much? You were pissed that Alisha closed it," he reminded his friend. "It was just one more thing that was making you mad at her."

Robert easily reached over and punched Dave in the arm. "Jerk," he said, but his grin belied his words.

Flushing, Alisha smiled apologetically. "Sorry, Robert. I really didn't know. But I am glad that I'm not on your shit list any longer."

Robert frowned. "I didn't say that, Alisha," he said sternly. "You've got a ways to go before—"

"Yes, Alisha, I'd be happy to review that pharma account with you," Dave cut in pointedly, making a motion over her shoulder with his eyes.

"Thanks, Dave," she said, playing along right away.

That's when she heard the footsteps behind her. *Click, click, click.*

"Well, Alisha, I would think you would be busy making appointments," Brittany said. "Not *flirting* with Dave and Robert."

Stiffening, Alisha stood up, pushing the chair back into position in the cubicle next to Dave. Clearly, Robert wasn't the only one who still hadn't forgiven her for falsely accusing Dave of sexual harassment less than two months ago.

"Thanks, guys," she said in a professional tone. "I appreciate your help."

Turning, she looked directly into her boss's eyes. The look on the older woman's face was a clear warning. "Just getting some info, Brittany, to help with those appointments."

"Glad to hear it." Brittany turned on her heel and strode away.

Alisha glanced over her shoulder and let out a huff of breath, but Dave and Robert had already turned back to their computer screens. She walked back to her cubicle, sitting down heavily in the chair.

*How long is everyone going to keep watching me like a hawk?*

# CHAPTER 2

# An Offer She Can't Refuse

Gemma Morrison's golden-brown eyes nearly popped out of her head when she saw the salary and possible bonus in her offer letter on her computer screen.

*Wow!* she thought, *I never expected to earn that much money—ever!* Every nerve in her body tingled with elation.

For a moment.

*"But is this what you really want?"* The little voice of her conscience asked, catching her off guard.

*Why wouldn't I want this?* she asked indignantly, albeit silently. The walls of her small office were glass, and she knew it was never a good look to be seen talking to oneself. Still . . .

*This is the opportunity of a lifetime.*

Gemma leaned back in her cream-colored leather chair, a luxury she had purchased herself for her corporate office, as she unconsciously ruffled her very short, auburn hair. After more than twenty years at Viva!, she had already achieved way more than she'd dreamed. She was the head of marketing for the luxury cosmetics company—already a coveted position. One more promotion and her responsibilities would expand to include sales and customer relations, in addition to a seat on the board of directors. Her boss, Charles, had recently implied that the in-house promotion might not be too far.

Certainly Gemma had not been thinking about leaving the company until a recruiter had called with an opportunity, hinting that it might be even bigger. The possibility of moving to a major online retailer had been too good not to explore, although secretly, she hadn't truly expected it to go anywhere.

Now, she was faced with the most difficult decision in her career.

Her personal cell phone rang just as she was reaching for it. The recruiter's name flashed on the screen.

"Hey, Nathan."

"Are you excited?" he asked in a deep baritone voice. "They want you, *bad*."

Gemma chuckled. "Yeah, so it seems. That offer was a lot more than I expected."

"So, can I tell them yes? The execs at Atrium want you to start as soon as possible. Next week, even."

"But I have to give at least a month's notice per my contract," she protested, her voice rising in dismay. "And I haven't made my decision yet."

"What's to decide?" Nathan challenged. "You can't possibly turn that offer down. There is no way that Viva! is going to match it. They can't."

"Nathan," Gemma chided, although she knew that was true. "Money isn't everything."

He laughed. "No, but it sure doesn't hurt. And . . . they are offering you the chance to create something bigger and better at one of the world's biggest online shopping company. You can shape the future of online cosmetic sales."

A thrum of excitement went through her at his words. *He is right, of course. I can make more of an impact there, but . . .*

"So, I can tell them yes?" Nathan prodded.

"No, not yet," Gemma said firmly. "I need time to think about this. Study the offer. Talk it over with—"

"Hey, this is all confidential. You can't talk it over with anyone," Nathan reprimanded her sharply.

"Don't be ridiculous," she retorted, sitting up straighter. "I can talk it over with someone I trust. No one can be expected to make a momentous decision like this in a vacuum."

"Well, be careful about that," he warned. "And don't take too long. They want an answer now or they'll move on to the next candidate."

"I'll give you an answer tomorrow, Nathan," Gemma's voice held its own note of warning. "I'm not going to let you or anyone else browbeat me."

She heard Nathan's huff of frustration.

"Call me in the morning," he said briskly. He paused. "Okay?"

"Yes, okay, although I have no doubt you'll call me anyway," she said tartly.

"Ha! You're right about that. Talk to you tomorrow, Gemma—and don't overthink this. It really is a great opportunity, and you know it."

He hung up before she could reply.

Gemma's teeth sunk into her lower lip. *Am I overthinking it?*

The alarm signaling her next meeting chimed on both her phone and her computer, and she turned her attention to the product launch material that her team would be presenting. She'd been very excited about this innovative new product line.

*But if I leave, this launch will no longer be mine.*

It was mid-afternoon before she was able to pause long enough to consider her dilemma again. The pre-launch material had been well received by executive leadership, and Gemma had been commended on the imaginative and thorough plan her team had created. Product launches were one of Gemma's favorite activities. *How many of those would happen at Atrium?*

It would be different, she understood. Atrium didn't plan to start their own line of cosmetics, at least not in the short term, but she would be curating and launching other companies' makeup-type products in the state-of-the-art Atrium platform, which could include Viva! products, although Viva! had always resisted mainstream distribution in order to maintain the prestigious image of luxury and quality. She wondered if getting Viva! on board was part of the impetus behind Atrium's offer, but she knew that would be a tough sell.

Viva! had always been a quintessential New York City luxury brand, even though they also distributed through high-end retailers worldwide. *The New York City flagship store and home office is a big part of the brand's allure,* Gemma ruminated. Although she wouldn't have to move for the new job; she would be working primarily from home. Certainly, she wouldn't miss the daily commute from New Jersey, but she would miss the energy and excitement of working in the city.

She glanced down at her chic black dress and red pumps. *I'll also miss dressing up.* She'd noticed right away that Atrium's dress policy was casual. Sometimes very casual, even for the executives she had met in person and via video during the interview process. *Do I really want to give all of this up?*

Picking up her phone, Gemma scrolled through her contacts. She had no idea who to call. Her shoulders slumped. *Which is a sad state of affairs.* Just six months ago, she would have called her husband, but no longer. As clichéd as it was, Kevin had left her for a younger woman whom he had met at the country club, for goodness' sake. He claimed that her focus was on her career and their two teenage children and not on him. He wasn't wrong, but he had been just as focused on his career, maybe more so. *Yet that doesn't count*, she thought bitterly. *He had to be the center of my world, even if I wasn't the center of his.*

Her two children would probably love for her to work for Atrium, she mused. Kevin, Jr.—KJ for short—and Annabel were into the latest trends of fashion, technology, and anything else that was "hot." But they were seventeen and fifteen respectively. She couldn't confide in them. *But then who?*

Gemma stared out the high-rise window without seeing the bustling traffic below. Her fingers toyed with the heavy gold pendant she wore. *I have no close female friends*, she realized sadly. Sure, she had friendly relationships with some of the kids' friends' parents, but no one close. Even the couples that she and her ex had socialized with had drifted away in the wake of the divorce. *The last time I had close women friends was in college, before Kevin, before KJ and Annabel.* She felt tears well in her eyes.

"Ms. Morrison?" The voice of her boss' admin interrupted her thoughts. "Mr. Tennot would like to see you for a few minutes."

Straightening quickly, Gemma smiled at the young woman who always greeted her with such formality. "Of course, Jean. I'll be right there."

She smoothed her dress and swiped a tissue beneath both eyes to remove any trace of moisture. One did not visit Mr. Charles Tennot with smudged mascara. Guessing that he wanted to debrief the recent meeting, she grabbed the appropriate folder and her laptop before hurrying down the corridor to his spacious corner office. Fortunately, the meeting didn't take too long.

The short meeting with the boss allowed Gemma to get home at a reasonable hour, in time for dinner. Standing at the butcher-block-topped island, she sorted through the vegetables she had pulled from the stainless-steel refrigerator to decide what went into tonight's salad. The island light shone from overhead, casting a warm glow on the white cabinets, marbled tan granite, and hardwood floor. She loved the warm and cozy feel of the kitchen.

Gemma smiled to herself as she listened with half an ear to her children interact at the long, teak table that filled the breakfast nook in the kitchen. Annabel, who preferred to be called Anna, had home-work spread out in front of her, although she was more focused on teasing her brother about a supposed new girlfriend. KJ was eating a pre-dinner snack and sidestepping his sister's attack. He had just come in from basketball practice smelling like he hadn't showered—again.

*They really aren't children anymore,* she thought wistfully. *They are both young adults.* KJ was a junior and Anna a freshman at the prestigious Blake Academy, the private high school Kevin had insisted they attend. Gemma was painfully aware that KJ would be headed off to college in less than two years. *Where does the time go?*

The fact that all three were home in time for dinner together was an unusual occurrence given their busy scholastic and social schedules, and Gemma was grateful especially tonight. She still felt unmoored and edgy because of the unexpected job offer—and the realization that she had no one to act as a sounding board for her, especially since losing her parents five years ago. Her thoughts continued to whirl as she defrosted a large portion of lasagna she had made a few weekends ago and toasted garlic bread to go along with the salad. It was a relief to be able to cook in advance these days. Kevin had flatly refused to eat anything that had been frozen, which made weeknight meals challenging. Fortunately, KJ and Annabel didn't share their father's snobbery when it came to food.

A prickling feeling of being watched ran down her spine, and she looked up to see two pairs of eyes staring at her.

"Mom, what's wrong?" Anna asked, a crease on her forehead marring her delicate features. Her daughter looked a lot like Gemma, although she had her father's light brown hair. She shared her mother's golden-brown eye color.

"Nothing. Why?"

"Because you were staring into space, Mom, instead of working on dinner," Anna replied, still frowning.

"Yeah, Mom, what's going on?" KJ added.

"Umm, I—" Gemma was about to change the subject when she paused. *Why shouldn't I talk to them? They are almost adults, and they will be impacted by any job change that I make.*

After the divorce, she appreciated that both kids seemed to be concerned about her and spent more time at home. They had chosen to live with her instead of their father, although they still saw him regularly. Gemma was careful not to be too dependent on them or put too much pressure on them though. She had seen other women put guilt trips on their children, and it had sickened her. Her children were not responsible for her happiness and never would be. She didn't want to burden them. *But does that mean not sharing my life with them either?*

"I had a job offer today, from a new company," she suddenly announced.

The identical looks of shock on her children's faces almost made her laugh as both sets of jaws dropped and they stared open-mouthed at her.

KJ was the first to recover. "Really, Mom? I thought you loved working for Viva!."

"I do. I wasn't looking for it," Gemma clarified. "But a recruiter called me a few weeks ago, and I decided to explore the opportunity. I didn't really expect to get an offer."

Anna, still wide-eyed, took a deep breath and plunged in with a barrage of questions. "Where is it? Do we have to move? Is it more money? Do you *want* the job?"

Gemma laughed, putting down the knife and moving to the table where she took a seat. "Slow down. No, we wouldn't have to move. In fact, I'd be mostly working from home. It's a remote position with an online retailer. The job would be in marketing, but it's very different than what I'm doing now."

"So, you'd work from here? From Dad's old office?" KJ inquired, raising the rusty eyebrows that matched his red hair.

"I guess so," Gemma answered. "I hadn't gotten that far, but yes, I'd be home more."

"I'd kind of like that," Anna added, looking wistful. "It would be nice to have you around when we get home, even if you are working."

"Does it bother you that I commute into the city now?"

"Not really. We're kind of used to that, but . . ." Anna's voice trailed off. She nervously tucked her shoulder-length hair behind her ear.

"It might be nice to have you around more," KJ concurred. "And, if you are making lots more money, you could buy me a new car?"

Gemma laughed. "Nice try, but no."

KJ grinned, flashing the even white teeth that years of orthodontics had created. He had his father's effortless charm.

"Mom?" Annabel's eyes lit up. "Could you go to more of my swim meets?"

"I don't know. I guess so. It's possible that my hours would be a bit more flexible. Maybe not at first, but yes, I could probably go to more meets." Her neck started getting a bit warm.

"And basketball games?" her son piled on.

Gemma felt a rush of guilt and love, taken aback at the direction of the conversation. Tears threatened but didn't fall. "Hey, I didn't realize you guys wanted me there! I'm so sorry," she cried. She had always made an effort to be an active part of their lives, but maybe she hadn't been as successful as she thought.

"Mom, it's okay," Annabel quickly assured her, coming around the table to hug her. "We know you're a Madison Avenue hotshot, and we're proud of you. You're not like the other moms who spend their time drinking and getting plastic surgery. You're real. We like that."

"But you wouldn't mind if I was around more?"

Her children shared a knowing glance. They both shrugged.

"Well, if you put it that way . . ." KJ said, a twinkle in his bright blue eyes.

Anna chuckled along with her brother, but her face quickly turned sober. "Seriously Mom, we just want you to be happy. We know it's been hard for you with Dad and all that nonsense. We're not going to be around much longer, especially KJ—thank goodness," she paused and smirked at her brother. "So, it's really your decision. We will support whatever you do."

Gemma gathered her daughter close and reached out her hand to her son. This time, the tears did fall. "You two are the best kids ever," she said quietly. "I'm so grateful to have your support."

Anna slid fully onto her lap, even though she was nearly as tall as her mother, and burrowed into her like she had when she was a small child. Gemma rubbed her back and smiled softly. The faint scent of chlorine filled her nose. *It would be nice to be able to attend more of her swim meets.* The sense of time passing swiftly with these two was real.

After a long pause, Gemma took a deep breath. "Okay, guys, I need to finish dinner, and I'm sure you both have homework tonight. Let's get moving."

Her statement was met with a pair of groans.

"And thank you. I do appreciate your perspective. I have to admit that I'm still torn about my decision, but you've given me other things to consider," Gemma told them.

KJ laughed a bit sheepishly. "It's weird to have you ask us for advice, Mom, but it's kind of nice too. I like that you respect us enough to ask; not all parents do, you know.

Gemma's throat tightened with emotion, but she held back her tears. Crying wasn't going to get dinner on the table or her decision made. She simply nodded at her handsome son and went back to chopping.

Later that night, alone in the large master bedroom that she had once shared with her husband, she sat at the pretty white escritoire that had been one of her indulgences when she redecorated. Kevin had given her the house in the divorce, wanting continuity for their children, thankfully, and she had kept things largely the same. Except for this room. She had needed to remove any trace of him from what was now her personal space. The bedroom, decorated in shades of blue, green, and teal now reflected her taste and style–clean and bright, but also warm and cozy. She loved it.

But she wasn't thinking about the décor now. In front of her was a list of pros and cons–stay at Viva! or take the job at Atrium. The lists were equally long, but she had felt the energy shift toward Atrium during her conversation with KJ and Anna. Yes, she only had a short time left with them at home. Was she going to waste that time commuting into the city most days and missing some of their big and small events?

*But will I still be happy with that decision when they're gone? After all, I'll be fifty next year,* she reasoned.

She knew that changing careers became that much harder as one aged. It was unfair, of course, but it was the reality, especially in a career like marketing where being young and hip was prized. Opportunities like the one at Atrium wouldn't come along much longer. It was now or never.

Or maybe it was already too late.

She sighed as she put down her pen. It was time to go to bed.

# CHAPTER 3

# A Bigger Stage Awaits

"Absolutely not," Joaquin Gonzales said firmly. "The last thing we need is more exposure on this investigation. It's not over yet."

Alex Thompson's boyish face creased in a frown. "She doesn't have to talk about the investigation—"

"No, no," Joaquin broke in, his normally faint Spanish accent more pronounced with his agitation. "She can't do it!"

Sheryl Simmons rubbed her temple with her right hand, ruffling her dark bangs. The three of them sat at the conference table in her large office, a perk of the Chief Information Office role she had attained last fall. The room, lavishly furnished with old-fashioned cherry furniture and faux oriental rugs, was still too ornate for her taste. However, the décor was a legacy from her former boss Carl Schmidt, and she hadn't had the heart to replace it. Nor did she want to spend the company's money to do it—not with all the recent budget cuts.

"Alex, it's okay. I don't have to give the speech," she said quietly. "I don't know if I even want to." Alex was her boss and the current, interim president of The Diamante, the boutique investment firm that she loved and fought for, for over fifteen years. She was glad for Alex's support, but as The Diamante's compliance officer, Joaquin had final authority over any public appearances by the company's staff, even the senior executives.

"Yes, you do," Alex countered, glaring at Joaquin. "It's a huge honor, and one you should be proud of."

"Yes, yes, it's an honor, no doubt about that, and I'm sorry to be raining on the parade," the younger man said, his deep brown eyes full of genuine regret. "But we can't take the risk, not with the ongoing investigation into Todd."

Joaquin was referring to Todd Fisher, former president and CEO of The Diamante, over whose head a cloud of suspicion remained, despite the fact that neither the Securities and Exchange Commission nor the FBI had been able to link him to the illegal activities that Sheryl and her protégé Keisha Smith had uncovered. Keisha was the lead designer and programmer for the pivotal Portal Project, a complete redesign of the company's customer interface. She had discovered the discrepancies in the database just over two months ago. *Was it really that recently? It feels like it's been much longer.*

"I understand, Joaquin. I really do," Sheryl said quietly. If she were honest with herself, she wasn't sure if she was disappointed or relieved. She had been astounded that she had received the invitation to give a speech to such an illustrious organization in the first place.

The email had been in her inbox that morning when she arrived at the office. "Dear Ms. Simmons," it had read. "The National Association of Information Technologists would like to invite you to be the keynote speaker at our summer conference on June 21 . . ."

She had been leaning back in her chair, studying the email with bewilderment, when Alex had appeared at her door. Sheryl had immediately shared the contents of the email with him, and he had been excited for her.

She had countered his enthusiasm with a flurry of questions. "Do you think so? I've never given a speech outside of this corporation, much less a keynote. Why did they ask me? And can I give it? Should I?"

Guessing that her poise and eloquence at the company's press conference in late December was at the root of her invitation, Alex had immediately called the compliance officer to discuss the pros and cons of her accepting it. Joaquin had taken the time to come down to her office, but then dismissed the idea out of hand, barely listening to Sheryl's explanation. Alex was pushing back. Now, the two were in a tug of war about what she was going to do.

*And why isn't it* my *decision?* she thought a bit resentfully.

"But wouldn't it be good publicity?" Alex asked Joaquin. "After all, it was Sheryl's team that found the problem. She made the company look good, and her talking about it only reinforces our position in the market."

Joaquin, ever conservative, shook his head. "No, Alex, no. The less said, the better," he stated emphatically, even though Alex was his boss too.

A tense silence fell in the room. Sheryl could see the wheels spinning in Alex's head as he tried to come up with a counter to Joaquin's arguments. She could hear the faint buzz of her computer and the distant murmur of conversation outside her door.

What seemed like a full minute elapsed.

"What if I talk to them and see what exactly they are proposing that I talk about?" Sheryl finally asked, surprising herself with the question. "After all, the invitation was quite vague. Maybe they want me to talk about something entirely different."

Joaquin looked pained, but Alex's light brown eyes brightened. "Yes, that's a great idea," her boss enthused. "It won't hurt anything to gain clarity."

Clearly reluctant, Joaquin nodded. "Yes, all right. Ask. But I have to approve the topic. No matter what it is. I shouldn't have to remind you we're still under intense scrutiny by the press and everyone else. Everything public counts. Everything."

Sheryl smiled gently. "Thanks, Joaquin," she murmured. She had grown fond of him during the hectic weeks of the internal investigation, when they had spent almost all their workdays trying to put the pieces of the puzzle together. She didn't like his taking control of this particular situation, but she did understand the predicament he was in. She also knew that he only had the company's best interest at heart. "I promise I'll run the topic by you . . . and Alex, of course."

"I've got to get back to work," the compliance officer stated abruptly, standing. She knew him well enough to know that he was irritated.

Alex rose too, as did Sheryl. She noticed he looked almost too thin next to Joaquin's stocky frame. Sheryl wondered if he had lost weight. His shirt looked a little baggy. It wouldn't be surprising given the stress of the last two months. She had lost a few pounds herself.

After watching Joaquin walk quickly away, she turned to Alex. "You didn't come here for this though," she observed. "Why did you pop in, in the first place?"

Alex sighed and motioned for her to sit down again. Sheryl's stomach dropped at the somber look that appeared on her boss's face.

"I got another call from the leaders of the activist investor group who took such a large stake in the company last year," he explained, a crease forming between his eyes. "They're on the warpath—again."

Sheryl frowned, feeling the tension spread across her shoulders. These new investors, representing a large block of shares and shareholders, had been trouble from the very beginning. "What do they want now? Don't they have enough other things to worry about?"

She had become Alex's confidante in the last month, despite the fact that she was technically his subordinate. While he had been appointed president and CEO of the company after Todd had been forced to resign, it was only temporary. Although Hank Turner and Anthony Russo, who had initially represented the activist investor group on The Diamante board, had been at the epicenter of the recent scandal, the group itself had taken no responsibility for the felonious behavior of the two. Nor had they changed their stance on the running of The Diamante. As they had from the moment they had purchased their stake, the cutthroat group continued to ratchet up the pressure for higher earnings and bigger profits. Sheryl wondered how much the principals of the firm had known about the Ponzi scheme Sheryl's team had inadvertently uncovered, but, as with Todd, there was no apparent evidence that they had been involved at all.

Alex shrugged. "Apparently not," he answered her second question first. "The group wants a board meeting before the end of January to review the year-end numbers. They implied that more cuts might need to be made, especially if we've taken a hit because of the scandal."

"The scandal that *their* people caused?" Sheryl said bitterly. She shook her head. "Sorry. Not helpful. I know."

She mentally reviewed the current board members. The three colleagues who were also employees of The Diamante were conscious of the impact of cost-cutting on the staff and productivity of the company, but there was one executive board position that was currently unfilled due to Todd's absence. That left the outside or nonexecutive members with potentially more influence. Three of these five outside board members, who had been with The Diamante for a long time, were mostly balanced but appeared to be open to the influence of others. It was the two from this crazy new investor group, one still yet to be appointed, who were the enemies, or so it often seemed.

"It's hard not to be angry," Alex interrupted her thoughts, sounding more defeated than upset. "But the principals continue to deny being involved or knowing anything about what Hank and Anthony were up to. They're just worried about their investment and the financial health of The Diamante."

Sheryl nodded. This was ground they had covered before. She wondered if they would continue to support Alex or make his role permanent. It seemed unlikely. Alex Thompson was too nice a guy for them, if she had to guess. The domineering investors were far more fond of aggressive cutthroats, although they didn't have all the shareholder votes. Still, they controlled a large enough block to make things difficult, especially if they influenced other shareholders and board members.

"Will the numbers be ready by the end of January?" Sheryl asked. "That seems awfully early."

"Blake said he can get solid projections, but the numbers won't be final." Blake Jones was the Chief Financial Officer, for whom Sheryl had put her career at risk during the hiring process.

Sheryl's hazel eyes narrowed as she studied her friend. He looked pale and tired. There were dark circles under his eyes, and his freckles, normally faint, stood out against his pallor. She knew from her own mirror that she didn't look much better, although she was only doing one job, not two. Alex was still the Chief Investment Officer too.

"We went over the preliminary numbers at the December board meeting," Sheryl commented. "No one said much then, although only Paul was there." Paul Haven was the board member who had replaced Hank Turner, when Hank was removed from the board because of his abusive treatment of Sheryl. Anthony Russo, Hank's cohort and partner in crime, had been eliminated from the board only a few days before that December meeting because of his arrest. There hadn't been time to replace him yet, as it had only been about three weeks since that meeting.

"I know, but everything was still in turmoil then." Alex swallowed hard, dropping his gaze. "They want more layoffs," he added quietly.

Sheryl cringed. "Not again!" she groaned, her pale face flushing with frustration. "Why? What could possibly justify that?"

Alex met her anguished gaze with his own. "They think that Artificial Intelligence can replace a lot of headcount."

Her jaw dropped as she gasped out loud. "You can't be serious!"

"But I am. Very. And so are they," Alex assured her.

"You know we're using AI where we can—where it makes *sense*. But we can't just start wholesale replacing people for a lot of different reasons," she argued heatedly. "Plus there's the SEC oversight to consider. Their guidelines are continually changing on how we can use AI, because no one fully understands all the implications."

"I know. I'm aware of all of that," he acknowledged. "Especially the restrictions on the financial analysts. But new investors, Alpha VC, have this bit in their teeth, so to speak, and they want to run with it," he paused, giving her a sardonic look. "They've been reading too much of the hype, in my view."

"So? Why don't we wait and see before doing anything drastic? There are no guarantees with AI, at least not yet, and you know I've done some extensive training on AI."

"I know, but Alpha wants to get ahead of the curve," Alex said with disgust. "They want a plan for a minimum of a 10 percent reduction in force by the board meeting on January 28, along with an explanation of which jobs will be replaced with AI now and in the future."

Eyes widening in shock, Sheryl leaned forward. "Are you kidding me? Ten percent? And which jobs? You know there's no way we can give them that with any degree of accuracy!" Her voice shook with rage and fear before another thought hit her. "And I suppose they want the Portal Project finished ahead of schedule too!" she added sarcastically.

"Well . . ." Alex said sheepishly.

Sheryl stiffened in her chair. "They do? Seriously? And just how do they think we're going to do that with even fewer people?" she demanded. "I guess AI is supposed to do that too?"

Her boss shifted uncomfortably in his chair. He looked her way but didn't quite make eye contact. She saw a faint flush creep up his cheeks all the way to his sandy brown hair.

"They think you're too soft on your staff," he confessed, his voice barely above a whisper. "Someone, I don't know who, told them about your memorial meetings. Paul indicated that, well, let's just say they weren't impressed."

Sheryl thought back to the meetings she had held with her teams, to remember and honor the employees who had been so unceremoniously laid off.

"But they helped!" Sheryl all but shouted. "Even Todd acknowledged that my team's productivity bounced back faster than any other department."

Alex shot her a sardonic look. "Todd's not exactly seen as the most reliable person right now," he reminded her. "They all but fired him, as you know."

"Is this nightmare ever going to end?" Sheryl grumbled, slumping as her defiance and anger seeped out of her. The enormity of the firm's problems washed over her again. *Every time I think things are going to improve, something else happens to prove me wrong.*

Alex shook his head, his face reflecting the same sense of hopelessness and frustration that she felt. In addition to Alpha Investment's relentless pressure, the SEC investigation still hung over all their heads. Todd Fisher hadn't been charged, but he hadn't been cleared either. Rachel Solowitz, the former Vice President of Client Services, was still insisting that Todd was involved in Hank and Anthony's Ponzi-type scheme, even though she had no proof. She had been indicted in the case, although she had made a deal with the prosecutor in exchange for her testimony against Hank and Anthony that would likely save her from any prison time.

The two former board members were set to be prosecuted to the fullest extent of the law, and the investigators from the SEC and FBI were still looking for more evidence and more potential conspirators. Sheryl had mistakenly thought that they had solved the case in December, but the whole situation continued to be a nightmare. She and Keisha Smith, the programmer who had uncovered the problem, were still being pulled into the investigation on a regular basis, which was yet another reason that the Portal Project schedule couldn't possibly be accelerated. *Why didn't anyone, besides Alex, understand that?*

This time, her boss did meet her gaze. "Yes, it will," he assured her in a voice full of sympathy. "I'm just not sure when."

Sheryl bit her lip. "What about you? Are they talking about replacing you as president?"

"Probably," he admitted, with a rueful look. "Although they haven't said so. They probably won't while the investigation is ongoing. It wouldn't look good."

"They are going to propose another board member to replace Anthony, I assume? Or have they already?" Sheryl asked, discouraged by Alex's assumptions.

"Yes, they have someone in mind, but they haven't shared who yet. They have to be very careful about their choice," he said gravely. "They still have mud on their faces with Hank and Anthony even though they don't admit it, so they'll need to find someone whose integrity is unquestioned."

"They will also want to find someone who is equally *ruthless*, won't they?" she asked, remembering Hank's insistence on hiring a totally inappropriate candidate because of that characterization.

Alex harumphed. "Well, they haven't said that either, but I wouldn't be surprised."

They sat in silence for a long moment.

"You'll have to draw up a list," Alex finally said quietly. "Along with the AI report. That's going to be mostly on you."

Tears threatened but didn't fall as Sheryl nodded tightly. "Yes, I know," she replied just as softly. "That's what you came to say, wasn't it?"

He nodded. "Yeah." He paused, looking at her with despair on his face. "I'm sorry. I don't like it either, but we have to be prepared."

"I just hope we don't have to use it."

"Me either," Alex agreed, standing. "But it's going to be a fight not to. We have to be prepared for that too."

Rising slowly, Sheryl felt a huge crushing weight descending on her shoulders—again. "Is this all this is, Alex?" she asked wearily. "This being on the executive team? Is it just fighting with the board, struggling to maintain your integrity, and trying to keep everyone's sanity?"

Alex returned her gaze with sympathy on his face. "It didn't use to be," he told her, "but it seems like that's what it is now." He paused, and she saw his shoulders slump. "I hope it doesn't stay this way. We used to work with the board, not against them. I'm sure it will turn around . . ."

"But you don't know when." Sheryl finished his sentence.

Shaking his head, Alex gave her a rueful smile.

She sighed. "I hope it turns around soon, but in the meantime, I'm not going to take more layoffs without a fight, you know. Nor am I going to agree to implement AI recklessly."

A brief smile crossed Alex's face as he turned to leave. "Somehow, I already knew that," he said as he walked out the door. "And believe me, I'm counting on it."

Sheryl's gaze lingered on the door long after Alex had left. She gritted her teeth and went back to her desk, her thoughts whirling.

*I took this job to make a difference.* She eyed the email from the technology association open on her computer.

Her jaw suddenly firmed. She typed in two sentences and hit reply. *Despite what Joaquin said, what's the harm in pursuing this further?*

# CHAPTER 4

# The Right Decision?

**Wednesday, January 12**

Nathan called while Gemma was still on the train.

"I can't talk now," she explained. "I'll call you when I get to the office."

"I don't need to talk. All I need is a 'yes,'" he said quickly.

Gemma noticed that "no" wasn't an option. She had learned this was typical of Nathan Hall.

"I have questions," she mumbled, finding it hard to hear in the crowded commuter car.

"Like?"

She succumbed to his pressure. "Why me? There's something about this fit that doesn't seem right."

"Does it matter?" he countered. "They want . . . They're willing . . . exorbitant salary and bonus . . .you."

"What? I can barely hear you with all the background noise, Nathan. But, yes, it matters. I have to do something to earn those things. They have to think I'm worth it."

Nathan responded, but she couldn't make out his words.

"I'm going to call you when I'm in the office and can hear," she said firmly.

"Okay, okay," he conceded. "Call . . . as soon . . . can." He didn't wait for her reply to end the call.

She sighed. After a mostly sleepless night, she wasn't in any position to make this kind of momentous decision, but she knew she had to. Still, the question she had asked him had been the main one that rattled through her brain during the night. It wasn't the only one, but it was the main one.

Yes, she was good at her job. Yes, she had a wealth of experience in the cosmetic industry but at the high end. She wasn't accustomed to targeting the mass market, which was where Atrium played. *How will my luxury experience help them?* Of course, Viva! had an online presence, so she wasn't inexperienced with online retail, but . . . It was the "but" that had kept her awake.

The people around her moved, alerting her that the train had reached her station. She joined the herd flooding onto the platform and up the escalators. Within ten minutes, she had reached the offices of Viva!, which were directly above the glamorous retail store on Park Avenue, her tote clutched tightly beneath her arm.

Once in her tiny office, she exchanged her sneakers for black, high-heeled pumps, hung up her coat and scarf, and checked her hair and makeup in a compact mirror. Satisfied that she looked okay, she swung the glass door closed for privacy and picked up the phone. *I might as well get this over with.* She hit the send button.

Nathan answered immediately. "Gemma, now are you ready to say yes?"

"No, not yet. I told you that," she chided. "You still need to tell me why they want me."

She heard his deep sigh, followed by the distinct sound of typing, then silence. She waited, biting her lip. She resisted tapping her fingers on the desk, barely.

After a long moment, he spoke. "I'm reading directly from their email to me. 'We would like to extend the following offer to Ms. Morrison. Her experience and background are exactly what we need to elevate our cosmetics offerings at Atrium. She can help us tap into new markets and reach a different set of customers.' Does that answer your question?"

"I guess so. It's what they said to me in the interview process," she answered slowly. "But it still doesn't make total sense to me."

"Well, are you going to take the offer or not?" Nathan said impatiently. "It's yes or no, Gemma. I don't think there's much to negotiate in their offer. They even agreed to your request for additional vacation time, something most firms don't do—as you well know."

Gemma tapped her fingers on the desk, spinning her chair around to look out the window. All she saw were KJ and Anna's faces all lit up with the idea of her being home more. That was the answer, despite her misgivings.

"Are you still there?" Nathan spoke sharply.

"Yes, I'm here. I guess I'll take it," she said reluctantly.

"Don't sound so happy about it. Are you sure?"

"Yes, I'm sure," Gemma affirmed, wishing she felt sure. "I'll talk to my boss and let you know when I can start. It will be at least two weeks." She paused, calculating. "Today is Wednesday. How about two weeks from Monday?"

"They'll want sooner," Nathan warned, "but I'll let them know. I'll send over the offer paperwork for you to sign later this morning."

"Okay, sounds good." She hung up.

Her chest felt tight, and she struggled to take a deep breath. "Please let this all work out okay," she whispered. She looked at the offer again. It was fabulous, and it would definitely help make up for what she had given up in the divorce settlement. She took a few more deep breaths to settle herself, then stood and headed to her boss' office. She was not looking forward to this conversation, but it had to be done.

"You're kidding me, right?" Charles stared at her, his jaw open. "Why in God's name would you do that?"

"Charles," Gemma protested his language, but it was half-hearted at best. "They made me an offer I just can't refuse. I didn't expect this. I wasn't even looking for it."

"You've been at Viva! for over twenty years. You're a valued member of our leadership team with a bright future ahead of you. And, you're well-compensated." He paused. His eyebrows drew together in a frown. "This isn't a ploy for more money, is it?"

"No, of course not," she retorted. "You know I don't play games like that."

"Well, what is it? I know you're not all about money. I thought we were happy here." He was obviously bewildered. His light gray eyes searched her face.

At that moment, Gemma felt bewildered too. *Why am I doing this?* She leaned forward, her eyes wide and intense.

"I am happy here. I wasn't looking for this," she repeated. "But it's something I have to do now. I have to take a chance and branch out. These kinds of opportunities don't come along every day. Plus, I'll be working mostly from home and be able to be there more for my kids."

"But Atrium?" Charles shook his head. "They'll eat you alive there. Working from home? You're kidding about spending time with your, might I add, teenage children. That's a whole different world–a much more cutthroat world than you're used to. Not to mention a younger world."

Gemma cringed, her stomach clenching. Trust Charles to hit on one of her biggest concerns. Younger world. Was she already too old for that type of job?

"Look, call the recruiter back. Say you've changed your mind. Gemma, I know you. You don't want to do this," her boss urged her. He got up and walked around his desk. A lean and handsome man in his mid-fifties, he was dressed in an expensive suit, the collar of his crisp white shirt open at the neck. He sat down next to her.

"Take a few minutes. Think about it," he said with a very serious voice. "Come back in an hour. I'm truly concerned for you." He smiled ruefully. "And Viva! too, of course."

Gemma sat up straighter in the chair. "Charles, I can't. I can't think about this anymore. I need to do this. No, I want to do this. It's important to me, and it's important to my family. With Atrium, I'll have the opportunity to work from home and be there more for my kids. I'll work for two more weeks. We can transition my projects to—"

"No, you can't. If you're going to Atrium, you have to leave now. I'll call Human Resources, but you can't go back to your desk alone." His face was harsh now, his gaze hard. He suddenly looked his age as he rose and stood over her. "I'm sorry, but that's how it has to be." He paused. "Are you sure?"

Every muscle in her body tightened in protest. This was not what she had expected. *To leave now? To be walked out like I have been fired?* She swallowed hard as she met Charles' gaze. Her stomach in knots, she nodded. "I'm sure."

"I'm disappointed," Charles said, but his tone lacked any warmth. In a few seconds, he had transformed from her formal, but kind boss to the cold, hard executive she knew he could be. She had never seen that persona directed at her. "Of course, I do wish you the best. We're going to miss you." He looked directly into her eyes. "But you're going to miss us more."

With that, he turned and picked up the phone. Gemma's time at Viva! was at an end—abruptly and unceremoniously. She bit her lip and blinked the tears away.

She went to her daughter's swim meet that afternoon. She slid into the poolside bleachers, already dressed in jeans and a lightweight green sweater. Anything warmer would be unbearable in the steamy heat, though it was not even thirty degrees outside.

"Mom! You're here," Anna cried from the pool deck before she even got settled, waving excitedly.

Gemma saw her tap one of her teammates on the shoulder and point. The other girl gave her a quick hug. The ecstatic look on Anna's face was a balm to Gemma's bruised emotions after the indignity of her exit from her long-term job.

The enthusiastic call she had received from her new boss Kushma had also helped. In light of Viva!'s response to her resignation, she had moved her start date up a week. Kushma had been thrilled with that news. The Atrium team seemed very excited for her to get started. Still, Gemma had wanted to take the rest of this week and next to relax a bit and convert Kevin's office to her own. She'd barely been in there since he moved out, and he had taken very little with him. He had wanted a "fresh start." *Well, now it's my turn for a fresh start. It's another room in the house I can now claim as my own.* She smiled.

The starting gun went off, followed by the splash of swimmers hitting the water. Gemma turned her attention to the pool. Anna wasn't in this race, but she joined in the cheering as the swimmer from Blake Academy surged ahead.

In between races, one of the other mothers, a woman Gemma had met a few times before, slid over to say hello. She asked about KJ and

Anna before inquiring about Gemma's job. "I'm surprised to see you here," she said. "Aren't you usually working?"

Gemma laughed. "Yeah, I'm actually between jobs as of today, but I should be able to get to a few more meets with my new job."

The woman, whom Gemma remembered was named Susan, smiled. "That's great. I'm sure Anna will love it. I know my daughter plays it cool, but she gets bummed out when I miss a meet."

"Does she?" Gemma asked, lowering her eyebrows. "I guess I'm slow on the uptake. I didn't think it mattered that much at this age, but Anna was sure excited to see me today."

Susan gave her a knowing look. "Yeah, they'd never admit to it, but they still like Mom's approval."

The start of the next race cut off the conversation, but Susan stayed where she was for the rest of the meet, making idle chitchat between races. *It feels nice to connect, even casually*, Gemma mused, trying to find more ammunition to justify her decision.

*But you are connected at Viva!—or you were*, said that little voice from inside. Her stomach clenched. She pushed the thought away.

She felt even better when Anna rushed over after the meet to beg for a ride home.

Anna peppered her with questions the minute they got into Gemma's Lexus SUV. "What are you doing home already, Mom? Did you leave work early just to come to my meet? Have you made a decision about the job? Did you see my race? I won the 200 IM today."

Gemma laughed. "One question at a time, young lady," she teased. "And yes, I saw your race. You looked great. You've improved so much since the summer. I'm proud of you."

"It was nice to have you there, Mom," Anna admitted. "But why *were* you there? What happened?"

"How about I tell you at home so that I can tell KJ at the same time?" Gemma suggested.

"But Mo-om, that could be hours!"

Gemma shook her head, her large dangling earrings swinging playfully. "An-na. It won't be hours. He might even be home when we get there. He didn't have a game today."

Anna pouted, sticking out her lower lip like she had done as a child. "But I want to know first."

"How old are you?"

"Okay, okay, I'll wait. I just hope he's home."

He was. He was sitting at the kitchen table, a bowl of Doritos in front of him. Susan inwardly groaned. He shot up as they walked in. "Mom, you're home. I got home, and your car wasn't here. Since you usually walk to the train, I didn't know what to think. You went to work this morning, and you never come home this early without letting us know." The words all came out in a rush.

"Hey, easy there," Gemma said. "Let me take my coat off at least." She pulled her gloves and thick, blue down jacket off. She only wore a hat when it was really cold. Tucking the gloves in her pocket, she hung the coat in the hall closet. A pointed look at Anna's swim bag sent the girl hurrying to the laundry room to hang up her wet things.

Gemma poured herself a glass of water and sat down at the table.

Anna slid into her chair moments later. "So, tell us," she demanded.

"I took the new job," she announced baldly.

Both kids froze for a moment, then started talking over one another.

"That's great, Mom—"

"I'm so excited. Was that why—"

"When do you start?"

"Who are you working for?"

"Why are you home today though? Didn't you have to give two weeks' notice?"

KJ's last two questions penetrated his sister's outburst. She stopped talking.

"So, you're going to let me speak?" Gemma asked humorously. She ran her fingers through her spiky hair, which only made it stand up more.

When they both nodded, she told them what had happened.

"They just kicked you out? Like you are a criminal or something?" Anna responded indignantly.

"That's what companies do, sis," her big brother informed her. "Right, Mom?"

"Yes, KJ, that's often what happens when you go to work for a competitor, which I am sort of doing. However, I wouldn't call them a direct competitor, more of an indirect one since they are in a different segment of the cosmetic market. Still, the company thought Atrium was close—"

"Atrium!" KJ and Anna spoke in unison.

"Wow! That's so cool, Mom! Wait till I tell the guys about that," KJ continued.

"Yeah, Mom. Awesome!"

"Whoa! Slow down. Let's not tell anyone until I have actually started," she cautioned them. "I need to get the lay of the land a bit before we make any grand announcements. Got it?"

"Aww man," KJ replied, scrunching his face in disappointment. "That stinks, but I get it. When do you start?"

"A week from Monday. That will give me time to get the office set up for me."

"Well, I'm proud of you, Mom, and excited you'll be home more," Anna told her earnestly.

"Thank you, sweetie, I appreciate that. Now, let's go out to dinner and celebrate—a little. Where should we go?"

After a somewhat heated debate, they settled on an Italian restaurant in nearby Summit and bundled up before heading out to the SUV. Gemma smiled as her children chatted excitedly about her new job as they drove there. *I'm fortunate to have such good kids*, she thought. *I'm grateful they are open and talkative with me, unlike so many teenagers.*

They were still smiling and laughing as they walked into the restaurant, and Gemma was able to put the embarrassment and anger about her final minutes at Viva! out of her mind. Just this time with her children was enough to make her feel good about her decision.

Until she opened the door and came face to face with Charles Tennot. She fought back a wave of nausea. Her old boss gave her an appraising look and turned away.

*What have I done?*

Suddenly, the last thing she wanted to do was celebrate, but she pasted a bright smile on her face and turned back to her children. At least they were unabashedly happy about her decision. In time, maybe she would be too.

# CHAPTER 5

# Déjà Vu

Sheryl's emotions were raw when she returned to her desk after personally visiting each of her direct reports that morning. The conversations had been painful, especially the one she'd had with Patrick. Like her, he had been shocked and dismayed when she told him that more layoffs were being suggested. His face had grown violently red, and she could tell that he had struggled to keep his red-headed temper in check.

Another one of the directors who reported to her, José, hadn't bothered. He had exploded with anger when she had visited him, condemning both the investor group and the board of directors for even entertaining the thought. The conversation with the others hadn't been any better. She could tell that the news was already starting to erode the goodwill and sense of peace she had worked so hard to establish with her team.

She herself felt like the worst kind of betrayer. She had stood in front of all of them—and the rest of her staff—in October last year, telling them no more layoffs were planned. Of course, they hadn't been at the time, at least not that she knew of, but still. It would be hard for them to believe her, not when requests for more layoff lists had to be made.

She was relieved when Blake Jones called. *Maybe he'll have better news.*

"Hey, Sheryl." Blake's warm and friendly voice raised her spirits immediately. They had rapidly become good friends in the month since he had started.

"Hey yourself," she breathed, tucking her dark, pageboy-cut hair behind her ear.

"Alex talked to me," he continued without preamble. "I just wanted to let you know that I'm going to do everything I can to find suitable ways to save money without instituting more layoffs. I already have some good ideas."

"Oh, Blake, that would be wonderful! I can't bear the thought of more layoffs."

"I know. Alex said you were upset, not that we all aren't, but knowing you, you're taking it very hard," he replied bluntly.

"I was. I am," she confirmed, leaning her elbow on the desk. "I just talked to most of my direct reports too. Some of them are breathing fire."

"Oh boy, I'll bet they are."

"I really hope we can find another way, Blake," Sheryl told him. "I'm afraid we're going to start losing good people."

"I know. I've seen it before, but I think I've identified a few ways we can tighten the belt, so to speak, without cutting off our circulation," Blake assured her.

She chuckled at his analogy. "That's a good one, Blake, because it truly feels like more layoffs would be damaging in more ways than one! May I cautiously share your thoughts with my team?"

There was a slight pause. Sheryl heard Blake take a deep breath. "Well, I guess, as long as it's in confidence and you're not making promises," he finally answered.

"Thank you. I will and I won't, respectively," she said, feeling her spirits lift. "I really appreciate you taking the time to let me know. I know from conversations I had before you were hired that you've been able to find unusual ways to save money."

Blake laughed heartily. "Oh, you did, did you? Now, I'd love to know who you talked to."

"I'll never tell," Sheryl countered lightly.

"Of course, you won't," Blake said, still laughing. "You're not one to reveal her sources."

"Nope, not a one."

"All right then, I'll let you go, but I'll be in touch, with you and Alex, as soon as I have something more concrete to share. We can strategize before the meeting. There's still time." Blake's voice was calm and full of conviction.

"Thanks, Blake," Sheryl responded, feeling much better herself. *At least this time, I have a team of people who are working with me rather than against me.* She thought back to her first board meeting when she alone had taken a stand on hiring Blake instead of Layla Arch. Others had followed her lead, thankfully, because she had certainly been proven right. Not only was Blake a great fit for the organization, Layla had also been implicated in Hank Turner's Ponzi scheme.

After hanging up with Blake, Sheryl turned back to her computer screen. Her email box was already full of new messages, accumulated during her visits with her team leads. She started to go through them methodically, but then the response from the NAIT caught her eye.

Sheryl quickly opened the email, suddenly anxious to know what they had to say:

Dear Ms. Simmons,

Thank you for your prompt response to our inquiry. To answer your questions, you were recommended by a member of NAIT who wishes to remain anonymous. However, some members of the event committee also saw The Diamante's press conference a few weeks ago, where you made statements with great clarity and eloquence. The invitation was based on both that recommendation and our observations.

With regard to the subject matter, we would leave that up to your discretion. However, the theme of this year's conference is "The Human Side of IT." We understand that you took some extraordinary measures in the wake of significant corporate layoffs at The Diamante. We would hope that you would share your methods, observations, and outcomes with our audience as a model for developing different approaches to corporate leadership.

I'd be happy to schedule a short call to discuss further.

*Carl.* Her former boss. *It had to be him. He was a major player in NAIT for years, and I'm sure he still has contacts there. Plus, I don't think anyone else would have told them about my memorial meetings . . . Would they?*

She picked up her cell phone and scrolled to Carl's name before remembering that he and his wife were off on a month-long cruise in the Mediterranean and Baltic Seas. She smiled at that thought, happy that Carl was embracing the retirement that had been foisted on him by the investor group that was still creating such angst.

*But wow. How awesome would it be to talk about my meetings? To share that with a large group of other CIOs and IT executives.* She was enormously flattered and encouraged by their interest. The memorial meeting she had held, over the objections of her husband and others, allowed her staff to recognize and "mourn" the loss of their laid-off colleagues, including Carl. The meeting had been hugely successful in restoring productivity and had been copied by other members of The Diamante management. *What if I start a whole new trend?*

Sharing her views on leadership outside of The Diamante had never occurred to her, but now that the idea had been planted in her head, she felt a rising excitement. She also felt a rising fear. She had no experience with public speaking, if one discounted the many staff and department meetings she had led. *Can I even do it?*

Stomach clenching, she picked up the office phone and dialed Joaquin's extension, hoping that he would relent on his no-speaking stance now that she had more information on the subject matter.

She held her breath as the phone started to ring, but still after a moment there was no answer. Disappointed, she dropped the phone into the receiver without leaving a message. She turned back to her inbox, but she couldn't concentrate.

*I have to talk to* someone *about this, but who?*

Her husband crossed her mind, but she knew Dave was busy and didn't want to bother him at work. She finally settled on her best friend Cindy. It was nearly noon in New Jersey, which meant that it was nearly 10:00 a.m. in Denver, where Cindy lived and worked. Grabbing her cell phone, she quickly dialed from her favorites list.

"Uh oh, you're calling during the workday," Cindy answered. "What's wrong?"

Sheryl laughed. "Nothing, for once," she replied cheerfully, momentarily forgetting the pending layoff request from the investor group. "But you won't believe what happened. I got invited to be the keynote speaker at NAIT, and . . ." She paused dramatically. "They want me to talk about my memorial meetings!" she finished with a flourish.

"No way! Really?" came Cindy's astonished response. "How did they even find out about those?"

"I don't know for sure," Sheryl said truthfully, "but I'm guessing Carl. Who else could it have been? He was very active in NAIT for a long time."

"Hmmm, could be. It sounds like something he would do. But wow. That's really exciting. Are you going to do it? No, forget that. Of course you are!"

"I don't know about that either," Sheryl cautioned, biting her lip. "Joaquin has to approve it, and he wasn't enthusiastic about it when I brought it up."

"Why not? It would be great for The Diamante."

"That's what Alex said too, but Joaquin is still all worried about the investigation and all."

"Yeah, I can see that," Cindy conceded. "But this has nothing to do with that, so why would he care?"

"I haven't reached him yet, not since I found out the topic," Sheryl admitted. "But Cindy, do you really think I should? I mean, I have zero experience with this kind of thing. What if I make an idiot of myself? I'm not sure I should say yes, even if Joaquin okays it."

"Are you crazy? First of all, you'd do great! Second, you have plenty of time to practice," Cindy shot back. "The meeting isn't until near the end of June, right? I remember getting some emails about it." As an IT professional herself, she was a member of NAIT and attended the annual conference occasionally. It was one of the ways the two women had stayed in close touch in the last ten years, after Cindy had moved to Colorado. They frequently met at the annual event.

"Hmmm . . . If you say so," Sheryl said doubtfully.

"Look how great you did at the press conference in December," Cindy reminded her, echoing the comments in the email.

Sheryl stood up and crossed the fifteen feet to her office door, closed it, then paced back to the desk. She didn't sit. Finding herself too restless, she turned around and paced around the perimeter of the room, skirting the small sitting area, conference table, and her overlarge desk. She nearly tripped on the oriental runner that lay under the chair in front of the desk but righted herself before continuing for around again.

"Oh Cindy, I don't know," she spoke as she walked. "That conference is so big. And to be the keynote? That's a lot of pressure. Plus, there is still so much going on here." The enormity of that statement hit her as she completed another lap, and she dropped back into her chair. "Oh God, Cindy, they're talking about more layoffs."

"What? No! Alex wouldn't do that," Cindy protested. She and Sheryl spent enough time talking that she was familiar with Sheryl's colleagues.

"No, he wouldn't," Sheryl agreed. "But the investors . . ."

"Oh, *them*," her friend said with disgust. "But one doesn't have any bearing on the other," she stated emphatically. "You should do this. Think about the impact you could have! It's amazing!"

"Really, you think I should?"

"Yes, yes, and triple yes!" Cindy was just about shouting. "I'll bet Dave would say so too. Have you talked to him yet?"

"No, not yet, but I will," Sheryl promised, albeit reluctantly. While they had reconciled after the debacle with Alisha, there was a level of trust that was still missing on her part. "But it won't matter what Dave or you or I think, if Joaquin says no."

"That's just not right," her friend replied loyally. "It should be your decision. As long as it's not compromising The Diamante or the investigation, which this won't, it totally should be up to you!"

"Yeah, but that's not how it works, as you well know, my friend," Sheryl reminded her. Cindy worked for an insurance company which was even more conservative than the investment firm that employed Sheryl.

"True enough, but listen, I've gotta run. There's a meeting I'm already late for. You let me know what Joaquin says." Cindy was gone before Sheryl could reply.

She placed the cell phone back on the desk and pushed her bangs back. Heaving a deep sigh, she shook her head. *I don't know; I'm a technologist, not a public speaker. I still think I could make a fool of myself.*

She turned back to her email.

*But what about the impact I could make?*

# CHAPTER 6

# The Hole May Be a Canyon

Alisha thanked yet another customer and clicked the end button. She pulled the phone away from her ear and gently massaged it. It was nearly eleven on Tuesday. She had been on the phone all morning, making appointments to visit the key clients in her new territory. Her calendar was filling up. She'd be on the road a lot for the next few weeks.

Her cell phone vibrated in her palm. Yet another unknown number popped up on the screen. "Alisha Carson!" she answered brightly, a smile stretched across her face. She had learned long ago that smiling while you were talking on the phone translated into a friendly tone in one's voice.

"I understand you're the person to call now," came a gruff male voice.

"That's probable if Mark used to be your account manager," she replied cheerfully.

"Well, he was, and I don't think it was right for him to retire in the middle of our project," the man stated emphatically. "It wasn't right at all."

"To whom do I have the pleasure of speaking?" Alisha asked politely, grimacing at the ire in the man's voice despite her best efforts.

"Walter Meeks, CPT Pharmaceuticals."

"Ah yes, Mr. Meeks. I'm just getting familiar with your account. I was planning to call you today," Alisha said, frantically typing the man's name into the CRM program. She scanned the notes quickly when the account appeared on the screen.

"Well, you should have called this morning. We're in the middle of a major project that's totally off-track," Walter grumbled. "I want to be at the top of your priority list, like I was with Mark. We spend a lot of money with LMS, young lady, and I expect to get better service than we're getting at the moment."

Alisha tugged on the end of her ponytail. "I'm so sorry, Mr. Meeks. I wasn't aware there was a problem. In fact, I don't see any notes to that effect in your account summary," she responded, careful to infuse sympathy in her tone.

"Hrmph," the man's deep gravelly voice was full of disgust. "I don't know how good Mark was at notetaking, but I'll fill you in now so you can jump right on this. I need answers, and I need them today." He went on to explain in great detail how the AI project that LSM was spearheading in their lab had gone awry.

While he spoke, Alisha accessed the company's central storage drive and found the project management documents for CPT. With a quick glance, she saw that the project timeline seemed to corroborate the client's complaints.

"I'm so very sorry, Mr. Meeks," Alisha said, as his tirade wound down. "I can see that the project plan reflects what you've told me. I'll get in touch with the project manager as soon as we hang up and get to the bottom of this. Is it all right if I call you back in a couple of hours?"

"You better call me Walter," he said gruffly. "And yeah, you can call me back. But it better be today, or I'll be calling you or your boss. I need answers, missy."

"Of course, you do," Alisha soothed. "I promise I'll call you back."

The faint background sound on the call ended abruptly as Walter disconnected. Shaking her head, Alisha slowly lowered the phone to the laminate desktop and studied the project plan. She didn't know the project manager, had never heard of her, but she recognized Robert Coleman's name. As the firm's primary AI specialist, it made sense that he was active with this account.

Swiveling in her chair, she found Robert's black curly hair poking above the low cubicle walls. Robert's height made him easy to spot, and she could tell from the lack of deep baritone murmurs that he wasn't on the phone at the moment. She rose and quickly crossed the floor to his desk.

Tapping him lightly on the shoulder, she greeted his cautious look with an open smile as he pivoted to face her.

"Hey there, I just got a call from Walter Meeks—"

Robert's groan cut her off. "Wow, I can't believe he found you already," he said, rolling his eyes. "He's a piece of work!"

"Well, he seems to have some legit complaints," Alisha responded with a quirk of her right eyebrow.

Robert's dark, dark eyes met her blue ones. "Yeah, he probably does, but the problems are more likely on his end than ours."

"Really? I couldn't tell from the project plan. I don't know Penny Forester, who's listed as the project manager."

"Penny's okay," Robert said, frowning slightly. He reached a long arm out to a nearby empty cube and grabbed a chair. "Sit," he commanded, pointing at the chair. "This is a bit of a long story."

Alisha sat, pushing a few stray tendrils of blonde hair back from her pretty round face. "This doesn't sound good."

The side of Robert's mouth quirked up in a half smile. "It's not," he replied frankly. "The basic problem is that Walter's team doesn't do their part. They are always missing deadlines, and Walter blames it on us. He drove Mark crazy. Wouldn't be surprised if Walter wasn't partially behind his retirement."

Robert went on to give examples of the kinds of issues Walter's team caused. Alisha had seen it before with other accounts. Clients love to blame the consultants for everything regardless of the cause. However, it seemed like Walter's staff was worse than usual, and Walter rarely would allow the true issues to surface.

"Great, just great," Alisha responded sarcastically. "So, how do we handle him?"

Robert's eyebrows shot up. "We? You mean you, or you and Penny? I don't deal with the diva types."

Snorting, Alisha rolled her eyes. "Yeah, right."

His full lips curving into a grin, Robert laughed. "Not if I don't have to, and in this case, I don't. That's your job."

"Yeah, yeah," she murmured before her gaze sharpened. "So, where can I find Penny Forester?"

Robert straightened in his chair and looked around the wing. Even seated, Alisha guessed that he could see as well as she could standing.

"I'd check the first floor," he finally replied, leaning back. "I don't see her up here. She has strawberry-blonde hair. You can't miss her."

"Will do," Alisha said, placing her hands on the arms of her chair.

She had just started to rise when she heard her name in a sharp tone coming from behind her. Startled, she whipped around and spotted Brittany marching toward them.

"What did I tell you about bothering Dave and Robert?" the older woman snapped. "Get back to your desk. I don't want to see you here again. Do you hear me?"

"But Brittany, I was—"

"Now, Alisha." Brittany's eyes were hard as she folded her arms across her chest.

Alisha bit back a sharp retort. Her face flushing with embarrassment and anger, she stood, pushed the chair back to its rightful place, and turned her back on her boss. She walked at a normal pace across the floor, her head high, refusing to give the woman the satisfaction of seeing her hurry.

She heard Robert's deep voice speaking in her wake, presumably to Brittany, but she couldn't make out the words. Bypassing her desk, she headed straight for the stairs and jogged down one floor. Finding Penny was as good a reason as any to avoid further confrontation with Brittany, and Alisha was fired up enough at the moment to say something she'd regret.

Entering the first-floor pod area, she immediately spotted strawberry-blonde hair cascading down a woman's back in gentle waves. *Penny*, she thought, striding over to her. She noticed as she approached that Penny had the CPT file open on her screen. *Walter must have called her too.*

Tapping the woman on the shoulder, she pulled a free chair closer with her other hand.

"Penny? I'm Alisha Carson," she introduced herself.

She saw the woman's shoulders stiffen as she very slowly turned around. Alisha took in a mass of freckles crossing a pale, oval face and lips drawn into a tight line. The pale blue eyes that met hers were not welcoming. If she had to guess, Penny was close to her age, but the harsh look on her face made her look older.

"Alisha." The tone was crisp.

"Did Walter call you too?" Alisha asked, nodding toward the screen.

"Yes. He did."

"I, uh, was hoping that you could get me up to speed on the account and the project?" Alisha said uncertainly, unsure of how to take the woman's hostility.

"I'm updating the project plan now," Penny replied. "You'll be able to see all my notes within ten to fifteen minutes."

"Oh, do you want to chat after I've reviewed them?"

"Not sure what we need to *chat* about." Her tone was close to a sneer, and there was no mistaking the heavy irony in the word "chat."

It took every ounce of Alisha's willpower not to recoil. "Well," she said as pleasantly as she could. "I thought perhaps we could strategize on how to best work together and with Walter? Being new to the account, I'd value your perspective."

Penny's eyes narrowed. "We'll see," she said enigmatically. "Read the notes and then call me if you think we need to talk." She spun her chair back around, effectively ending the conversation.

Alisha felt a hot flush climbing into her cheeks—again. Suppressing the urge to force the project manager to talk, she mutely pushed the chair back to the cube and squared her shoulders. Ignoring a few curious looks from coworkers in the area, she walked confidently toward the stairs with her back straight and head tall. All the while, she could feel waves of humiliation crashing over her.

*Why does she hate me? And Brittany too?* In the past, Alisha had been accustomed to having challenging relationships with other women. Her blonde good looks and bombshell figure made her very popular with the guys but had engendered a significant amount of tension with other women. Her friend Julie was one notable exception. However, in recent years, she had worked hard to maintain at least cordial relationships with her female coworkers. This blatant hostility was, frankly, a new experience in the workplace.

*Is this because I moved here from California? Or because of Liam?*

Unable to maintain her composure, she bypassed the stairs and headed to the first floor ladies' room instead. She pictured Brittany's stony stare as she pushed open the door. *No, I was talking to Robert then.* Alisha sank into one of two small, rather cushy chairs strategically placed near the entrance to the bathroom.

Understanding abruptly dawned. Oh. *This must be because of Dave, and what I did to him. There's no other explanation, is there?*

The door swung open, and two women entered the room, both laughing heartily. One of them was Penny. The laughter stopped abruptly when they spotted her, and both women gave her a wide berth as they made their way into separate stalls.

Alisha put suddenly icy hands on her flaming cheeks. *This is a nightmare. How am I going to do my job?*

Her interactions with Brittany had been bad enough, upsetting enough. But were her relationships with everyone else going to be worse? *Especially the women?*

For the first time, she grasped the enormity of the hole she had created for herself. Despite her reconciliation with Dave, his wife Sheryl, Robert, and even Elizabeth in Human Resources, her relationships with everyone else in the home office-and maybe the entire company-had sustained a lot more damage than she could possibly have imagined.

She wondered suddenly if her days at LSM were numbered. She could already feel her mother's disappointment and her father's disgust. *Oh God, I hope I don't have to move back to California and start all over.*

Horrified, she shot up out of the chair and rushed out of the restroom, anxious to get away before the two women emerged. She felt tears prick her eyes as she climbed the stairs. *I have no idea what to do to fix this. Or who to turn to for help.*

Dave and Robert were out of the question, clearly, and her boss appeared to be more of an adversary than a supporter. There was her friend Julie, but Julie was in California and didn't work for LSM. She would be sympathetic but hardly helpful.

*Who in the world can I turn to for help?*

For the life of her, the only name that she could conjure up to help her was the one person she had absolutely no right to ask.

# CHAPTER 7

# Help Is on the Way, Maybe

**Thursday, January 13**

"You have an appointment with your new executive coach at 4:00 p.m. tomorrow," the head of Human Resources said bluntly.

Sheryl Simmons' hazel eyes widened with shock. "What? What executive coach? I haven't hired—"

"No, the board has hired one for you," Janine cut in. Sheryl could hear the heavy irony in her voice even through the phone line.

"I don't understand," Sheryl said, pushing her bangs back from her face.

"The board has decided that you need an executive coach to help you assimilate to your new role," her friend explained.

"But I've been in the role for over three months now. I know it's not long, but still. Am I doing that terrible of a job?" Sheryl protested, her grip tightening on the phone receiver. She had been appointed as The Diamante's Chief Information Officer when her former boss decided to "retire" the previous fall, although Sheryl knew it had hardly been his decision at all. Despite the challenges her team had been having with the redesign of the company's customer portal, a high-profile project, Sheryl felt she was doing a good job. Although, she grudgingly acknowledged that she still had things to learn. Carl hadn't been able to stick around long enough to ease her into her new, high-stress, high-stakes position, and that was before she and Keisha discovered foul play regarding forces inside and around The Diamante.

Janine sighed. "Yes, but the board feels that you could use some guidance so that you can meet their expectations."

"Guidance?" she asked a little hotly. "How am I not meeting their expectations?" Then she paused. "Are they getting ready to fire me?" Sheryl asked, a tremor of fear creeping into her voice.

"No, of course not," Janine assured her.

"Then why? And who is this coach anyway?" she snapped, her fear morphing quickly back into frustration.

"John Hargrove," the CHRO (Chief Human Resources Officer) replied. "He's considered one of the top coaches in the financial services sector. He's known for grooming leaders to be successful executives and board members."

"Never heard of him," Sheryl said. "Was this Alex's idea?" It didn't seem like something her temporary friend and boss would suggest.

"No, of course not. Alex loves you. He thinks you're doing a great job."

"Let me guess. It's the new board member, Paul, the one who replaced Hank representing the evil investor group," Sheryl said with disgust. "How can just one board member have that much influence? Did the rest of the board even weigh in? I didn't, and I'm on the board."

Her comment was met with silence.

"No answer, Janine? Then, I'm right, damn it." Sheryl spun her chair around to face the windows that lined the back of her large office, the office that had once belonged to Carl. The investors who had put Paul on the board were the same ones who had driven her former boss and mentor from the company. *Am I next on their list?* she wondered.

"I can't answer that," Janine admitted, her tone conciliatory. "I just found out. John called me a few minutes ago to ask me—"

"What? How is that possible?" Sheryl's dismay quickly escalated into an uncharacteristic anger. "Didn't they go through Alex? He would have told both of us. Does he even know? Or is this John coaching him too? How did anyone know if I was even free to meet with this guy?" she sputtered. "And why a guy? Why not hire a female executive coach? But no, they only want to turn me into one of the guys. Right?"

"Sheryl, calm down," Janine said sharply. "I don't know what Alex knows. I haven't spoken to him. John only mentioned coaching you. In a way, you should be flattered that they are taking an interest in developing you."

"Flattered?" Sheryl huffed. "Well, that's one way of looking at it, I guess. It's better than kicking me out." Her gaze caught the tops of the trees swaying outside her window. Her heart felt like the bare, icy tree limbs she witnessed. *It seems that my supposed victory in November in defeating Layla is going to come with a big price tag.*

"You have too big a media profile for them to do that now," the CHRO reminded her. "You made a bit of a name for yourself at that press conference last month. After all, you were responsible for bringing down their guys."

"Which might be why they'd want to get rid of me. I embarrassed them."

"No," Janine said firmly. "Hank and Anthony embarrassed them. You made the company look good by exposing the fraud. You're a hero. Don't forget that." Janine's tone was now encouraging.

Pondering her friend's words, Sheryl watched a flurry of brown leaves fly across the open lawn below her second-floor window and guessed that the temperature had dropped. *Maybe it will snow tomorrow, and I won't have to meet with this guy.*

"Sheryl? Are you there?"

"Yeah, I'm here. Just thinking. I'm not sure what to make of this, but you're right. I need to keep an open mind. I don't know why this got to me so much," Sheryl admitted.

"It would have been nice if they had been more upfront about it," Janine noted with an edge of resentment. "I can see why you feel ambushed. I know I did when he called. After all, I've arranged for executive coaches on the rare occasions when they've been needed."

"Really? I didn't know that—although that makes more sense than board members hiring them."

"Yeah, it does, but there's not much we can do about it now," the CHRO agreed. "Let's just see how it plays out. John asked me for the company's coaching contract, which I sent over to him. Ultimately, he's answerable to me because I'll be the one who approves his fees."

"You? Why wouldn't I approve them? I'm his client, right?"

"No, the company is his client," Janine corrected.

Sheryl sat up straighter in her chair. "What? Does that mean he's going to report on what we talk about? That the board will know every-thing I'm telling him?"

"No. Your conversations are confidential. I already checked on that and reinforced it to him. Even with the company paying him, he has to respect your privacy." She paused. "However, he will be expected to report on your progress."

"My progress?" Sheryl's voice pitched up in disbelief again. "What does that even mean?"

"That's something that you'll have to work out with John. I'm sure much of your first meeting will be to work out the goals of the coaching, both from your perspective and the company's. I don't know what objectives the board gave him. You'll have to ask him that yourself."

Sighing, Sheryl leaned back again. "You're right, of course. I just wish someone had talked to me first. This doesn't feel good, and I don't trust that it's all that well-intentioned." It was her turn to pause, thinking back on all the negative things that had happened since these new investors had taken a significant stake in The Diamante. From mass layoffs to executive dismissals and unethical behavior and now this. *I wonder if I still belong here*, she thought, not for the first time recently.

"Me know in advance too."

Janine's indignant voice brought Sheryl back to the present.

"Yes, I know this is upsetting to you too, Janine," Sheryl assured her friend, catching the gist of the older woman's comments. "I'm going to call Alex and ask him what he knows. I'll call you back later," she finished decisively. "I need to know where Alex stands on all of this."

"Good idea. Let me know what he says."

Sheryl slowly lowered the receiver into its cradle. Instead of calling Alex, she opened her email to see if there was any written commu-nication from him, one of the board members, or this John person. There were several emails regarding the investigation into Hank and Anthony's alleged Ponzi scheme, and several more from Alex, but none that appeared to be related to the coach.

She started to minimize Outlook when a new email popped in. The sender was John Hargrove. She clicked it open.

> Dear Ms. Simmons,
>
> I hope that you've already been informed that I've been hired to coach you by the board of The Diamante. While I would have preferred to have talked with you before accepting this engagement, I understand that there is some urgency for our work to begin due to the recent unfortunate events and your increased public profile.
>
> I think it will be easier for me to go over the board's expectations for your coaching tomorrow, but I'd like you to consider your own goals in advance of our first meeting. While I was hired by the company, my primary concern is your career development and growth. I also want to assure you that our discussions will be 100 percent confidential, although I will outline for you what I will be required to report to your employer.
>
> I'm looking forward to meeting you tomorrow at 4:00 p.m. in your office.
>
> John

Somewhat mollified by its content, Sheryl forwarded the email to Janine without comment before reaching for the phone. *I'll reply after I talk to Alex.*

The acting company president answered on the first ring. "Sheryl, to what do I owe the pleasure?" he asked warmly.

Sheryl smiled at Alex's enthusiastic greeting. He had become a good friend even before his temporary promotion. She hoped that it would become permanent, although she still wasn't sure that Alex was cutthroat enough for these crazy investors.

"Hey Alex, how are you?"

"I'm hanging in there. Still spending way too much time with the SEC and FBI investigators," he replied, his tone turning grim.

"I know. Me too," she commiserated. The ongoing investigation was also consuming a lot of her time and that of several key members of her team, including Keisha Smith who was pivotal to the high-profile

Portal Project.

"But that's not why you called?" he guessed.

"No, I was wondering what you knew about this executive coach the so-called board has hired for me."

Alex groaned. "You're kidding, right?"

"No, I'm not kidding. You didn't know?"

"I knew some of the board members were talking about it. None of the internal ones, of course. Paul Haven asked me what I thought, and I told him emphatically that you didn't need one. I thought that was the end of it. Clearly, I was wrong."

"Wow. I wish you had given me a heads-up. I still don't know why Paul has the authority to do this in the name of the board when all the members weren't consulted."

"I'm sorry, Sheryl. I should have, but I really thought I had killed the idea. I didn't think Paul would go ahead and do it after what I told him. At least, I assume it was primarily Paul. How were you informed?"

"Well, Janine called me first, thankfully. Apparently, the coach called her to get the contracts signed. Then, I just got a short email from him. Our first meeting is tomorrow."

"Whoa, tomorrow? That's fast," Alex said incredulously, his voice reaching a pitch she had never heard from him.

"I know. Too fast. This guy's email implied that the board told him it was urgent. They told him that they're concerned about my new public profile," Sheryl replied with a trace of bitterness.

"Yeah, that's what they told me too. Ridiculous. You did such a great job with that press conference, even better than Joaquin," Alex concurred, referring to the company's Compliance Officer who had shared the stage with Sheryl and Alex when The Diamante had released the result of their internal investigation to the press a few weeks ago on December 17.

"Well, I guess they didn't listen," Sheryl said unnecessarily. "It looks like I have no choice except to see what this John Hargrove is like, or I'll appear hostile."

"Let me know if there are any problems. I'll get rid of him if you are in any way uncomfortable," Alex promised sincerely.

"Thanks, Alex. I will," Sheryl said gratefully, but she wondered if Alex had that power. The activist investors still appeared to be calling the shots through their proxy on the board, despite the illegal behavior of their previous board representatives. She had assumed that would make them back off a bit, but to her surprise and dismay, it had only seemed to make them more aggressive.

Pushing back her dark brown bangs, she turned back to her computer and opened a reply to Mr. Hargrove. *What are my goals for coaching?* she thought as she typed a cursory reply. *I've never thought about getting coaching. Prior to his sudden departure, Carl was always enough, and now I have Alex, Janine, and even Blake as sounding boards.*

Sheryl sent the email and turned her attention to her growing inbox, spending the next few hours working her way through a myriad of small problems and requests. But her concentration was off, which is why it took so much longer than normal.

*What do I want from this coach? Nothing? If he were truly on my side-not that I trust he will be-what areas do I want to grow?* The invitation from NAIT crossed her mind. *Is that something he could coach me on?* She laughed quietly. *I don't even know what a coach does!*

Of course, more sinister thoughts crept in as well. *Is he going to report everything I say to the board? And if so, precisely to whom on the board? After all, I'm on the board with eight other people.* The board was normally ten people, but they currently were down two as Todd and Anthony's spots had yet to be filled. *Only the outside board members? Only Paul? Or the investors that he represents directly? I'm going to have to watch every word, but then will he tell them I'm uncooperative?*

Her thoughts continued to swirl as she closed the latest email from Patrick, the director in charge of the Portal Project, without reading it. It was unlikely to be good news, and she couldn't handle any more today.

Disregarding the fact that it was not quite four o'clock, she shut down her computer and left the building, heading for home.

Whatever issue Patrick was bringing to her attention could wait. Her sanity couldn't.

# CHAPTER 8

# Truth and Consequences

**Thursday, January 13**

By nine o'clock the next morning, it was obvious to Gemma that the news of her departure had made the rounds at Viva! Not that there was much communication; there wasn't. And the messages she did get from her now former colleagues? *Well, they certainly aren't very supportive.* She grimaced. After all these years.

The one from her second-in-command was particularly distressing. Carithia Raleigh was her protégé and most ardent supporter—or had been. Gemma had been grooming her for years, recognizing both her talent and her fire. Today, that fire was directed at her.

Disappointed in you, girl.

Gemma had slumped in her chair at the kitchen table at those unexpected words. The text itself had arrived before 8:00 a.m., while she was finishing her coffee and enjoying the moments of unexpected leisure time. All the joy went out of her. Gemma guessed that Charles had given Carithia the news when she arrived at the office. *Did she get my job? I hope so, but wow!* She felt another pang in her chest. *That text really hurt.* Not knowing how to respond, Gemma simply had not.

A few other messages arrived just before 9:00 a.m., some from people in her group and some from others scattered around the organization. Enough to know that everyone knew. While not as blunt as Carithia, the message was more of the same. No one wished her well. No one.

Shocked that you left, from one of her team members.
Wow! I never thought you'd leave here, from a colleague in product development.

Atrium? Are you kidding?, from a colleague in accounting.

I'll miss you, from another team member. The friendliest message of the bunch.

Gemma scrolled through the messages again and again, still seated at the table, unable to move as the enormity of her decision hit her hard. Her auburn hair stuck up in spikes because of her repetitive head rubbing; her eyes, last night so bright and shiny with her kids, were now red with tears. These were people she had known, worked with, and trusted for a long time . . . even as friends.

Trust. The word sat heavily in her gut. *Have I truly betrayed their trust in me? What about me and my needs? Do they not trust me and my decisions?* Her heart skipped a beat, and her thoughts went off on a tangent. *Is this how Kevin felt when he "betrayed" me?* Her stomach churned and she attempted to reel in her wild thinking.

Just then, the ringing phone reclaimed her attention.

"Nathan! What's up?" It was a relief to focus on something else.

"I heard that Viva! let you go early," he said briskly.

"How did—never mind. I don't want to know," she said wearily.

"For someone who has just taken an amazing new job, you don't sound so good," he noted with what she considered a rare display of empathy, and she didn't like it. Not now.

"I'm not," Gemma snapped. "I didn't expect leaving Viva! to be this awful."

"It can sometimes be that way," Nathan said. "But Atrium is excited! They want you to start Monday now."

"Monday? But it's already Thursday!" she cried. "I can't be ready by Monday. How can *they* be ready by Monday?"

"If they can be ready, you can be ready," Nathan quipped, reverting to his normal pushy self.

"No, not Monday," Gemma said firmly, straightening in the chair. "A week from Monday. I'll have time to get things ready here by then."

"They won't be happy," he warned.

"Hey! It's still three full weeks earlier than they expected," she retorted. "Take it or leave it."

"You don't really mean that. They'll drop you like a hot potato with that kind of attitude."

Gemma's own fire was back in her voice. "Yes, I do mean it. You don't have to say it like that, but I'm not starting this Monday. Period."

"Okay, okay. I'll let them know," he soothed. "I'm sure they won't be *too* surprised. I'll send over the paperwork this afternoon, and from then on, you'll deal with them directly. Got it?"

"Yes, you're washing your hands of me," Gemma responded testily.

"No, no. You can call me if you need me. But I don't need to play middleman with the administrative stuff."

Gemma huffed, then realized that she was being too snippy. "Sorry. That makes sense."

He sighed. "I know this is a big deal, Gemma. You're right to take a little time to get your head around all of this. You'll need to have your sh*t together when you start there. You know that, right? So, take this time but be ready to go a week from Monday."

"So, you do have a heart," Gemma teased, relieved by his recognition of her feelings.

"I'll never admit to it," he laughed. "But seriously, call me if you need anything. I know I'm on retainer for them, but I take care of both sides as much as I can. After all, I may have something even better for you in the future."

"Thank you," she replied, this time sincerely. "I'll look forward to getting the paperwork."

"You bet."

Determinedly, Gemma got up, rinsed out her coffee cup, and marched to the home office. Located off the front foyer, it had always been Kevin's room. Now, it was another space for her to lay claim to. She was full of creative ideas for how to transform it from the edgy masculinity of its mirrored cabinets, dark gray walls, and slick, glass-topped desk to something she loved. *To start with, everything needs to go!*

Pulling a pad of paper from the built-in wall unit, she started making a list. If this office was going to be ready to start working in a week from Monday, she had a lot to do.

By the time KJ and Anna got home from school and their respective sport practices, Gemma had been to Lowe's, ordered new cabinet doors—thankfully, they were stock sizes—and picked out a lovely paint color. She had also ordered a new desk and chair, area rug, and comfortable-looking accent chair from West Elm. The deliveries were scheduled for Monday and Tuesday.

The activity kept her mind off the messages and lack of messages from her Viva! colleagues. There were several people that she had considered friends from whom she had not heard. Just thinking about Viva! made her stomach roil. She pushed the thoughts away.

"Mom!" Anna practically shouted, as she rushed in.

"Anna!"

"Mom, I made the varsity freestyle relay team! I beat Dina Masters in a swim off," her daughter said proudly, her dark blond hair still damp from the pool. "Can you believe it?"

"That's fantastic," Gemma crowed. "This is now happening for the meet tomorrow?"

"Yes! We're swimming against Monroe Academy. As you know, they're our biggest rival. Are you going to be there?" she asked hopefully. "Although it's at Monroe?"

"Yes, of course, I'll be there," Gemma assured her. "I don't start at Atrium until the week after next, so I plan to spend extra time with you and KJ until then."

"Awesome! I'm so excited. I can't wait to tell Kaitlin!" Anna practically bounced out of the room.

"Dinner in forty-five minutes," her mother called after her.

"Okay," echoed a distant reply. Anna was already in her room.

Gemma smiled, pleased that her daughter was happy. She wouldn't even have been able to think of going to Monroe tomorrow had she not agreed to the job move. *Yes, this is going to be a good thing,* she reminded herself. *Although driving an hour to see an afternoon swim meet is probably not going to be possible most of the time. Still, I can get to as many of the home meets as I can.*

Of course, she discovered an inevitable conflict with KJ's schedule, who had a big home basketball game at the same time tomorrow. He'd strode in shortly after his sister, and was now in a bluster. "But Mom, it's at home. You don't have to drive. You can see Anna's next home meet," he protested. "I'm going to be starting tomorrow."

Shaking her head, Gemma laughed. "But you always start," she scolded gently. "And I already promised Anna."

"But Mo-o-m," he grumbled.

"Anna's meet is earlier than your game. I'll try to get to the second half," she promised rashly.

His blue eyes, so like his father's, lit up. "Really? That's great. We're also playing Monroe, and they beat us earlier in the season. This game is important."

"I know. I'll try. Now, go get a shower," she ordered. "You stink!"

Making a face, he trudged out of the kitchen.

Gemma grinned and turned back to making dinner. Focusing on her children was the right thing, she told herself.

*But what about me?* a little voice chimed in. She shushed it.

# CHAPTER 9

# Whose Goals Count?

**Friday, January 14**

"The board feels that you prioritize people over profits," John Hargrove said solicitously.

Sheryl gasped, her spine straightening in outrage. Her hands slammed down on the wide arms of her maroon leather armchair.

"Hold on," she interjected sharply. "Let's get one thing straight right now. The *board* did not hire you, nor are you speaking for *the board*. Am I correct?" Her eyes were steel.

The executive coach had arrived at her office a mere ten minutes prior, knocking at her door promptly at 4:00 p.m. as scheduled, despite a light afternoon snowfall. They had settled in the comfortable seating area of her office. So far, he had done his best to put her at ease and establish himself as her coach with her best interest at heart. Until now.

Until she had asked the all-important question in her mind as to why he was there.

The older man dropped his gaze momentarily and cleared his throat. "Well, uh . . ." As he did, his head dipped, his full mane of gray hair slipping forward over his broad forehead. Sheryl was struck again by his unfortunate resemblance to Hank Turner, the former board member who had tormented and belittled her so openly. John had the same burly build, thick white eyebrows, and florid complexion. His appearance did not engender her trust. Nor had that last statement.

"If you have *any* hope of me trusting you, which is what you said earlier that you wanted, then you'd better answer truthfully," Sheryl warned in her best executive voice. "After all, I am on the board and was not consulted. The acting president and chairman of the board did not approve. You said the company is paying you, but I'm not even sure about that."

John's gray eyes shot up, and he looked at her with what appeared to be surprise before narrowing in a speculative manner.

"You're correct," he replied briskly. "I was hired by the Alpha Venture Capital Group."

"Specifically, Paul Haven," Sheryl stated firmly.

John nodded. "Yes, specifically Paul," he confirmed.

Some of the tension in Sheryl's body eased. *At least he's answering honestly.*

"How do you know Paul?"

"He's a former colleague from another company."

"So, you were an investment banker at some point?" Sheryl guessed, curious now. John hadn't mentioned that fact when he talked about his coaching credentials.

"I was," he affirmed. "But I had some health issues a while back and realized that I couldn't keep up that frenetic pace. I still had a lot to offer. Coaching was the next, logical step."

"So you can help others keep up that pace?" Sheryl quipped.

His face lost some of its harshness as he laughed. "No, not at all. Quite the opposite, in fact."

"Well, I can't imagine the companies your clients work for like that. Why would they pay you to have their executives work less?"

"Work-life balance, although a misunderstood and overused term, is more potent than people realize. Many of my clients pay me themselves, rather than go through their companies," he confessed. "But in the cases where the company pays, they've rarely been unhappy with the results."

"And when they are?" Sheryl asked, now intrigued in spite of herself. This was an aspect of coaching she hadn't considered.

"It's usually because the client decides he or she doesn't want to work at that place of business anymore." He shrugged and half-smiled.

"Yeah, I can see that being a bit of a problem."

"Let's get back to you," John suggested, his face turning serious again.

"Yes, and my tendency to prioritize people over profits," she responded sarcastically.

He held both hands up in self-defense. "Their words, not mine."

"Understood," Sheryl acknowledged with a nod. "But to be clear, I do not prioritize people over profits. That would be suicidal to any company. In my view, though, people are the means to profits. Taking their needs into consideration only makes good business sense—although I realize that not every executive believes that."

"Yes, and even fewer act on it," he paused and leaned forward in the matching maroon chair across from hers. "You did. I admire that."

Sheryl's hazel eyes widened. Both his tone and facial expression were full of sincerity. A warm glow spread through her chest at his praise. But just as quickly, that cynical little voice dampened the pleasure. *Does he mean that or is he just buttering me up?* This time, it was her eyes that narrowed.

"Thank you," she finally said. "I appreciate that." Then she paused. "I assume that you've been told about the meeting I held with the staff to honor their colleagues who had been laid off."

"Yes, I was told." John's voice was heavy with irony. "The memorial meeting."

"And that's why you were hired?"

"It's among the reasons," he confirmed, his tone once again frank, which she appreciated.

Sheryl tucked her hair behind her ear and gave him a long, assessing look. *How much do I share with him?* She let out a slow breath.

"Do you know that I've been invited to speak about that meeting and its outcome to the National Association of Information Technology in June? The keynote speech, I might add."

His eyebrows shot up. "I did not know that. That's impressive. Are you going to do it?"

"If Joaquim approves it."

John gave her a quizzical look, cocking his head slightly to the left.

"He's the compliance officer," Sheryl explained. "With the recent turmoil that has taken place inside The Diamante, I am sure you can appreciate that all communication must go through proper channels."

"Do you want to do it?" John asked. The question threw her a bit.

"Yes, I think I do," she said at last. "I feel very good about those meetings because there ended up being more than one of them—and I feel even better about the positive impact they had. Although I'll bet Paul didn't mention that part, did he?"

"Paul's not a total villain, you know," the coach chided gently. "He did say that there appeared to be an improvement in productivity following the meetings, but he was skeptical about that."

Sheryl raised one shoulder. "I don't know Paul that well. My experience with the previous representatives of Alpha wasn't a positive one, as you know. I could be making assumptions about Paul, but they aren't totally unfounded."

"So, what did you want to get out of our working together?" John asked, clearly finished with the topic of Alpha VC.

"I don't know," Sheryl replied frankly. "I've never considered hiring a coach before and don't know much about how you work."

"It's pretty simple. What are your career goals? Or your personal ones, for that matter? What do you want or need support to accomplish? Where are you stuck or confused? Where are you holding yourself back? Those are the kinds of questions that I can help you answer and then help you create a plan to get beyond the obstacles to reach your goals. Plus, I will help you identify where you might be sabotaging yourself."

Sheryl leaned back in her chair, her forehead wrinkling as she considered his words. "Those are some pretty heavy questions," she observed. "I'm not sure where I'd start to answer them." *And the personal ones have implications. Paul could use them against me. It's been done before . . .*

"Why don't we start with your leadership? You clearly have some idea of what kind of leader you want to be. You've already demonstrated that. But what do you want to do with your leadership? What do you want to accomplish?"

Sheryl thought about the speaking invitation and her desire to make an impact. "I want to make a positive difference," she answered slowly. "Although saying it out loud, it seems cliché. I want the company to be successful, and in the same breath, I also want the people who I work with to feel respected and fulfilled—not that a job can do that entirely, but it has the ability to be foundational." She thought for a moment. "I don't want people to be afraid of me, but I do want to be respected. I hate leaders who rule through fear. That's not leadership in my book."

He nodded. "And how do you feel you're doing with that?"

"It's tough," she admitted, "especially since Alpha has gotten involved. They appear to be all about the bottom line with little to no thought about the employees—or the long-term implications of their decisions. Right now, I feel like I'm holding my own, but barely."

"You managed to derail their candidate for CFO," he observed.

Her look hardened. "Another reason they want you to coach me? So that I support the 'right' candidates in the future?" She paused before turning the tables on him. "Why did you take this coaching assignment? Do you agree with Alpha about my leadership? What is *your* leadership philosophy?"

The coach started and shifted uneasily in his chair for just a moment. "My philosophy doesn't matter," he answered finally. "I'm here to help you define yours and help you make it effective."

"That doesn't answer my question about why you took the assignment. Is it just about money? Do you agree with Paul? What kind of leader do you think is *effective*?"

John cleared his throat. "To be honest—"

"We already agreed that is of utmost importance," she interjected.

"I took the job partially as a favor to Paul. To be fair, when he worked with me, I was probably a lot more like him and the others at Alpha than I am now. I don't know if he's aware of that. I discovered I like coaching women leaders, mostly because they tend to be introspective and quite concerned about truly being good leaders. Candidly, I was intrigued by what Paul told me about you because I don't see many people take the kind of risks you've taken, especially so early in their executive careers. You had the guts to stand up to Hank Turner, of all people, at your very first board meeting. How could I not be impressed by that?"

"The guys at Alpha clearly weren't," she replied dryly.

"I'd like to play a part in helping you to really live up to the potential you've shown so far, whether Alpha likes it or not."

"So, you're doing a bait and switch with them, not me?"

His bushy white eyebrows shot up again. "You don't pull any punches, do you?" He chuckled. "But no, I told Paul that I wouldn't bully or badger you into being something you're not. I also told him that there were different styles of leadership that were also very effective. He did concede that point, by the way."

Sheryl nodded briskly. "Fair enough."

"So, tell me more about this speech. What's the main point that you want to make?"

"That we should prioritize people over profits," she replied with a broad grin on her face.

After that, the conversation settled into a real discussion of what and how she could present during her keynote speech, if Joaquin agreed. Sheryl found John's advice to be sound and very helpful, and she was surprised when he indicated that their session was at an end.

"We'll meet from now on with Zoom. While I like to have our first meeting in person," John explained, "it's more practical to use video going forward for busy executives like yourself."

Together they settled on a regular schedule, subject to her availability, and Sheryl walked him out of the building, as per policy. Glancing at her watch as she briskly returned to her office, she marveled to find that it was nearly 5:30 p.m.. The session had obviously gone longer than their scheduled hour. *Was this typical for a first session?* she wondered.

Deciding that it was too late to dive back into her emails, she packed up her laptop and headed home. Plus, it was Friday, and her husband Dave might already be home from his latest business trip.

The normal thirty-minute drive from the outskirts of Piscataway to their home in Lebanon took closer to fifty minutes that evening. When she finally pulled her luxury sedan into the garage, she saw that Dave's SUV was there. Her stomach clenched. Lingering misgivings about her husband flashed across her mind, and she gripped the steering wheel tightly as she maneuvered into position and shut the car off.

*When are these doubts going to end?* she thought impatiently.

But the cynical voice answered quickly. *When you are sure you can trust him again . . . and you're not ready for that.*

Sighing, she slipped out of the vehicle and trudged into the house, stopping on the way to hang her coat in the mudroom. Dave, a warm smile on his handsome face, was waiting in the kitchen. His lean athletic form leaned against the granite counter; a glass of red wine already poured for her in his hand. She smiled inwardly at the gesture, but the doubts remained. *Is there something he is making up for now?* asked the taunting voice. She inwardly groaned. *God, I am tired of that insidious voice.*

"Hey, sweetheart," he greeted her, his dark brown eyes warm and sparkling with welcome. "I started dinner. Take this up with you while you change. It should be ready by the time you get back."

It wasn't unusual for him to cook when he was home. Not that either of them cooked on weeknights. Preparing the meal usually meant defrosting something they had already prepared the prior weekend and making a nutritious salad.

"Thank you, Dave. I appreciate that. It was a lousy drive home." She smiled as she took the glass from his hand, careful—still—not to touch him.

He leaned over for a quick kiss, but he had just grazed her cheek before she turned away and quickly headed upstairs to change. She felt what she suspected was a very worried gaze follow her out of the kitchen.

By the time she had changed into comfortable but stylish sweats, Dave was putting the food on the table. He held her chair—a new habit—and she sat down at the table, her back to the large island that dominated the spacious, cozy room. Eating at the table was also new, but she had to admit that it was more comfortable than eating at the island as well as easier to make eye contact and conversation, which they needed in order to reacquaint themselves with each other.

"How was your day?" Dave asked pleasantly. "Didn't you have your first session with your coach? How did it go?"

Sheryl's eyes widened. "I'm surprised you remembered that," she murmured.

"You told me last night when we talked," he reminded her.

"Yeah, well . . ." She left the rest of the sentence unsaid. "I guess it went okay. He admitted that he was hired by Alpha, although I put him on the spot. He seems sincere, but I'm still not sure I can fully trust him."

"Is he reporting back to Alpha on your progress?"

"He says he has to, although just in the broadest terms, which is good, or I wouldn't talk to him at all. In fact, we spent most of the time talking about my speech at the NAIT conference."

"What would make you trust him?" Dave asked, looking at her intently.

Sheryl knew instinctively that Dave wasn't really asking about John Hargrove. *He is asking about himself.* While she had been relieved and happy in the immediate aftermath of resolving his situation with Alisha, it had nearly cost him his career and certainly his relationship with Sheryl. She had quickly realized that her trust in her husband had cracked, if not completely broken. Since then, she had found it hard, particularly after the dust settled, to be as warm and open with him as she had always been in the past. She wanted to be, but something inside her was still holding her back.

"I don't know," she replied, sticking to the topic of the coach. "I guess it's going to take time. I really need to see what he's going to tell Alpha and/or Paul Haven. Apparently, he used to work with Paul. Maybe they are closer buddies than he let on."

"Time, huh," Dave said, running his hands through his light brown hair, a clear indication of his frustration with her answer.

"Yeah, time," Sheryl echoed, although this time her firm hazel eyes were filled with compassion.

They both turned to the chicken stew on their plates, eating in an uneasy silence. A silence that was broken moments later by Sheryl's ringing phone. She looked over her right shoulder at her purse, which was just visible, lying on the narrow bench in the mudroom.

Glancing at Dave, she settled back in her chair. Another new rule. No cell phones during dinner. The ringing subsided, and she went to take another bite, only to hear it start up again immediately. She looked anxiously toward the phone. So much had been going on at

The Diamonte. Was it an after-hours private update from Keisha? Had information been finally ferreted out about Todd or any of the others who pretended not to get caught red-handed?

Dave sighed. "Go."

Sheryl rose from the chair and hurried to the phone, reaching it just in time. Just as she swiped up to answer, she caught a glimpse of the caller's name and frowned.

"Hello," she answered cautiously.

"Sheryl, I'm sorry to bother you, but I have a problem. A really big problem, and I need your help."

# CHAPTER 10

# The Black Cloud Gets Darker

The black cloud that had plagued Alisha all week followed her home on Friday night. It was only seven o'clock when Alisha pushed open the door to her new condo, but she had no more energy for socializing or nightlife. Not that she knew anyone in New Jersey anyway, outside of the coworkers who hated her.

She tossed her keys and cell phone on the kitchen counter in disgust. Dropping her computer bag and coat on one of the two stools positioned next to it, she reached over and turned the phone, which she had deliberately and unusually turned off upon leaving the office, back on.

Her condo had an adjacent dining room, but the peninsula separating the kitchen from the den served as the only casual eating area. Not that there was a formal one yet—or anything filling that area for that matter. The dining room was empty. She groaned out loud and it echoed in the space.

*And it's obviously going to be empty for a while with that stupid bonus cap,* she thought bitterly.

Slipping off her black, high-heeled pumps, she padded down the short hallway to her bedroom, a large square room that thankfully *was* fully decorated. It was her sanctuary, a reminder of her more abundant past in sales in California and adorned in her favorite colors and items that quietly comforted her.

Alisha was exhausted from the whole day. She had gone straight from work to a local pub, hoping to meet some new people and distract herself with a drink or two from all the issues at work. The pub had been crowded and busy. While she had met a few people, no one had held her interest. So, she had left. Before 7:00 p.m. On a freaking Friday.

She sighed. The young woman knew it wasn't the pub crawlers. *It was me.* Unable to summon the least bit of energy and enthusiasm, she was pretty certain that her momentary drinking mates had been just as bored with her as she had been with them. Maybe more.

*I was way more fun in California!*

Just then, Alisha's phone rang. She jogged back to the kitchen and picked it up. A cold thrill of fear shot through her. *Brittany. What in the world does she want?* Especially this time of night.

"Hi Brittany," she said as cheerfully as she could muster.

Without preamble, Brittany burst in. "I need to know what you said to Walter Meeks, and I need to know now!" her boss all but shouted into the phone.

"About what?" Alisha asked, and she hated that her voice was shaking. Sliding down onto the floor, she leaned back against the cabinet.

"About the project. What else?" came the impatient response.

"I sent him an update on the project. Penny filled me in—but she wouldn't send an email to Walter, so I did."

"And you blamed all the project's problems on him and his team!" Brittany summarized furiously.

Alisha's mouth dropped open. She had a vision of the woman's tanned face turning purple with rage, and she could see it because Brittany's voice was just that angry.

"I didn't!" Alisha defended herself. "Although that's certainly true. I was as diplomatic as I could be, and I put the blame on both sides. I tactfully suggested—"

"You weren't tactful enough. Walter called me two hours ago, threatening to pull out of the whole project and not pay his bills." A shiver went down her spine at Brittany's words as she listened. "I've been trying to reach you for TWO HOURS," Brittany screeched. "JUST WHERE HAVE YOU BEEN?"

"I . . . I was at dinner, and it was crowded and loud so I turned off my phone. It was—"

"You are a salesperson, Alisha. You are to be in touch at *all* times, especially given the thin ice on which you are skating," Brittany ground out.

Alisha was shaking all over now. *I never turn my phone off, damn it. Why did I do that tonight?* She wrapped her free arm around herself and tried desperately to stop the tears from falling. Brittany's voice was as cold and hard as the tile floor under her bottom.

"I'll send you a copy of the email—"

"I already have it."

"I was tactful!" Alisha repeated again, trying to defend herself. "You can see that."

"You weren't tactful enough," Brittany countered sourly. "And Walter says that some of the things in here aren't even true."

"I only repeated what Penny put in the notes. She wouldn't—"

"Don't you dare blame Penny for your mistakes! Penny is a great project manager, one of the best we have."

"But Brittany, I'm not blaming her. I just—"

"I want you to fix this and fix it NOW. Walter is waiting for your apology—both in writing and via phone. He's probably home by now, but you can leave him a very, very respectful message. Tomorrow, you will review the project notes again and write another *correct* email that I will approve *before* you send it to Walter. Got it?" There was complete silence on the line as Brittany waited for the only answer she would accept.

Alisha paled. Even Liam, that chauvinistic jerk, had never talked to her like this! "Yes, Brittany," she said dutifully. "I could do it tonight."

"No, you need to do this when you're fresh," her boss ordered. "Get some sleep AFTER you apologize to Walter. Tell him that you want to take your time to review the project plan again and make sure that you have everything correct before you send him anything else. He'll be okay with that. We've already discussed it. You can call Penny if you have any questions tomorrow," Brittany said, her voice finally calmer and quieter but still brisk.

"Okay. Does Penny know that I may call her?" Alisha asked hesitantly. *The last thing I want to do is call Penny on a Saturday . . . or any day.*

"Yes, she does. I called her when I couldn't get a hold of you." Brittany paused. "She at least answered."

"I'm sorry, Brittany. It won't happen again," Alisha said quickly, mentally chastising herself again for turning off the phone. "I'll call

Walter right now, and I'll cc: you on my apology email. I'll take care of this. I will." Alisha prayed that the older woman couldn't hear the quaver in her voice.

"You'd better."

The line went dead. Alisha's hand dropped into her lap, still clutching the phone. *What now?* She felt hot tears trickle down her cheeks. This had never happened to her before. In the past, she was always on top of her accounts. *And I know I gave Walter the correct information—at least according to what Penny had put in the notes.*

Penny. Alisha shuddered, remembering the women's laughing at her in the ladies' room. A frisson of alarm suddenly went down her spine for the second time that night. Her whole body stiffening, she pressed her back against the cabinet. *What has Penny done? She wouldn't really . . .*

Horror filled Alisha's body from head to toe.

*No. No. No.*

She pushed herself up and grabbed her computer case, opening it as fast as she could and almost dropped it with her trembling hands. Catching it in time, she forced herself to breathe.

*Deal with Walter first*, she reminded herself as she anxiously waited for the laptop to boot up—feeling like she was going to throw up. She forced herself to open the customer relations management tool on her phone where she accessed Walter's contact information. Her heart racing, she pressed the call button.

The call went right to voicemail. Alisha breathed a huge sigh of relief as she listened to Walter's abrupt message. She left a short, but heartfelt message apologizing for the incorrect information she had sent him earlier and promising to take care of it directly in the morning. Bile rose in her throat as waves of humiliation crashed over her, but she kept a smile on her face and the tremor out of her voice during her apology. When she hung up, all she could think was, *please don't let him call back.*

Hands still trembling, Alisha typed an email with a similar sentiment. Her cheeks burned as she abased herself again, but now, anger was mixed with the humiliation. *I know I didn't misinterpret what Penny wrote. I know I didn't!* She typed quickly, suddenly determined to see if her growing suspicions were correct.

The email sent, Alisha opened the project management software. She pulled up Walter's project with a sense of dread. *Had Penny purposefully put false information in the file? But there would be a record of that, wouldn't there?* She wasn't sure what kind of tracking was in the database.

Scrolling down to the latest set of notes-the ones Penny had entered after talking to Alisha on Wednesday-she saw that Penny had taken her time, not providing the updates until late on Thursday, despite Walter's request for an immediate update. Alisha had had to dance around that already with Walter, but she thought she had appeased him.

The comprehensive update Alisha prepared for her client had been sent early this morning, Friday morning, because she had wanted to make sure that she had every fact correct and prove to Walter he could count on her. In fact, she had emphasized that in her email to him. *Which would partially explain why he's so mad. Late and bad news. Not a good combination.*

Finally, Alisha found the notes dated yesterday and approved by Penny. At first glance, it seemed like the notes were the same, and Alisha's shoulders started to relax.

*But then why?* She read the notes again. *No*, she realized, *something is different.* She wished she had the original notes. These were so similar and time-stamped . . .

*Wait. These are time-stamped today! Are these new notes?*

Squinting at the screen, Alisha went through each word carefully, and it finally dawned on her, seeing precisely what Penny had done. The facts were largely the same, but a number of carefully chosen key words had been changed. Just enough to completely throw someone off who was not deeply entrenched in the project. *Someone like me.*

Alisha reared back, forgetting she was on the kitchen stool, and just barely kept herself from falling. Her gut felt as tight and painful as if Penny had reached out and punched her. The air left her lungs in a whoosh. *What the hell? Why would she jeopardize an account like this? Just to hurt me?*

The screen blurred, and Alisha realized that her eyes were full of hot tears. In the moment, she couldn't tell if they were sad tears or angry ones. Maybe both. The fact that this woman, who didn't even know Alisha, would put a major account at risk to make her look bad was unbelievable. Even on her worst days with Liam and her desire for retribution, she would *never, ever* have considered doing something like this.

*And what can I do about it?* Alisha dropped her head and rubbed her shoulders, which were suddenly tight and very painful. She stared at the screen. Penny had added a few things to the bottom of the notes, nothing consequential, but enough to say she had just updated things today, not changed them.

*I can't accuse her anyway. Brittany would never believe me. Of course, if she reads these notes, she's not going to understand how in the world I got the email to Walter all wrong either.*

Alisha stared at the screen, willing the words to change back to the way they had been. She pressed her fingers against her eyelids as if she could hold back the tears.

*I'm screwed. Totally and utterly screwed.*

Slamming the laptop shut, she laughed harshly—almost hysterically shaking her head in reluctant admiration for Penny Forester. The woman had gotten her revenge for Alisha's treatment of Dave and Sheryl, even if neither of them had wanted it.

Alisha picked up her phone. *I need help, and I need it badly.*

Scrolling through her contact list, she selected a name and hit send. At the same time, she sent up a silent prayer that her call would be answered.

CHAPTER 11

# Loving Thine Enemies

The caller ID had not been mistaken, although Alisha's voice was raw and distorted with what seemed to be hysterical tears. Sheryl's hand tightened on her cell phone, fighting the desire to hang up this very second. She took a deep breath, then deliberately turned to face her husband.

"Alisha? What's going on?"

She watched Dave's eyes widen and his jaw drop open. *So, he didn't know*. Her shoulders relaxed momentarily as she listened.

"Everybody . . ." Sob. "Hates . . ." Hiccup. "Me," the younger woman wailed.

"Alisha, calm down. I can't understand you very well," Sheryl responded soothingly, her compassionate instincts taking over.

She slowly crossed back to the kitchen table and sank into her chair. She saw Dave's eyes, full of questions, follow her movements intently.

"I'm sorry . . ." Alisha sobbed again, "To bother you and Dave."

"Take a deep breath," Sheryl urged Alisha. "Slowly, breathe in. Good. Now, breathe out."

Sheryl nodded subconsciously as the breathing on the other end of the line deepened. She could still hear the occasional sob, but Alisha seemed to be getting control of herself.

"Okay," Sheryl said calmly. "Now, tell me what's going on." She heard another breath, then it all came in a rush.

"Oh, Sheryl, I'm so sorry to call you," blurted the young woman, "but I didn't know where else to turn! And you are so . . . so . . . wise."

"Well, I don't know about that," Sheryl said dryly.

"You are!" Alisha insisted. "I really need your, uh, wisdom now. I'm in such a big mess, and you helped me, well, you know."

"I helped you out of the mess you made with *my husband*?"

"Yeah, that. But it's so much worse now. I don't have any idea what to do!" Alisha's voice pitched up into a wail again.

"Okay, okay," Sheryl soothed, noticing that Dave was leaning in intently, as if trying to listen to Alisha as well as Sheryl. Despite herself, a spurt of anger shot through her, and she abruptly pushed back her chair, stood up, and swept out of the kitchen, shooting her husband a dirty look as she left. She stomped up the stairs, clutching the cell phone, relaxing a tiny bit only when she reached her office.

"Sheryl? Are you still there?"

"Yes, I am. Sorry. I wanted to go somewhere more private." Sheryl settled on the daybed, leaning back against the plump pillows and kicking off her house shoes.

"Oh. Okay." Alisha's voice was small and timid.

"So, you said something about everyone hating you?" Sheryl prompted. "At least that's what I think you said."

Alisha sobbed again. "Yes, yes. That's what I said. And they DO!"

"Tell me what happened," Sheryl heard herself say, astonished that she was actually comforting this young woman who had caused her so much heartache. But, she reminded herself, she had seen something of her younger self in Alisha in December, even in the midst of the terrible and false accusations she had made against Dave. She knew, even then, that Alisha was . . . *lost, not evil.*

Listening carefully as Alisha poured out the story of the last few weeks at LMS, Sheryl put herself in Alisha's shoes and could understand her distress. She actually felt great sympathy for her. At the same time, another side of her, a more malicious one, couldn't help but feel a little vindicated. Yes, she and Dave had decided not to punish Alisha, but apparently everyone else at LMS was doing it for them! Now she was the one who took a breath and recentered herself.

"Wow, that's unbelievable," Sheryl murmured as Alisha recounted the way the project manager had sabotaged the account. She pushed her bangs back and shifted uncomfortably, reminding herself that Penny's act wasn't illegal.

"It is unbelievable!" Alisha agreed. "But I don't have any proof. It's not like I took a screenshot of what she had written." A little fire crept into her voice. "Although I damn well will the next time."

"That does sound like a good idea, but it doesn't solve the problem now, does it?"

"No, it doesn't." Sheryl heard the defeat in Alisha's voice. "I think I'm going to have to quit, aren't I?"

Sheryl sighed. "Maybe. Maybe not. But you certainly have a big hole to climb out of. Although I have to admit that it's nice to hear that my husband is so well liked." There was a pause.

"Yeah, he is," Alisha said despondently. "He's such a nice guy."

"Alisha," Sheryl warned.

"I know. I know. But he is. That's just a fact."

"Hmph." *But is he really?* Sheryl shook her head to clear *that* thought.

"Anyway. I don't know what to do. Brittany is on my butt all the time, and now this with Penny. How can I get *them* to forgive me, like you did?" Alisha asked, a tremor in her voice, as if she didn't quite believe that Sheryl had forgiven her.

"I'm not a saint, Alisha," Sheryl protested. "And, well, forgiveness isn't always very straightforward."

"You haven't forgiven—"

"Yes, I've forgiven you, Alisha, but I haven't forgotten, and neither have your colleagues. Still, you apologized to me, profusely, and Dave. Have you apologized to Brittany or Penny or anyone else at LMS? You know you did your female colleagues a big disservice with your false accusations. They might be angry in Dave's defense, but did you ever think that there might be more to the whole picture than just that?"

"Uh, well, yes and no," Alisha mumbled. "I sort of didn't think that part through, totally, though I know you know that. I acted rashly."

Sheryl didn't respond, letting the younger woman ponder this new aspect of her ill-advised actions. She closed her hazel eyes and breathed deeply, settling deeper into the cushions as she willed her rigid body to relax.

"I guess I can see how they would be angry both at what I did to Dave and how my lying might cause other women not to be believed in the future. Maybe even the second one more," Alisha finally said. "Because that's worse, isn't it?"

"It is just as bad," Sheryl concurred, opening her eyes again.

"But how can I apologize? It's not like I can write the whole company an email and send it out!" Sheryl heard agony in Alisha's words as again, she started to cry.

"Why not?"

Sniff. "Why not?" Sob. "What?"

"Why not send a company-wide email?"

"What? Are you kidding? Maybe not everyone even knows about this. And I could absolutely humiliate myself like that!" Alisha snapped indignantly.

"Okay, maybe just the US-based staff," Sheryl said, ignoring the outburst.

"I'm *not* doing that!"

"What are you going to do then?"

Silence. Sheryl waited with surprising patience, focusing on keeping her own breath deep and even. She was slightly tempted to sit up and light a candle in the dark but couldn't find the energy. She grabbed the hand-knit blanket from the bottom of the daybed instead and pulled it over her legs.

"I don't know," the younger woman finally admitted.

"Well, frankly, I don't have any other ideas," Sheryl said briskly, although not unkindly. She suddenly wanted to get back to her half-eaten dinner, her patience with the conversation and this woman who had caused so much trouble at an end.

"I'll think about it," Alisha said sullenly. "I just hoped . . ."

"Yes? You hoped?"

"I hoped you'd have a magic answer."

"Ha! Well, I'm all out of those today," Sheryl replied, sitting up and swinging her legs down. She paused and softened her voice. "But Alisha. I am sorry. I know this isn't 100 percent your fault, but you are the one to bear the brunt of it. Unfortunately, that's the way of the world—still. Your boss did a number on you and you were innocent. Then you pulled a number on someone else. You are going to have to do something to fix this—to rebuild trust with your colleagues. And just time, while it *will* help, obviously isn't going to be enough in the environment you created."

"Rebuilding trust is hard," Alisha stated.

Sheryl thought about Dave. "Yes, it is," she agreed simply. "Yes, it is."

Alisha sighed. "Okay. Thank you for listening. I know, well, I know you don't have to, and I'm probably the last person you want to talk to. You are amazing, Sheryl, because you probably hate me as much as they do. I'll think about what you said. You're probably right, but . . ." Another sigh.

"Alisha, I don't hate you. Am I still angry at you and Dave? Yes. I am. But I understand you more than you realize. I told you a few weeks ago that you could call me if you were facing trouble, and I meant it. I know you're in a really hard place."

"Thank you. I, well, I'll think about what you said."

"Good, and, Alisha, let me know what you decide to do. I *am* interested," Sheryl said sincerely. "But now, I'm going to go finish my dinner."

Alisha laughed. "Whoops! I'm sorry again, and thank you, Sheryl." She paused. "Really. Thank you."

Sheryl heard the line go dead and chuckled, shaking her head in disbelief at the whole conversation. "I must be crazy," she said out loud, before sliding her feet into her shoes and heading back to the kitchen.

The first thing she noticed was that Dave's wine glass had been replaced with a tumbler filled with an amber liquid and ice. *Scotch*, she guessed, knowing his after-dinner preferences. He had moved from the table, his plate cleared, and was slouched on the large leather sofa in the adjacent great room, which was open to the kitchen. He threw her a disgruntled look as she walked in.

She returned his gaze steadily as she strolled by but didn't join him. Instead, she picked up her bowl of stew from the table and stuck it in the microwave. She turned and leaned against the counter while she waited for her food to reheat.

"You didn't have to leave the room," Dave said truculently after a moment of silence. His eyebrows were drawn together, deepening the vertical creases between them.

"I did," Sheryl said firmly. "It wasn't a conversation you needed to listen to."

"She's my colleague," he objected. "And my fri—"

Sheryl felt a sharp pain between her shoulder blades. "*Was* your friend," she shot back angrily, turning away to hide the sudden rush of tears. Thankfully, the microwave started beeping, and she retrieved her food.

She heard the swish of leather followed by Dave's heavy footsteps.

"I'm sorry," he whispered, touching her shoulder.

Resisting the urge to shrug it off, Sheryl turned.

"I didn't mean . . . I keep . . ." Dave huffed. "I'm screwing this up, aren't I?"

Seeing the glint of tears in his eyes, Sheryl softened. Compassion warred with anger as she pushed herself away from the counter and walked to the table. She sat down and put the blue linen napkin back on her lap.

Dave followed, sitting down next to her.

"Sheryl?"

"Yes, you keep screwing this up!" she replied tersely, without meeting his eyes.

"You know she's not really my friend anymore," he said decisively. He leaned back. "I just, well, I was just curious, damn it. Why in the world would she be calling *you*?"

Sheryl audibly blew out her breath. She put her spoon down and raised her hazel eyes to his dark brown ones. "Because I told her she could," she answered softly.

Her husband blinked. "You what?"

"I told her she could call me if she needed help," she explained.

"But why?" The creases on his forehead were back.

"Because she's lost, and honestly, I don't think she had a lot of good role models." She paused. "*Female* role models, especially, as well as male."

"Hmmm. I can see that," he agreed thoughtfully. "The other women seem to, um, avoid her."

Sheryl rolled her eyes. "Exactly."

"That's why she wanted to be friends with me and Robert," he breathed.

Another eye roll. "It's one of the reasons, I'm sure." Sheryl looked her husband squarely in the eyes. "But my question is why did you want to be friends with *her?*"

A red stain crept up Dave's neck and into his cheeks. "Well, she seemed so, uh, so . . . helpless. Like she needed me. She looked up to me."

"And that's appealing to you. A helpless woman?" Sheryl snapped, shaking her head in disgust.

"No, but . . ." Dave's voice trailed off as his eyes widened in what seemed to be surprise. "But, damn it, Sheryl, she respected me, asked me for advice. And you don't do that anymore!"

He nearly shouted the last sentence.

Sheryl sat there, stunned. She felt her mouth open, but no words came out. It was as if he had stolen the air from her lungs.

Dave abruptly pushed his chair back from the table and stood up. "The bottom line, Sheryl, is that you have *all* the answers. What in the world do you need me for?"

He turned and stalked from the room, his footsteps heavy and loud as he crossed the kitchen into the hallway. A moment later, she heard his office shut loudly and firmly.

*What in the world, indeed? What does he mean?* Shoulders slumping, Sheryl looked at the food on her plate and shoved it away. Her thoughts continued to swirl.

But the one question that came to her again and again was: *How is his behavior with Alisha suddenly all my fault?*

# CHAPTER 12

# Is This the Only Way Out?

Alisha resisted the urge to hurl her phone across the room. *Write an email to the whole company! Was the woman crazy?*

She respected Sheryl. Hell, Sheryl was the one who had saved her job when Elizabeth Curtis, LSM's head of Human Resources, had been ready to throw Alisha out on her ear in freezing, freaking December. But this? This suggestion was just nuts.

*Wasn't it?*

Grinding her teeth, Alisha paced back and forth across her new kitchen and empty dining room, all her pent-up anger now directed at Sheryl Simmons. *Dave's wife. The one who kept me from realizing all my dreams. The woman who stood between me and the love of my—*

She jerked to a stop, realizing just how ridiculous her spinning thoughts were. "Stop it," she said aloud. Shuffling across the open area to her living room space, she flopped onto the navy-blue sofa, which happened to be the only place to sit. Picking up her phone, she scrolled through her contacts, rejecting one after another as someone else she could call.

Pausing when her friend Julie's name popped up, Alisha frowned. *Julie is likely to agree with stupid Sheryl*, she thought, her finger hovering over the name. She stared at the phone, trying to conjure someone else she could talk to. She continued scrolling, until the phone suddenly vibrated in her hand. She looked closely at the screen in surprise.

*Julie. Of course.*

"Hello," Alisha answered huffily, annoyed that her friend had reached out first.

"I'm surprised you're home on a Friday evening," Julie replied cheerfully. "I didn't think I'd catch you. I haven't heard from you in a couple of weeks and wanted to hear how things are going at work. How's your new boss?"

Alisha growled.

"Whoa! That doesn't sound good!"

"It's not," Alisha ground out. "In fact, things could hardly be any worse." She launched into a lengthy description of how badly Brittany was treating her and the perfidy of her coworker Penny. "So, how's that for a great week?" she finished defiantly.

She heard a low whistle from Julie. "Man, oh, man, that's rough, Alisha. I'm sorry. That's pretty unbelievable—especially what Penny did."

The sympathy in Julie's voice undid her, and Alisha felt the tears begin to fall again.

"It's so unfair," she sobbed. "I'm just trying to do the right thing . . . and . . . well . . ."

"I know," Julie soothed. "I know all this has been hard on you."

Alisha knew that Julie meant more than just this particular situation. They had been friends for a long time. She knew about Alisha's old idiot boss, and she knew her dreams—or rather fantasies—about Dave Simmons, but more importantly, Julie knew about her friend's history with her father and stepbrothers.

"It's not fair," Alisha reiterated, stifling another sob.

"Alisha, life isn't fair. You know that," Julie chided gently. "When are you going to stop fighting that?"

"I'm not," Alisha retorted with a pout. She tugged the ponytail holder out of her hair and wrapped a length of blond hair around her fingers. Her blue eyes filled with tears—again.

"What are you going to do?" Julie asked softly.

"I don't know. Sheryl seems to think this is all my fault."

"Sheryl? As in Dave's wife Sheryl?" Julie's alto voice pitched high with incredulity. "When did you talk to her?

"Yeah, her. We talked a few minutes ago. I was desperate. I *am* desperate. I thought she might have some good advice since she kind of bailed me out with HR before."

"What did she say?" Julie sounded curious now.

"She said it was no wonder they were all treating me like this after what I did to Dave and that I should apologize," Alisha paused dramatically, "to the whole company!" she exclaimed, her tone reverberating with disgust. "Can you believe that? Like I'd send an email to the whole company. She's such a goody-two-shoes. I bet she'd do that if she screwed up. Not that she ever would."

Julie sighed. "Oh Alisha."

"Oh Alisha, what?"

"Well," Julie took a deep audible breath, "it's not really that bad an idea."

"WHAT? Not you too! God, I think you are as crazy as she is," Alisha snorted.

"Well, you *did* falsely accuse Dave. It kind of makes sense that people who like him want to defend him. You would, if the roles were reversed. Wouldn't you?"

Alisha twirled her hair some more, thinking of what she would do if some other woman falsely accused the man she knew to be so good. Her claws would have probably come out, but she wouldn't admit that to Julie.

"I know you're not a bad person, Alisha," Julie encouraged. "You would defend Dave. You wanted to defend him against Sheryl when you thought she was treating him badly. Didn't you?"

"Yeah, but I wouldn't have sabotaged a customer account."

"Of course not. But who knows what's on the rumor mill at LSM. You know how things get blown out of proportion. Penny and Brittany might think you did a lot worse things than you really did, although . . ."

"Although what I did was bad enough." Alisha flung herself back on the sofa so she was lying down, her head resting against the bright geometrical print accent pillow. "Maybe I should just quit and find another job. Move back to California. I could always live with my mother. She'd *love* that. And my dad could say 'I told you so' again and again and again."

"Alisha. It wouldn't be that bad."

"It would. You know it would. You know my parents. Mom would try to set me up with all her friends' sons and get me a job selling real estate, for God's sake."

Julie laughed.

"You know I'm right," Alisha insisted.

"Yeah. About your mom. I could see that," Julie admitted, still chuckling. "But I'm sure you could get a job with another tech company. Surely, LSM would give you a reference, but Alisha, is that really what you want to do?"

"I don't know what I want to do," Alisha replied sullenly. "But I know I don't want to send an email to everyone at LSM *apologizing* for my bad behavior. Geez!"

"Why don't you talk to the head of HR about it? What's her name? Elizabeth? After all, it was her staff member, Barbara, who created some of this problem. Maybe she could help you out."

Alisha snorted. "Like she's going to admit that someone in HR did something wrong!" she scoffed.

"Is Barbara still there?"

"Yeah, I think so," Alisha replied, pulling another pillow under her legs with her feet. "But I think she's doing something different now. Maybe benefits? I don't remember."

"Well, it might not be a bad idea to talk to Elizabeth. Tell her what Sheryl suggested and see what she thinks. Tell her you want to make amends in some way," Julie said firmly.

"Make amends? As if I haven't already done that with Dave and Sheryl?"

"Yes, you have, but you hurt more than just the two of them. The 'Me Too' movement was encouraging everyone to believe women making those kinds of accusations, but you lied. It makes it harder for people to listen during the vital times when women *aren't* lying," Julie said bluntly.

"Ugh, Sheryl implied something similar, but she wasn't as mean about it as you are."

Julie sighed again. "I'm not being mean, Alisha. It's about integrity and trust. You respect that about Sheryl, don't you? You said you did."

It was Alisha's turn to sigh deeply. "Yeah, I did. I do."

"Well, Sheryl gave you an idea—"

"It was actually my idea," Alisha broke in. "I just wasn't serious when I said it, but Sheryl jumped all over it."

"Terrific! It's a great idea, Alisha, and you should be proud of having it. Despite what happened with Dave, you are not without integrity. You know, you've always talked about how important trust is with your customers. That's why you would never do what Penny did, no matter the motivation."

"Oh my God. You sound just like Sheryl now. I can't stand it. I have to hang up," Alisha grumbled. The hair twirling intensified again. *Nothing like having your own words thrown back at you.*

Julie laughed out loud. "I'll take that as a compliment," she said happily. "But seriously. Think about it. It's really a good idea, but I would definitely talk to Elizabeth first."

"All right, all right, I'll think about it." Alisha rolled over, nearly falling off the sofa, even though it was a wide one. "But not now. I need to get some rest so I can fix this problem tomorrow, if I even can on a Saturday, and then try to do something to entertain myself this weekend." She paused, a new emotion welling in her eyes. "Damn it. I miss you, Julie."

"I miss you too, my friend. I'll let you go, but I'll check on you later this weekend. K?"

"Yeah, thanks. Talk to you later." Alisha tapped on the screen to end the call, then dropped the phone on the vinyl wood floor. She pulled one of the throw pillows over her head and groaned. *How did I get myself in this mess?*

But Julie's words continued to echo in Alisha's mind. *You are not without integrity.*

Maybe she had given up on herself as much as everyone else in the office seemed to. Maybe she had started buying into the narrative that she was the bad guy. *Not that what I did was right,* she scolded herself, *but maybe one—or two—bad things don't make a bad person.*

Something had to change, and it seemed like that something was herself. Brittany and Penny, and probably many others, had already convicted her. For what crimes, she wasn't sure because Julie was right about the company grapevine. Even in the California office, rumors from the home office had reached them regularly, and Alisha knew from experience they were often wildly exaggerated.

She rolled onto her back, covering her eyes with her forearm as she continued to wrestle with herself and what to do next. Going back to California would be the easiest thing—but was it the right thing? And writing an email to the whole company apologizing? *Damn it, that is just a really, really bad idea.* She huffed.

*Or is it?*

# CHAPTER 13

# Open Minds and Open Hearts

Gemma felt a bead of sweat roll down her cheek and wished she were anywhere but in this hot, humid indoor pool area. She raised her right hand to wipe the moisture away. She had forgotten just how hot it could get in this environment, even in the middle of the winter.

The sound of cheering diverted her attention. Her daughter's team had won another race. They were dominating opposition. Gemma grinned, but it was short-lived. She was happy for them, but she really, really wanted to go home. She was hot and tired, and the delayed start of the meet meant that she had not even had dinner, even though it was after 8:00 p.m. on a Friday evening.

She pulled her sticky sweater away from her stomach, wishing she had a fan. One of the other mothers scooted over to her. *Barbara? Carol? No. Ah yes, Rhonda.*

"You look miserable," Rhonda said. "I made the mistake of wearing jeans a few times last season." She shuddered. "Never again."

Gemma looked woefully at her dark wash jeans. "Yeah, this is tough. It wasn't this bad at the meet the other day."

The other woman, dressed in a light blouse and khakis shook her head. "No, it wasn't. They do a better job of controlling the temperature at our pool. Some of the other schools, well, not so much. I can tell you which ones are bad in advance, if you'd like."

Eyes widening with surprise, Gemma nodded. "That would be great! I don't know how much my schedule will allow me to get to away meets, but I'd love to know when not to wear jeans and a sweater."

"Are you starting a new job? My Emily said you might be," Rhonda probed gently. "Didn't you use to work in the city?"

"I did," Gemma confirmed briefly, not wanting to talk about Viva! "And I am starting a new job soon, working remotely, so I'll have more time to come to Anna's meets."

"That's great! Maybe we could carpool sometime."

Rhonda looked to be about her age, Gemma guessed, but she was at least twenty pounds overweight and wore way too much cheap makeup. Her eyeliner was drooping at the corner of her eyes and fanning out into her laugh lines. *But she seems friendly, more so than the other women who are just covertly staring at me.*

"Yeah, maybe. I really have to wait and see what kind of flexibility I have, but let me give you my number."

The bottle-blonde woman promptly produced her cell phone, opened the contacts app, and handed it to Gemma. She dutifully typed her number in and was rewarded with a big grin.

"Great. I'll touch base before the next meet. It's so nice that Emily and Anna—oh! They rhyme," she tittered, "are in the same class and on the team together."

"Mmm," Gemma agreed, wondering why Rhonda wasn't moving back to her own seat. Uncomfortably, she pulled at her sweater again. Then she stopped.

*This is why I changed jobs,* she reminded herself. *To spend time with Anna and KJ. To make new friends.* She shot a sidelong look at the plump woman next to her. *And to be open to new experiences.*

As Rhonda chattered away about the swim team and the back stories of all the girls, Gemma listened with half an ear, not sure she wanted what she was certain was gossip. She made what she hoped were appropriate *mmm's* and *ah's,* while trying to focus on the swimming and keep her mind off her discomfort.

Finally, the event was over. Anna had won all her races easily, including the relays. Gemma was so proud of her—and all the time she'd been putting into the sport. After enduring congratulations from Rhonda, Gemma eased away and headed toward her car. Anna would take the bus back, but Gemma would meet her at the school to take her home, preferably after obtaining something for dinner.

Her daughter's enthusiasm more than made up for Gemma's sticky clothes and growling stomach when she picked her up an hour later.

"Mom! Did you see? I won all my races, and I did a PR in the 200

IM. It was such a great meet. Did you love it?"

Gemma laughed softly. "Yes, Anna, I loved seeing you swim so well. I'm very proud of you because I know how hard you work at your swimming."

"Thanks, Mom! I'm so happy to have you there, but Mom, uh, did I see you sitting with Mrs. Conroy?"

"Conroy? Is that Rhonda's last name? I couldn't remember. Yes, she was nice enough to sit with me." There was a pause as Anna stared out the window, then glanced at her.

"Mom, you need to be careful with her. None of the other mothers like her or will sit with her. And Emily, her daughter, is such a loser. I'll tell you who to sit with next time."

"Anna!" Gemma retorted sharply, shocked at her daughter's attitude. "That's not nice. Emily may not be someone you prefer to hang out with, but to call her a loser? When have you become so judgmental?"

Her daughter's face flushed pink, making her look even prettier. "Mo-om! You know what I mean."

"I *don't* know what you mean. I know I taught you not to talk about people like that! How would you like someone to call you a loser?"

"But I'm not!" Anna exclaimed indignantly. "I'm one of the nicest people at school, even when other people aren't!"

"What? What does that mean?" Gemma had a sudden instinct that there was more to that statement.

"Nothing. I'm just nice, but that still doesn't mean that Emily isn't, uh, not as much fun to hang with," her daughter retorted, clearly on the verge of calling her teammate a loser again.

"That's fine. I'm not asking you to hang with her. I am asking you to treat her with respect, like you would anyone else. And Mrs. Conroy too."

"Oh Mom, you know what I mean. You saw Mrs. Conroy. She's a mess," Anna retorted with disgust.

"Anna!"

"I'm sorry, Mom, but you have no idea what goes on at school. I have to be so careful that—" Anna cut herself off.

"Careful about what?" Gemma probed.

"You know, my image. You always talk about how important managing my 'brand' is," the teenager shot back.

Gemma shot Anna a dark look, wishing she hadn't taught her daughter about personal branding, but turned her attention back to driving. Moments later, she pulled her late model SUV into the garage and shut off the engine. She turned to face the now sulking teenager.

"Anna, this is serious. I don't know anything about Emily, but her mother was very pleasant to me—more than the other mothers were, I might add. You don't have to be friends with Emily, but you do need to show her some respect. Every human being deserves that," she said firmly, although guiltily remembering her own judgmental thoughts about Rhonda Conroy. "We've always talked about keeping open minds and open hearts, even when we don't want to . . . or it's not a popular stance."

Hanging her head, Anna nodded. "I know, Mom, but the other girls—"

"Are not you, are not my daughter."

"Mo-om! Next you're going to ask me if the other girls jumped off a bridge, would I jump with them," Anna replied sarcastically.

"I'm glad you do listen to me sometimes," Gemma responded smugly. "Now, I don't know if Mrs. Conroy and I would ever be friends, but I can be polite and respectful to her. And I will. Of course, I'd like to get to know your friends' mothers too. It's something I hope I have more time for now."

Anna suddenly looked excited and horrified. "You're not going to become a helicopter mom, are you? I mean, I want you around more, but . . ."

Gemma laughed heartily, her shoulders shaking. "Oh my goodness, Anna! Of course not. I probably won't even be able to get to all your swim meets. I will be working, and it's such a big job I'm finding out. A really big job."

She watched her daughter's shoulders sag with relief. "Phew! That's good."

"Is there something that you're not telling me?" Gemma asked, her eyes narrowing with suspicion. "Something you don't *want* me to know?"

She thought about what Anna said about managing her brand. *Is there something more going on?* Her maternal instincts suddenly on alert.

It was Anna's turn to laugh, her green eyes sparkling with mirth. "Ha! Of course not, but I'm sixteen, you know. I need my space."

Gemma rolled her eyes, imitating the look that Anna often gave her. "Space. Oh boy, I've heard that before." She grabbed the handle and opened the car door. "But I'm starving, and you must be too. It's late. Let's eat. We can continue this conversation later, if we need to."

"Great idea, Mom! I am starved." Anna jumped out of the car and was in the house almost before her mother had time to move. Shaking her head, Gemma grabbed the food and followed at a more sedate pace but still moving briskly. The food in the bag, from her favorite Thai food, smelled too good to dawdle.

But she wondered as she walked into the kitchen: *What do I need to be keeping an open mind about?* Because she knew from experience that the lessons she taught Anna and KJ were often ones that she needed to learn or relearn herself.

# CHAPTER 14

# Double, Double, Toil, and Trouble
## –from Shakespeare's *MacBeth*

**Saturday, January 15**

Dave was gone from the bed when Sheryl woke up the next morning. An ominous silence suggested he was gone from the house as well. Groaning, she pulled herself up, grabbing a robe and hoping that he had made coffee before he left. She needed it, after the restless night she'd had.

They hadn't spoken again before retiring, although he had pulled her close, spoon-style, when he did lie down. She had resisted the urge to pull away, allowing herself to lean against his warm, athletic body. But she had not relaxed, even when his breathing lengthened and he slept.

*Coffee first*, she thought, already alarmed by her whirling thoughts. *What did he mean by saying that I have all the answers? He knows I don't!*

The rich aroma of coffee greeted Sheryl when she entered the kitchen. Pouring herself a cup from the insulated carafe and adding a dollop of cream, she shuffled to the small mudroom separating the kitchen from the garage. Dave's jacket and running shoes were gone, which meant that he had headed out for his morning run despite the frigid weather and risk of black ice. *Crazy man.*

She wandered back into the kitchen, indecisive and unmoored. Her stomach roiled at the thought of food. *As if all the drama at work isn't enough.* She rolled her shoulders, unsuccessfully trying to ease the tension. *Maybe I should work out too.* But she rejected that thought immediately with an outward sigh. *I don't have the energy.*

Pacing back and forth between the kitchen and the large open family room, she settled at the French doors overlooking the backyard. Watching the barren trees at the edge of their property sway in the wind, she felt buffeted herself. She and Dave had been navigating a minefield for months, and, although there were moments of calm and connection, they didn't seem to be able to get back on stable ground. Alisha continued to stand between them.

*But it's not her, is it?* Sheryl thought as she went back over the conversation from the previous evening for what seemed like the thousandth time. *Dave seems to think it's something I'm lacking.*

As if conjured by her thoughts, Dave burst through the mudroom door, breathing heavily, his nose and cheeks bright red from the cold. He pulled an orange stocking cap from his head, leaving his dark brown hair in disarray. He took a long pull from his water bottle before setting it on the counter.

"Good morning," he said gruffly when he spotted her.

Flushing, she muttered a response.

He poured a cup of coffee for himself, running his hand through his hair, which did nothing to smooth it. Silence permeated the air for several minutes. Finally, Dave broke it.

"Do you want to go out to breakfast?"

Sheryl looked up, startled. They used to go out to breakfast on Saturday mornings, a long time ago. It had been kind of a connection ritual, romantic even.

"To Katrina's?" She named the little French-inspired café in neighboring Clinton, which sat on the south branch of the Raritan River.

"Yeah. I need to get showered first."

"Okay," she agreed reluctantly, wondering if she was ready to talk.

He waved his coffee cup in her direction. "We don't have to. It was just a suggestion," he said defensively.

"No, it's a good suggestion," she forced herself to say despite her reluctance. "But I need to get dressed too."

"Half an hour?"

She glanced at her watch. Something told her that she needed to process first, but he would be hungry after his run. "Sure," she conceded.

He nodded and strode out of the kitchen. She heard his footsteps on the stairs.

Although she knew she needed to get ready herself, she felt pulled toward her small office in an upstairs bedroom, the room they had always thought would be perfect for a nursery. She remembered Dave's cutting words from a month ago about wanting children—with Alisha—and shuddered. Still, she continued up the stairs and into the warm and inviting room.

The gentle smell of lavender wrapped around her as she entered the room, and she sank onto the daybed and pulled her journal out of the end table drawer. Opening, her eyes widened when she noticed that she hadn't written anything since New Year's Day. Her journal was one of her anchors. *No wonder I am so out of sorts.*

Knowing she didn't have much time, she picked up her pen. Nothing came to her to write. It all seemed so overwhelming, she didn't know where to begin with all her swirling thoughts. Dave. John, the new coach. Paul Haven. Even the invitation to speak. The pen and journal dropped in her lap.

She closed her eyes, forcing herself to breathe deeply and from her belly. *Focus on the sensation of the breath,* she told herself falling back on years of practice to center herself and clear her mind. She realized that she hadn't been meditating any more than she had been writing in her journal. She brought her attention back to her breath and felt her body relax.

"Sheryl?" Dave's voice penetrated her semi-conscious state. She realized by his tone and volume that it wasn't the first time he had called her name. She didn't even have time to open her eyes.

"Sheryl!" His voice was sharp now with an undertone of irritation.

Her eyes fluttered open quickly. He stood in the doorway to her office, one hand braced against the doorframe, twin deep creases between his eyes.

"You're not ready to go," Dave nearly growled.

"I'm . . . uh, I'm sorry. I sat down for a minute to relax while you were in the bathroom, and I guess I slipped into a deeper meditation than I planned." Sheryl blinked again, rising to her feet.

"Well, I'm ready to go. I'll wait for you downstairs," her husband said, the corners of his mouth turned down. He turned on his heel and walked heavily down the hallway.

"I'll be quick," she called after him, moving lightly toward the master bedroom. Her body felt freer and looser than it had in weeks. Even Dave's irritation didn't lessen her state of calm. *Wow. I need to get back to meditating more often.*

Five minutes later, she was downstairs, hair and teeth brushed, dressed in wide-leg jeans and a marbled, mauve sweater. She smiled, pulling her coat on even though Dave glowered at her.

"I'm ready," she announced cheerfully.

He grunted and opened the door to the garage. "Let's go then."

Fifteen silent minutes later, they were seated at a window table with a white tablecloth and bright blue napkins. Sheryl looked out at the ice forming a pristine border between the dark water and rocky shoreline. It seemed a good metaphor for the icy boundary that lay between her and her husband.

A young woman poured fragrant coffee and took their order. French toast for Dave, an omelet for her. Dave picked up his mug with two hands and drank deeply, regarding her solemnly over the rim.

"When are you going to forgive me?" he asked bluntly. "I feel like you're half in, half out of this marriage, and I'm waiting for your verdict." He leaned in, his voice low but full of meaning. "I thought we had everything sorted out in December, but since then you've been . . . well, cold. Or cool, maybe." He leaned back out, awaiting her response.

Stung, she sipped her own coffee, stalling for time. She knew he was right, but she also didn't know the answer to his question, even for herself.

"I don't know," she finally said quietly. "Trust is a hard thing, especially after it's been broken."

The creases between Dave's eyebrows deepened and his lips tightened. "But I didn't betray your trust," he protested, suddenly on the defensive. "I didn't do anything wrong with Alisha, well, not really."

Sheryl felt her heart contract. She took a deep breath, consciously expanding her belly. "Alisha thought you were leaving me for her," she countered, keeping her tone neutral.

Dave pulled back as if he had been struck. "Yes, but I can't help what she thought!" he shot back.

"No, but she didn't pull those ideas out of thin air." Again, her tone was quiet and matter of fact, as she desperately held onto the sense of calm she had achieved with her meditation.

The waitress brought their food at that moment, and Dave, seeming grateful for the interruption, dug into his French toast. Sheryl watched him for a moment and then started picking at her own food, deliberately tasting each bite and taking deep breaths in between. After a few moments, she felt her heart rate ease again, and settle into a slow, steady rhythm.

She looked up to find Dave watching her. "What are you doing?" he asked abruptly.

Sheryl shrugged. "Consciously calming down again. The meditation this morning really helped, but it's hard to maintain that calm when we are having these difficult conversations."

"I don't know why they have to be difficult or even why we're having them," he stated bluntly, his eyes boring into hers accusingly. "We've talked about all this. I've apologized. It's over and done! Why can't you let it go?"

Resisting the urge to slam her fork on the table, Sheryl set it carefully on her plate, but now her hand was shaking. "Because I don't understand why this happened or what needs to change, and until I understand, I don't know how to trust you again."

Dave's face reddened and let out an explosive breath. "Geez, Sheryl. We've been married for over twenty-five years. It's not like I cheated on you. I didn't sleep with Alisha, and most of what happened was in her mind. So, I flirted with her more than I should have. So what? I'm a guy. I'm not dead yet. But when it came down to the nuts and bolts of the situation, I backed off. At least she listened to me, took my advice, treated me with respect. You're so busy crusading at your company that you didn't. I'm not even sure what you want from me anymore. You seem to have it all together. Your damn meditation is clearly more important to you than I am. You couldn't even get ready for breakfast this morning."

His voice was accusatory, and he didn't even bother to keep it low now, she noticed, flushing.

"I'm sick of being treated like I've committed some big crime. I didn't, and I'm not going to apologize to you anymore. If you can't trust me after all these years, that's your problem." Glaring at her, he was the one who slammed his fork on the table and stomped out of the restaurant.

Silence fell over the room as the other diners openly gaped at her. An older couple, seated two tables away, smiled gently at her, the woman subtly nodding as if she understood the humiliation that Sheryl was feeling. Two men having coffee at the counter, on the other hand, gave her a scathing look. Sheryl swallowed hard, picked up her coffee mug, and forced herself not to sink under the small table.

After a moment, the low hum of conversation and clinking of silverware resumed as the other diners returned to their meals and she just . . . kept . . . breathing, waiting for Dave. The server appeared and freshened Sheryl's coffee with a sympathetic smile.

Murmuring a muted thank you, Sheryl looked down at her omelet, which she had barely touched. Her stomach rebelled at the thought of eating more. "I'll take a box for this, please," she said softly.

The waitress shot a questioning glance at Dave's half-eaten food. Sheryl nodded, and the server slipped the check onto the table before turning away. Cheeks now flaming, Sheryl pulled out her purse and counted out the cash to cover the bill with a generous tip.

Dave still did not come back.

Returning, the young woman deftly boxed up both meals and scooped up the payment with a brief smile. Sheryl gathered her belongings up as quickly as she could and hurried out, conscious of the eyes following her. She wasn't sure the last time she had been so embarrassed.

*And Dave wants me to trust him.*

But even as she exited the restaurant, his words reverberated in her mind: "I don't know what you want from me anymore." *What do I want? What will make this better?* The sad thing was that Sheryl had no idea. *How do we rebuild the trust in our relationship? Because there's clearly distrust on both sides now.*

Dave was waiting in his large, black SUV, the engine running, when Sheryl made her way to the parking lot. She stowed the food in the back seat and pulled herself into the leather passenger seat. Dave put the vehicle in motion the minute she fastened her seatbelt. He neither looked at her or spoke.

The pit in Sheryl's stomach grew.

"Dave . . ." she began tentatively.

"I'm not talking about this anymore," he declared, not even glancing her way.

"But we have to talk," she protested. "How else—"

"Sheryl, STOP." His gloveless hands clenched the steering wheel so hard that his knuckles were white.

"But—"

"No," Dave ground out through gritted teeth.

Sheryl tightened her jaw to hold back a sharp retort. There was no sense trying to talk to Dave when he was like this. She swallowed hard as tears of frustration and anger started to fill her eyes, and she deliberately turned to look out the window.

The rest of the drive over the snowy terrain was accomplished in silence, even as Dave pushed the limits of the large vehicle. Sheryl sagged with relief when they safely pulled into the garage. Dave slammed the door as he lunged out of the car and stalked into the house, leaving her to follow.

Sighing, she gathered the food containers and walked slowly through the mudroom into the kitchen. Her husband was nowhere to be seen. He was in his office, she guessed.

Biting her lip, she slid off her coat and placed the food containers into the refrigerator. Noticing that the coffee pot, which Dave had turned off before their venture, was still half full, she poured a full cup and heated it in the microwave. Blinking back tears again, she crossed the open space to the family room and plopped into her favorite corner of the couch.

*What now?* She wondered, knowing from experience that Dave was unlikely to re-engage for hours. Not that she was anxious to re-engage herself. *How did we get into this mess? And how do we get out of it?* A disturbing thought niggled its way into her mind. *Or do we?*

For the first time, Sheryl had to face the fact that her marriage was again in real trouble. Worse, she hadn't the foggiest idea how to fix it.

# CHAPTER 15

# The First Step to Restitution—or Not

**Monday, January 17**

Dressed uncharacteristically in a dark navy suit and pale pink blouse, Alisha hurriedly dropped her belongings in what had become her "usual" cubicle on Monday morning. Before she could change her mind—again—she determinedly marched into the adjacent wing to Elizabeth Curtis' office. After spending much of the weekend debating her options—and after she had managed to calm both Brittany and Walter down—she had come to a terrifying conclusion: Sheryl was right.

Alisha truly couldn't afford to wait for people to "forgive and forget" what she had done. Elizabeth was her first stop to rectify the situation—if indeed, she could.

A stone-faced admin greeted Alisha coldly when she walked into the secluded suite that housed the Human Resource department.

"May I see Elizabeth, please?" Alisha asked pleasantly, masking the frisson of fear the woman's attitude invoked.

"I'll see if she's available," came the stiff reply. The woman, whose name Alisha couldn't remember to save her life, marched off in the direction of Elizabeth's office.

Moments later, Elizabeth herself walked over the reception desk and greeted her warmly. "Alisha! It's nice to see you. Carol said you need to speak with me?"

"Yes, please," Alisha replied politely, a little surprised at the greeting. She hadn't been treated this way by anyone for weeks. "Uh, I need your advice," she admitted to Elizabeth.

The older woman's smooth forehead wrinkled in an inquisitive look, but she waved Alisha to follow her and strode back into her office, despite her narrow pencil skirt and high-heeled pumps. Sitting down in a comfortable-looking chair at the end of her desk, Elizabeth indicated that Alisha should take the matching one.

Feeling welcome, Alisha unbuttoned her suit jacket and leaned back in the chair, as she glanced around the office, noticing the variety of plants and colorful artwork that gave warmth to the otherwise sterile room.

"So, how can I help?" Elizabeth asked, her brown eyes warm and curious.

"Things have been really bad for me since word got out about what I said about Dave Simmons," Alisha said bluntly, tugging on the end of her blonde ponytail.

Elizabeth frowned. "I see," she said. "That's very unfortunate, but the grapevine is always alive and well here, despite our best efforts."

"Everyone hates me!" Alisha blurted, her voice rising in distress. She immediately flinched. *Damn, I didn't mean to say that.*

Rather than disputing Alisha's words, Elizabeth pursed her lips and tilted her head with compassion. "I'm sure it seems that way," she murmured.

Clearing her throat, Alisha continued in a more modulated tone. "It more than seems that way. There are some people, and no, I won't say whom, who are actively sabotaging things for me."

Elizabeth sat up straight. "That's unacceptable!" she said. "You need to tell me who. That has to stop."

Alisha snorted softly. "I don't think that will help, Elizabeth, although I appreciate the sentiment. I think I need to take a more proactive approach in making, um, amends, I guess." There was no mistaking the thoughtful look from the woman across from her.

"What do you have in mind?"

"Well, I was thinking that it might be a good idea to apologize publicly for what I did. I mean everyone knows about it already. Maybe I just need to come clean and admit that I messed up and that I'm sorry."

Pursing her lips, Elizabeth steepled her hands in front of her chest and looked thoughtfully at Alisha for a long moment.

Alisha shifted uncomfortably at the older woman's gaze but didn't drop her blue eyes.

Finally, the Human Resources executive smoothed her nearly black hair, which was pulled sleekly back from her narrow face, and let out a long breath. "I can't say that I've ever seen anyone do that before," she observed. "But it's not a bad idea, although it's not without risk. It could backfire." She paused. "Why are you willing to put yourself through that?"

Having asked herself that exact question all weekend, Alisha answered quickly, "I value my job at LMS. Other than Liam, nearly everyone else has been great to work with, and I really like what I do. I have been looking forward to the challenges of moving to the East Coast, and I want a fair chance to be successful here. Right now, I don't think I'll have that chance unless I do something."

"Because of whatever this mysterious person did?"

"In part," Alisha conceded. "But it's more than just that."

"Brittany Mollier?" Elizabeth guessed.

Alisha nodded hesitantly. "But I don't want you to talk to her!"

"I understand," Elizabeth said slowly, pursing her lips again. "And I promise I won't. Brittany has always had a strong sense of right and wrong. I admire that about her, but I also know it can be a shortcoming when one sees the world only in black and white."

Her shoulders dropping in relief, Alisha leaned forward. "Thank you," she said simply. "But will you help me with the email? I thought maybe it should just go to the US-based staff? I mean, the people in the overseas offices don't need to be involved, do they?"

Elizabeth chuckled. "Well, I suspect many of them have heard the story anyway," she noted. "But they can get your apology via the grapevine too."

"Ugh," Alisha grimaced. "So, how does this kind of thing work?"

"I've never done it before, but I can give you access to the email list for the US-based employees for this one time." Elizabeth wrote one word on a notepad, then looked up. "And I think I'd like to see a draft of the email before you send it, if you don't mind. Both for my peace of mind and to make sure that you are presented in the best light possible. I'm aware of the role that Barbara Montgomery played in your accusations and feel somewhat responsible. I do want to help you make things right."

"Oh, thank you, Elizabeth!" Alisha nearly gushed in relief, realizing she had an unlikely ally in this. "That would be great. I have some ideas, but I'd truly appreciate your feedback."

"Okay then, we have a plan," the older woman said, rising gracefully. "I admire you taking responsibility, Alisha, and I'm happy to support that. I'll look for your email later this morning?"

"Yes, I have a rough draft already written," Alisha confirmed, the tension in her shoulders significantly less than it had been. "I'll go through it again and send it to you in a little while."

"Good. In the meantime, I'll think this through so that I can give you the best possible feedback," Elizabeth said with an encouraging smile. "Let's see if we can clear things up for you."

"I'm so grateful for your help," Alisha reiterated before turning to almost bouncing out of the office, feeling hopeful for the first time in weeks.

Brittany, in a stunning mauve silk dress, was waiting for her when she arrived back at her chosen cubicle for the day, her bejeweled arms crossed and a scowl on her face. "Where have you been?" she demanded.

Alisha felt her shoulders sag. "I needed to see Elizabeth Curtis about something," she replied calmly, despite the heat rising in her face.

"You had better not be telling lies about me or Penny!" her boss snapped, her scowl darkening. She leaned toward Alisha, nearly baring her teeth as she did so. "If you can't take the heat of this job, then you can just take yourself right back to California."

Rage fought with humiliation, even as tears filled Alisha's eyes, and she bit her lip. "It's not like that," she protested quickly, hating how her voice sounded like a whiny little girl's.

"It better not be," Brittany snarled, a dark flush on her perpetually tanned face. "You've caused enough trouble around her with your prima donna attitude. I don't care why you needed to see Elizabeth. You need to be at your desk working. Now, what's the status with Walter? Have you talked to him this morning? We need to get out to see him today, tomorrow at the latest."

"Brittany, it's only 8:45 a.m.!" Alisha cried, holding up her hands in self-defense. "No, I haven't talked to him since Saturday, but I will. I told him I'd call later this morning, after he's had a chance to review things with his team. I'll make an appointment to see him then. If he wants to."

"Don't give him an opportunity to say no to the appointment," Brittany ordered sharply, "and I'm going with you. I've cleared my schedule through the end of the day tomorrow." With that, Alisha's boss turned on her very high stiletto heel and clomped across the floor to a cubicle as far away from Alisha's as it could be, although Alisha noticed, while still having a clear view of what she was doing.

Silently sighing, Alisha pulled off her suit jacket, draped it on the back of her chair, and flopped into it. All the hopefulness she had felt with Elizabeth had evaporated under her boss's attack. *Brittany's never going to forgive me or believe that I don't usually lie, no matter what email I send. Maybe I do need to go back to California.*

But the specter of her father's disapproving face and her half-brother's jeering ones made that option seem just as unpalatable as dealing with Brittany. She blinked back hot tears that showed up, unbidden for the second time that day. *Stop it with the damn emotions! The last thing I need is mascara running down my face.*

Squaring her shoulders, she turned to her laptop, which was connected to a large, stationary monitor, and quickly pulled up the email she had written. In light of Brittany's latest assault, her accountable email seemed weak and mewling. A shot of anger went through her as she remembered Elizabeth's words about Barbara Montgomery. The Human Resources staff member *had* been the one who had twisted Alisha's story about her confrontation with Dave Simmons that had led to Alisha's allegations against him. *False accusations*, to put the matter bluntly. Alisha knew in her heart that she wouldn't have done that without Barbara's encouragement, but the older woman, who had to be in her fifties, had seemed so offended on Alisha's behalf that Alisha herself had bought into the fact that Dave was in the wrong.

*That doesn't justify you lying*, Alisha reminded herself sternly. *Being swept up in Barbara's drama doesn't excuse you for taking the steps to actually file a complaint against Dave.* She sighed, tugging on her ponytail. Her friend Julie would be so proud of her. Taking a breath, she looked at the email and went to work strengthening the language. She resisted the temptation to throw Barbara under the bus by naming her complicity, although a part of her really wanted to. Her more rational side prevailed. *I'm afraid it will dilute the message.*

Scanning the document one more time and addressing it to Elizabeth, she clicked send. The gentle swoosh sound told her the email was on its way. Cognizant of Brittany's watchful eyes, she pulled up the CRM program and went back to the task of calling the important customers in her new territory. But her stomach continued to be in knots as she awaited Elizabeth's reply.

About an hour later, Alisha had just hung up from making an appointment with a greatly mollified Walter when she saw Elizabeth's response pop into her inbox. Glancing around to make sure no one was looking over her shoulder, she eagerly opened the email.

> Alisha, Great job with this email. You have shown impressive maturity in taking responsibility for your actions, especially since you didn't mention Barbara at all. Thank you for that. I made a few suggestions in the body of your email below. I hope you'll take them. The email address to use to send it is: lsm_us_all@lsm.com. It's a restricted email address, but I have added you to the approved sender list for now. You have my permission to send it when you feel ready. Good luck, and please know that you have my support.
>   Warmly, Elizabeth

Swallowing hard, Alisha found herself blinking back tears again. She was so heartened by the HR executive's support, although she knew it would only go so far. Alisha glanced at the changes Elizabeth suggested and was shocked to see that she had added an oblique reference to faulty advice given to her when Alisha consulted with a trusted advisor. *Of course, Elizabeth can't publicly acknowledge what Barbara did without destroying people's trust in the whole department, but this is a great compromise.* A small smile tugged at the corner of her mouth.

The rest of Elizabeth's changes were more cosmetic, but Alisha acknowledged that they made the whole email stronger. The only question was whether she really had the guts to send it. Sensing that she was being watched, she looked up to see Brittany eyeing her from across the floor, a full forty yards away. Even at that distance, she could feel, if not see, the narrowed eyes and tight mouth of her boss. *Not sending the email isn't really an option. At this point, I have nothing to lose and everything to gain.*

Since it was getting close to lunchtime, Alisha debated the timing in her head. If she sent this email before lunch, people would have their whole lunch hour to dissect it with their friends and coworkers. If she sent it afterward, maybe they'd be too busy to talk about it until later in the day or the next day. She sighed. *I might as well get it over with.*

She copied Elizabeth's version into a fresh email with the address provided and made a few additional tweaks. Satisfied that it was the best she could do, she leaned back and took a deep breath.

*Am I really going to do this?*

Alisha hit send before she could back out.

Realizing a copy had landed in her own inbox, she opened it and read anew the words she had painstakingly written.

Dear LSM coworkers,

I'm sorry.

In late December, I made a serious error in judgment when I falsely accused one of my colleagues of something he did not do. At the time, I was hurt, confused, and obviously not thinking clearly. I have no excuses, although I received some misguided advice from a trusted advisor. I understand that I have not only let down my immediate colleagues, but also my female coworkers whose future safety might be negatively impacted by my behavior.

Lying violates not only LSM's culture but also my own values. As a salesperson, I know that trust is paramount in business relationships, and I have broken yours.

I have made amends with the people directly impacted by my accusations, but I also want to apologize to all of you. I'm truly sorry, and I promise that this won't happen again.

I humbly request your forgiveness and forbearance as I work to re-earn your trust.

Alisha Carson

The buzz started less than five minutes later, and she knew from the growing tide around the office that people were reading her email. She even heard a few gasps, as if people were shocked. She had no doubt they were. Certainly, she had never seen an email like it before, and she doubted that anyone else had. Alisha could only hope that it was a positive shock. Still, she didn't dare look around.

Knowing that she once again would be the subject of intense gossip, she focused on her computer, shaking her head. *If only I had had the foresight to schedule some appointments this afternoon!*

The next thing she knew, Brittany was standing over her, waving a sheet of paper, an inscrutable look on her face. "Did Elizabeth Curtis give you permission to send this?" she demanded. "I've never seen anything like it!"

Startled, Alisha looked up, trying to figure out if Brittany was angry or something else.

"Well?" her boss prompted.

"She did."

Brittany's eyes widened. "C'est incroyable."

"Excuse me?" Alisha recognized the words as French, but she had taken only Spanish in school.

"It's incredible," the older woman answered. "Just incredible."

Alisha tugged on her ponytail. "Is that a good incredible or a bad one?"

# CHAPTER 16

# Early Warning Signs

Gemma's phone chimed again with an incoming text. Putting the paint roller down, she saw that it was Kushma again. Her new boss. And she hadn't even officially started yet. That was a week away. *A week!*

Groaning, she stretched and rubbed her lower back. In between texts, she had been continuing the work on redecorating Kevin's old office that she had started over the weekend. It had been quite a while since she had done renovation-type work by herself, and she could feel it. *Probably in my twenties*, she thought ruefully. *And forty-eight is a long way from twenty-five.* Yet, when she looked at the progress she had made, she gave herself a virtual pat-on-the-back.

The gray walls had been covered in primer, a recommendation from Pete at the local paint store, and the mirrored cabinet doors were gone. She'd get KJ to help her remove the rest of the furniture that evening, as Habit for Humanity was scheduled to pick it up tomorrow.

Her phone chimed again. Kushma Panjari, a dynamic woman who Gemma guessed to be around thirty-five, was obviously excited about getting her new marketing expert on board. She had been texting Gemma all morning with information for her to read in preparation for her first day. Kushma was anxious for Gemma to hit the ground running, and while she appreciated the chance to get a head start on her new job, she had hoped to have a little time for herself this week.

Responding with a quick acknowledgement, Gemma turned back to the office. She hadn't planned to paint the trim, but she had noticed how scuffed it was as she was priming the walls. Nodding briskly, she added another trip to the paint store to her list. Maybe she could get that done before the kids got home from school.

The phone rang.

"Hello?" Gemma answered without looking at the caller ID.

"Gemma, it's Kushma here," came her new boss's lightly accented voice. "I really wish you had agreed to start today. There's so much to be done." A brief chuckle softened the harsh words.

"I know Kushma, and I'm excited to start too," Gemma responded cheerfully. "But I need the time to get my home office set up. I'm used to commuting to the office, remember?"

"Yes, yes, I understand. You need a good place to work away from interruptions and your family, don't you. My husband is always interrupting me. It's frustrating."

"Oh, does he work from home too?"

"No, no. But he's usually home earlier than I'm able to stop working. He keeps wanting me to watch television with him. Ha! As if I have time for that," Kushma said dismissively.

Gemma could picture her waving an elegant hand as if to shoo a fly away, and the knot in her stomach that had been growing all morning got bigger again. *No television?* She hardly watched TV herself but still. *Does the woman do nothing but work?*

"Uh, yeah, I guess that would be frustrating," Gemma murmured.

"I've scheduled a meeting for you and your entire staff next Monday right after your orientation with HR. I made it mandatory, so they'll all be there," Kushma went on briskly.

"But isn't that going to be rough with all the different time zones?" Gemma had been told that her team members, although largely based in the US, were scattered all over the world. She was to have seven groups reporting to her, each team comprised of between four and twelve people. Three of the teams were outside the US, but there were six people or less.

"Oh, they're used to that. We vary our meeting times so that everyone has a chance to be on calls during their daytime. Of course, the US time zones take precedence since most of the people are there, but we all do 2:00 a.m. calls from time to time." Kushma laughed. "Fortunately, not too often."

Gemma blinked, stunned by this new information. "Wow! That's good. I'm not sure how well I'll function in 2:00 a.m. meetings."

"Ha! You'll get used to it," Kushma assured her. "So, the other reason for my call is to tell you about a meeting with the executive team later next week. You'll need to prepare a presentation, which is why I'm sending you all this stuff now. I'll give you the details next Monday, but make sure you're familiar with Atrium's offerings as well as the current marketing positions for them."

"Next week? That's fast," Gemma said. She sat down hard in Kevin's office chair, a sleek ergonomic number, now covered with a drop cloth, which Gemma found dreadfully uncomfortable. But she was afraid if she didn't sit that her legs would buckle. She was getting the idea that "hitting the ground running" had an all-new meaning at Atrium.

"Yup, no grass growing under anyone's feet here," Kushma replied. "But I'll let you get back to your office and your reading. I'll be sending more things along as I find them. Text okay? Or would it be easier in email?"

"Uh, email would be easier to read," Gemma said, thinking of the six or eight text with information that she had already received.

"Done! I'll talk to you later this week, I'm sure. Ciao."

The line went dead. *Ciao? Clearly Kushma is going to take some getting used to,* Gemma thought, running her hand through her short auburn hair again. Suddenly, her laid back week of redecorating and spending time with the kids seemed like it was going to be much less relaxing.

She glanced around the room, assessing the word that needed to be done and rethinking the necessity of painting the trim. *Maybe I'll just go shopping instead.*

Her afternoon trip to Short Hills Mall proved to be a pleasant distraction from the morning's work and Kushma's call. Keeping her new boss's commentary in mind, she chose furniture and accessories that were designed to be soothing and stress-reducing. She especially loved the little fountain that gurgled gently when the water flowed over beautiful blue stones. She had a feeling she'd need that kind of peacefulness on her desk.

By the time she got home, her optimism had been somewhat restored. Until she opened her email. *Twenty-seven emails from*

*Kushma. Twenty-seven!* Gemma had a sudden feeling of being engulfed by an avalanche. *How in the world am I going to get through all of these this week? If this is even all of them?* Her heart sank.

She leaned back in the pretty white chair that matched the writing desk in her bedroom and closed her eyes. An image of Charles' face, full of disapproval, formed in her mind's eye. She wondered now if there hadn't been concern on that face too. *Did he know something I didn't?* He was so well-connected in the industry. More so than she, although she had her fair share of contacts. *But I didn't talk to a single one of them,* she suddenly realized. Her heart plummeted.

*Did I let Nathan push me into this too quickly?*

Hearing the garage door slam, she pushed her doubts aside, closed her laptop without looking at a single email, and hurried downstairs toward the kitchen.

*Focus,* she told herself. *This is for KJ and Anna.*

*And yourself,* the little voice of her ego whispered.

Anna rushed past her on the stairs, sobbing in the way that only teenage girls can sob.

"Anna, what's wrong?" Work forgotten, Gemma's motherly instincts kicked in.

"I don't want to talk," her daughter sniffled, continuing up the stairs without looking at her mother.

"But honey—"

"Mom, not now!" Anna practically ran the rest of the way up the stairs and disappeared around the corner. A moment later, Gemma heard her bedroom door slam too.

Gemma stood looking after her for a full minute, debating whether it was best to follow her or wait it out. Deciding to respect her daughter's "not now," she made her way to the kitchen. *Anna will come down when she is ready, and in the meantime, I can provide some enticement.*

Smiling, finally, Gemma pulled open the door to the walk-in pantry and stepped in. All the ingredients were there. Anna never turned down her favorite butterscotch, dark chocolate cookies, and the cookies had never failed to encourage her daughter to talk.

Putting her phone on the counter and grabbing her recipe book, Gemma set to work.

An hour later, cookies were cooling on the table, and their aroma filled the kitchen and wafted, Gemma knew, throughout the house. As expected, she heard a door opening upstairs and Anna's light tread on the stairs. Her daughter, with red and swollen eyes, shuffled into the kitchen doorway.

"Mom, you made cookies," she half wailed, staring longingly at the plate. "For me?"

Gemma walked over to her daughter and wrapped her in a big hug, savoring the feel of Anna's slim but muscular body against her own. It wasn't often she got to hug her nearly grown offspring anymore.

As usual, Anna pushed her away all too quickly and shuffled over the table. She sat down in the closest chair and grabbed several cookies. "Can I have some milk too?" she asked her mother before stuffing the first one in her mouth.

"May I," Gemma corrected gently, moving to the cabinet to get a glass. Filling it with cold milk, she went to the table and sat down next to Anna.

"Wanna talk about it?" she asked.

"No," Anna mumbled through a cookie-filled mouth. "It's just stupid stuff with Kylie. The cookies help."

Gemma smiled. Kylie was Anna's best friend since kindergarten, but they frequently had rough patches. Both girls were competitive and fiercely independent, but they were also loyal and the fallings out didn't last long.

"If that was a 'thank you,' you're welcome," she prodded Anna.

"Thank you, Mom," Anna replied dutifully. "This is nice. Will I get cookies more often now?" she added hopefully.

As if on cue, Gemma's phone chimed. *What? Yet another text from Kushma?* Studying her phone, Gemma also noticed that ten more emails had arrived from Kushma along with three texts while she had been baking. She groaned out loud.

"Who's blowing up your phone?" Anna asked.

"My new boss."

"But you haven't even started yet, have you?" Her daughter's voice rose with incredulity.

Gemma sighed. "No, I haven't, but it seems she wants to make sure that I get up to speed quickly."

"Now? Before you are getting paid?"

"Yes, now," Gemma confirmed. "Work in the real world isn't like your summer job. I don't clock in and out and only work my scheduled hours. A salary basically means that you're on call 24/7."

"Well, that sucks. No one can do that." Anna took another cookie. She waved it in front of Gemma's face. "I'm not going to do that when I grow up," she pronounced.

"I hope not," Gemma murmured, but she knew it was a nearly futile wish. The pace of the world was speeding up, not slowing down. "Some of the younger people at Viva! pushed for shorter work hours. They didn't last long," she told her daughter. *And based on what Kushma had said about Atrium, it might be worse there,* she added silently, the doubts creeping back in.

"Good for them," Anna said grandly. "My generation isn't going to be defined by work like yours is."

Gemma cleared her throat and managed not to roll her eyes. "Work isn't all bad, you know," she reminded Anna gently.

"Yeah, yeah, I know. I just hope I get more cookies now that you're working from home. These are the best!" With that, Anna grabbed three more cookies, her half-full glass of milk, and bounced out of the room. "Got homework to do," she called over her shoulder, whatever had been bothering her earlier clearly forgotten.

This time Gemma did roll her eyes. *Ah, the resilience of youth,* she thought, as her phone chimed again. Ignoring it, she stood, preparing to clean up the kitchen and put the cookies away. *I have another week before I really have to answer Kushma,* she reminded herself. *There will be time enough to be chained to my devices again.*

But she wondered if she would be able to make cookies or go to Anna's swim meets as much as she had thought with her new job. Her ever-chiming phone told her she wouldn't.

# CHAPTER 17

# Unrealistic Expectations

Sheryl's Monday morning started with a disturbing email from Patrick Kerrigan about the Portal Project. Despite everyone's best efforts, they were falling behind, and it was largely because the ongoing SEC investigation was taking so much of Keisha's attention.

Grimacing, Sheryl typed a quick reply requesting a meeting with Patrick and Keisha to review options to get back on track. She sighed. Because he was her least senior director, she had been working with Patrick to strengthen his leadership skills. Unfortunately, he still needed a lot of her guidance.

*This is the last thing I need this morning*, she thought, rubbing her already sore neck. Things were still unresolved with Dave. They had barely spoken the rest of the weekend, and he had left early this morning for another business trip to California. *At least Alisha isn't there anymore.* Feeling guilty at that thought, she sighed and turned back to her email. *I can't do anything about Dave right now, so I might as well work.*

She had just opened the next email when Paul Haven strode into her office. Despite his relatively short stature—Sheryl guessed he was five-foot, nine-inch at best—Paul had that charismatic something that filled whatever room he was in. His brown hair was expertly cut, and he was dressed in what looked like a hand-tailored shirt and dress pants.

"Paul, good morning. This is a surprise," Sheryl said pleasantly, despite the fact that her stomach was already churning.

"Sheryl," Paul acknowledged her greeting, his unusual charcoal eyes peering at her alertly and coolly. He perched comfortably in one of the two armchairs in front of her desk.

"What can I help you with?"

"I am here to meet with Alex about the next board meeting," he replied. "I thought I'd check in on you first. You had your initial meeting with John Hargrove last week," he stated curtly. "How did it go?"

Sheryl bristled, sitting up straighter in her chair. "Fine," she said briefly. "He seems like a, uh, knowledgeable guy."

"He is," Paul nodded. "One of the best in the biz. You can learn a lot from him. I hope you take his advice seriously."

"Of course," Sheryl murmured, appalled as usual by the man's arrogance. Paul was probably around her age, but he was sleek and polished in the way powerful men often were. One thing she knew about him for certain was that his goal was to intimidate. Sheryl grudgingly admitted to herself that he was good at it.

"We're going to need a report on the Portal Project next week too," he went on. "I assume that you're on schedule with that?"

Shifting uncomfortably, Sheryl thought of the email she had just read. "We're doing our best," she hedged.

"And your best means that it will be on time," Paul stated unequivocally. There was a clear warning in the man's voice.

Sheryl nodded and maintained eye contact as she did so.

"Good," he said, rising.

Sheryl stood up too, not wanting to give him the chance to tower over her.

"One more thing," he said casually, but Sheryl noted that his eyes were intent. "We'll also want a report on how The Diamante is leveraging, and going to leverage, AI. I assume you have some familiarity with Artificial Intelligence?" The last was said with a great deal of cynicism in his voice.

Putting her hands on her desk, Sheryl leaned forward. "That was unnecessarily insulting, Paul," she replied coldly, grateful that Alex has forewarned her about Alpha's AI salvo.

He smiled and raised one hand in a dismissive gesture. "No insult intended. You've been here a long time. I don't know how much exposure you've had."

"I have several certifications in AI," Sheryl assured him smoothly, her jaw tight.

"Good, then you'll be able to give us a good assessment of how much headcount we can replace with AI. From what I understand, it can replace most, if not all, of our entry level jobs, and maybe more than that."

Sheryl gasped. "What? Are you kidding? Of course, it can't do that. For a lot of reasons, not the least of which is developing new talent."

He shrugged. "We can *buy* talent with all the savings we'll get."

"Do you know how expensive AI is to implement? And that despite all the progress being made, 80 percent of AI projects fail?"

Paul merely shrugged again. "It's your job to see that they don't fail here."

Stunned at his callousness, Sheryl's jaw dropped.

"This can't be a surprise to you," he continued. "The rest of the industry is doing it. We can't be left behind. In fact, we're small enough to be able to be ahead of the competition, Sheryl. We can be on the leading edge of AI in the investment industry if we act quickly enough." The gleam in his eyes was one of triumph. He was deliberately pushing her buttons, and she knew it.

"We're already using AI," Sheryl shot back, her cheeks flushing with anger. "But to supplement our *talent*. Plus, there are the SEC guidelines that we have to consider. We have to stay in control of the AI, and that means having people to work alongside it to guide, educate, and *monitor* it. You must know that the AI has to conform to current SEC regulations, especially when it comes to fiduciary responsibility!"

Paul matched her stance, leaning forward so that they were eye to eye. "By all means, we have to stay within the SEC boundaries, especially since we are still under investigation, but we expect that you'll walk as close to those boundaries as you can. Alpha didn't invest in this company to be a second-tier player."

Pausing, he gave her another hard look and then turned and calmly strode the fifteen feet to her door as if it were his office. He paused there and looked over his shoulder. "This isn't a debate," he said flatly and continued walking without waiting for a reply.

Sheryl fell back in her chair, stunned by the exchange. Even though Alex had warned her, she wondered if he knew just how far Paul Haven wanted to go. *And what about the rest of the board members?* Alpha had a significant investment in The Diamante, but they were not the majority shareholders by any means. Despite Paul's assertions, there were other board members and other investors to consider. *Or,* she thought with alarm, *has Alpha recruited a big block of shareholders to their cause?*

Her stomach churning, she reached for the phone to call Alex but stopped herself. Paul said he had stopped by her office first. The last thing she wanted was to have Paul in the room when she called Alex to complain about him. She decided to wait until later to talk to Alex, after she was sure Paul was gone.

She pushed her bangs back from her face. She had better deal with Patrick and Keisha first because it was clear that the Portal Project had to get back on track and fast. The question was how to do that without increasing headcount or hiring consultants. After Paul's visit, she knew without a doubt that either of those options was completely off the table.

Laughing bitterly, she acknowledged that Paul was right about one thing. AI was going to be a necessary tool in that fight. The question was how much. *Thank goodness for Keisha,* she thought, not for the first time. *She'll have a good handle on that.* The SEC investigation popped into her head. *At least I hope so.*

Sheryl lifted the phone and called Patrick. There was no time to waste. She needed him and Keisha in her office *now,* and the SEC investigators could damn well wait.

Ten minutes later, a red-faced Patrick hurriedly entered her office. To Sheryl's dismay, Keisha wasn't with him. He held a single white envelope in his hand instead.

"Patrick?" Sheryl questioned, her heart in her throat as she grasped the implications of that envelope.

The younger man hung his head. "I'm sorry, Sheryl, I really am." The color of his face now almost matched his bright copper hair. "It's not you. I promise, it's not you."

Sheryl's shoulders tightened. "What's wrong, Patrick?"

He handed her the envelope. "That's my official resignation letter," he said. "For you. I have another version for Human Resources."

"But why? And why now?" Sheryl asked, compassion warring with a bright anger at his timing.

"We're moving back to Georgia," he replied sheepishly. "My wife's family is there, and, well, we're expecting a baby. She'll have more support there. It's cheaper, and I got a job that, um, is going to be, uh, less . . . pressure. I think."

Despite her sense of betrayal, Sheryl felt genuine delight at his news. "Oh Patrick!" She rose from her chair, rounded her deck, and gave him a hug. "I'm so happy for you. A baby! That's great."

He flushed again with pleasure. "Thank you. We're excited."

Stepping back, Sheryl looked at him appraisingly. "Less pressure, huh?"

Patrick had the grace to look abashed. "Yeah, I hope so anyway. I know you trusted me with this Portal Project, and I appreciate that, but it's too much. Keisha is a rock star, and honestly, she's been carrying me. I feel bad about that," he confessed. "Even with you and her helping me, well, I'm not sleeping at night, and my wife started to become really frustrated with me."

*Join the club,* thought Sheryl, quickly pushing the notion away.

He shrugged his shoulders helplessly. Sheryl couldn't help but compare Patrick's authentic gesture to Paul Haven's arrogant one. The rest of her anger vanished.

"I understand, Patrick. I really do. Nothing about this project has been easy, and it would be a lot even for someone with more experience than you," she conceded. "It's just that . . ."

Her words hung in the air.

"I know. With the layoffs, you didn't have many choices," he finished for her. "I do appreciate your confidence in me, and I'm sorry it's been misplaced. I did my best, but, honestly, I just can't handle it."

"Oh, Patrick. Don't be so hard on yourself," Sheryl said. "Yes, you haven't had any experience with a project of this size and importance, but I've seen how you handled other projects. You do have the capability. You're smart, organized, and have a good sense for people. This was a big leap, and you've handled yourself well. Don't think that you can't work up to this kind of project in the future. You can."

The freckles on Patrick's face disappeared under his bright red blush. "Thank you, Sheryl," he responded sincerely. "I can't tell you how much I appreciate your faith in me. I wish . . . well, anyway, thank you. That means a lot to me."

"You're welcome. I'm quite sure your new company is lucky to have you."

He dipped his head in a grateful acknowledgment.

"About my replacement . . ." he began slowly.

Suddenly, Sheryl was struck by the limited number of options open to her to get the Portal Project on track and keep it there.

"Can Keisha do it?" she asked abruptly. The young woman was the obvious choice, but she knew what others' arguments would be: Keisha was young and more inexperienced than Patrick. She had had little supervisory experience, but she was bright and had a good way with people. Still . . .

"I think so. She's really, really smart," he admitted, "and she's been doing a lot of the project management already."

"What about the rest of the team?"

Patrick nodded slowly. "Most of them will be okay. They like Keisha and respect her."

"But?"

"Chang-Ho might have a problem working for a woman," he answered cautiously, naming a male Korean staff member who was the team's AI expert.

"Why do you say that?"

"Well, he's challenged her a few times in meetings, although she handled it great! But he's also made comments about her and some of the other women in the group privately to me. I get the feeling that he thinks men are superior." He paused. "Not to be biased, but it might be a cultural thing? He moved here from South Korea only a few years ago."

Sheryl recalled an article she had read recently about an unspoken misogyny problem in that country. Yet, it wasn't fair to judge Chang-Ho on that alone. She didn't believe in stereotyping one bit. She'd have to dig deeper to find out what was going on with him.

"Okay, thanks for telling me that. Anyone else?"

Patrick shook his head.

She glanced at the envelope in her hand. "When's your last day?"

"At the end of the month," he replied, his eyes downcast. "I tried to give you as much notice as I could." Sheryl was aghast.

"That's still only two weeks, Patrick!"

Sheryl watched his face turn red again. With his fair skin, he couldn't hide his emotions at all.

"I know. I'm sorry, but my wife's parents . . ."

"I get it. I guess I'd better talk to Keisha," she said briskly. "And it sounds like you need to make a trip to HR."

"Thanks, Sheryl," Patrick said earnestly. "I really do appreciate everything you've done for me. I'm sorry I couldn't live up to your expectations."

"Patrick, stop it. We already agreed this was a really tough assignment, and you did your best. I'm sure you'll excel at your next job. I've already seen how much you've grown in this role. And you have. Really! It had to be a great learning experience." She smiled gently at him, taking the time to reassure him again despite her impatience to talk to Keisha. "Don't let this job erode your self-confidence. You're an excellent programmer, and I've seen your potential as a leader. Remember that!"

He stood a little straighter at her encouraging words. "Thanks, Sheryl. You're a great boss, you know. You really are."

Laughing self-consciously, Sheryl pointed to the door. "Get out of here. For now. We'll still need to meet with Keisha, but let me talk to her first."

He grinned and hurried out.

Sheryl returned to her chair and sank down in it.

*What in the world am I going to do now?*

Between her unresolved issues with Dave and Paul Haven's unrealistic expectations, she had enough problems. The muscles in her neck and shoulders contracted further. And now this? If Patrick wasn't up to the challenge, would Keisha be? She was only what? Twenty-seven? Twenty-eight? A lot younger than most of the other directors. Promoting her would be a big leap and a big risk.

*But what other choice do I have?*

Paul Haven's parting words echoed. "This isn't a debate." *He'll probably want me to replace Patrick with an AI bot.* She paused, abruptly sitting bolt upright as panic shot through her. *Oh no. Will I even be able to replace Patrick at all? Even with AI, we'll need . . .*

She dropped her head into her hand.

*Maybe this Portal Project is doomed,* she thought fatalistically. *And if that's the case, then I'm doomed too.*

# CHAPTER 18

# Earning Respect

Alisha waited, the lump of fear in her throat restricting her breathing. Still, Brittany didn't respond, just stood and stared, an indecipherable look in her whiskey eyes.

The older woman shook the paper in her hand again. "Was this your idea or Elizabeth's?" she demanded.

"Mine," Alisha squeaked.

"Incroyable," Brittany muttered again. "Who would have thought that you had such gall, although given what you did in the first place . . ."

Feeling her breathing ease a bit, Alisha took a deep inhale. She met her boss's gaze squarely for the first time since the woman had approached her.

"People are talking all over again," Brittany informed her. "You know that?"

Alisha nodded. Of course, she had heard the buzz. "Yes, I expected that, but, well, what do you think, Brittany?" she asked abruptly, tired of waiting for her boss to explain herself.

One shoulder rose in a classic Brittany gesture. "It was a bold move. I didn't think you had it in you. Lying is a coward's way. This," she shook the paper again, "this is not."

"It was probably the hardest thing I've ever done," Alisha confessed, then mentally kicked herself. *Why did I tell* her *that?* The last thing she wanted to do was to give her boss more ammunition.

To her surprise, Brittany nodded. "No doubt. Humility is not easy for anyone. Confession even less so." She paused, giving Alisha another assessing look. "If you really meant what you wrote, I'm impressed."

Alisha released the breath she didn't even realize she was holding. Brittany being impressed was a big step forward. A leap compared to anything before.

"But don't forget that actions speak louder than words!" With that trope, her boss turned and started walking away.

Blinking back fresh tears, Alisha willed her shoulders not to sag.

Yet, she noticed, Brittany stopped after only two steps. Her boss looked back over her shoulder, her eyes kinder than Alisha had ever seen them. "But the email is a really good start," she said gently. "And I know Elizabeth wouldn't have approved this if she didn't think you meant it. It *is* well done, Alisha. Very well done."

With that, she continued back to her own cubicle, leaving Alisha gaping after her in disbelief. *Did Brittany just say something nice? Encouraging? That in itself is incroyable, or however you pronounce that.* Tears filled her eyes again, and Alisha turned back toward her desk to hide them. But for the first time, her tears held relief and gratitude. *Maybe there is hope.*

Still hearing the flurry of conversations across the open-floor plan, Alisha decided to escape for lunch. She grabbed her handbag and cell phone, checking carefully to turn the ringer on the latter back on, and headed toward the stairs. Hurrying down, she kept her head down and eyes averted, not wanting to engage in another conversation about her email. Not yet, anyway.

Alisha made it as far as the first-floor lobby, when someone latched onto her arm. She looked up, startled, only to see Robert's dark face grinning down at her.

"Well, if it isn't the woman of the hour!" he exclaimed, loudly enough for several people walking by to turn their heads.

Blushing, Alisha snatched her arm back. "Robert, stop it! You're making everyone look."

He quirked one eyebrow. "I think everyone is already looking. And why not? That was quite an email you sent. I have to hand it to you."

"Can we not talk about this here?" she whispered urgently, tugging him toward the door.

Robert laughed, his big, booming laugh, which of course, made everyone stop now and gawk openly at them. Alisha hung her head. *I should have known. This is Robert,* she thought with a mix of dismay and affection for the older man.

"There's nothing to be ashamed of, Alisha," he disclosed in a softer voice, but one that could still be heard across the lobby. "You took responsibility for your actions in a very public way, and that's admirable. I, for one, am proud of you."

Grateful tears shining in her eyes again, Alisha reached out and gave him a hug, propriety be damned. *There is just something so endearing about this man!* Yet, he had been one of her harshest critics when he had first learned what she had done to his friend. She would do well not to forget that.

"Hey! It's okay," he said, clearly caught by surprise. He gave her a quick squeeze and gently pushed her back to arms' length as his gaze swept her face.

Alisha could now feel a half dozen curious eyes still on them, but when she looked around, she saw only good-natured smiles on most of the faces. A few even gave Alisha respectful nods as they walked by.

"Thanks, Robert. I appreciate the support more than you can imagine," Alisha told him earnestly. "That email—"

"Was the biggest piece of mewling drivel I have ever read in my life," a woman's sneering voice interjected. "You've missed your calling, Alisha. You should be writing fiction for a living."

Gasping aloud, Alisha spun around. Penny stood there, flanked by the two women who had been laughing with her in the ladies' room last week. All three had the same disdainful expression on their faces.

Robert stepped forward. "Penny, you—" he began gravely.

"Thank you, Robert, but don't," Alisha laid a hand on his arm to stop him, the lump back in her throat. "You don't have to defend me. Penny and her, uh, friends have a right to their opinions," she finished with much more bravado than she felt. She forced herself to look Penny in the eye.

The project manager directed a scorning look at Alisha. "After all, there's no defense for more lies, Robert," she spat out. "And we *all* know that that email was just another set of Miss California's lies."

Alisha felt Robert go rigid, and remembering Penny's own deception, she stiffened in rage herself. She pulled herself up to her full five-foot, six-inch height, her deep blue eyes shooting fire.

"It takes a liar to recognize a lie," she said vehemently, pitching her voice so that the words didn't reach any ears outside their little group, but they hit home.

Penny blanched, but she kept her pale blue eyes on Alisha's. The two women stared at each other for a long moment, the other women shifting uncomfortably as they watched.

Finally, Robert cleared his throat, and Penny dropped her gaze, tossing her head toward her friends. "Let's go," she said and swept across the floor, the other two women following in her wake. Alisha stared after them, noticing that the woman with long, dark hair peeked back over her shoulder, sending Alisha a brief, curious look.

Only after they were out of sight, did Alisha turn her attention back to Robert.

"What was *that* all about?" he asked bewildered by the exchange.

Alisha sighed. "You really don't want to know," she assured him. "But thank you. Thank you for standing up for me. I know I haven't been your favorite person, for good reason, but I appreciate what you tried to do just now."

Robert nodded, a small, puzzled frown still on his face. "You're welcome," he said quietly. "The truth is, I think that email showed you taking accountability, and I believe that you've learned your lesson. Dave told me that you even talked to Sheryl. Brave of you, but smart. Sheryl's a wise woman."

Feeling her eyes start to fill with tears once again, Alisha simply nodded. *When did I become such a watering pot? This is getting old.*

Glancing at his watch, Robert gave her a quick smile. "Gotta go," he said. "But keep up the good work."

He crossed the lobby in a few long strides and disappeared around the corner. Alisha turned and walked the other way through the doors to the outside. She prayed Penny and her friends were long gone. Having Robert by her side had given her a measure of strength, but she wasn't at all sure she was capable of taking Penny and her entourage on again on her own. *At least not yet.*

When Alisha got back to her cubicle a mere half hour later, she sat down and pulled up Walter's account in the CRM program. She had spent her lunch time driving around, her stomach in too many knots to contemplate eating. After fruitlessly trying to banish her encounter with Penny from her mind, she gave up and decided to get back to work.

The project manager, who Alisha guessed was about five years her junior, had updated the file late that morning. The new input showed progress from Walter's team, which someone from CPT Pharmaceuticals had recently supplied. Alisha smiled. These changes should make the all-important meeting with Walter and Brittany—scheduled for early tomorrow morning—much easier to navigate.

Taking no chances, she captured screenshots of all the key information, along with the date and time stamps that indicated that Penny had made the updates. Penny was clearly still angry, very angry, and Alisha didn't trust her not to pull another stunt like she had on Friday.

*Trust. There's that word again.* Alisha had never given it as much thought as she had in the last few days. Yes, she had always known that it was her job to build trust with the company's clients, but beyond that? She certainly had never really thought about how much trust was needed between colleagues and coworkers. *Not until I started violating that trust.*

"Is that the information we need for tomorrow's meeting?" Brittany's voice, surprisingly warm, interrupted her thoughts.

"It is," Alisha confirmed, glancing up at her boss. "I want to make sure that there is as little room for misunderstanding as possible."

But Brittany was frowning at her screen. "Why are you taking screenshots of the CRM notes?" she asked.

Alisha looked back at her screen, realizing with sudden horror that the screenshots were still visible on the left edge of the extra wide monitor—right in Brittany's line of vision! She wracked her brain for a plausible explanation.

"Uh, I just wanted to make sure I had them ready in case, uh, we, uh, can't get to the network when we're at CPT," she finally said. *Phew! That is a good reason.*

Her boss nodded. "Good thinking," she affirmed. "You never know when technology will fail. Send copies to me too."

"Sure, no problem, Brittany."

"Is there anything we need to go over with Penny?" Alisha almost cringed at the name.

"No, she made a bunch of updates this morning, which are all straightforward," Alisha replied honestly. "I don't have any questions."

"Are you sure?" Brittany asked. "I thought maybe the three of us should talk before the end of the day."

"I really don't think that's necessary, Brittany," Alisha assured her. *The last thing I want to do is meet with Penny today.*

Brittany narrowed her eyes. "Is there a problem with you and Penny?" she questioned abruptly.

Alisha looked at Brittany with what she hoped was a surprised look on her face. *How does Brittany know there's a problem? And how do I answer without lying again?*

"Um, not really. We, uh, don't really know each other that well yet," she hedged.

"'Not really' means there's a problem," Brittany stated flatly. "Tell me."

Glancing around, Alisha didn't notice anyone paying particular attention to them, but there was no privacy either.

She lowered her voice. "Okay, Brittany, in the interest of being honest, Penny has made it very clear that she doesn't like me. Obviously, she's rightfully upset at what I did in December," she paused. "I'm sure we'll be able to work through it," she finished hopefully, although she wasn't sure of that at all.

Her boss pursed her lips. "I don't like the sound of that. Do you need me to intervene?"

Alisha frantically shook her head. "No, no. Please don't do that. You'll only make it worse, especially if she thinks I've run tattling to you. I told you because you asked, and I really do believe in honesty. But please, don't."

"Hmph. All right, I won't. For now," Brittany agreed. "Thank you for sharing. But if this situation between the two of you starts impacting our customers, I'm going to step in. You can trust me on that."

Thinking about how it already had impacted Walter, Alisha paled. "Yes, I understand, Brittany. And you're 100 percent correct. I promise, I won't let it interfere with any customers."

"I know you won't," Brittany shocked her by saying, "but you can't control Penny. Or anyone else."

Knowing what her boss said was true, Alisha could only nod.

"Okay then," her boss said, clearly done with the subject. "Now, who else are we visiting this week?"

Alisha pulled up the schedule and talked the older woman through the week's sales calls. Brittany's demeanor was noticeably warmer, but a certain wariness remained. Sighing inwardly, Alisha remembered what both Sheryl and Elizabeth had said. *The email was a first step, not a total cure. Time was a necessary element in rebuilding trust.*

An image of Penny's disdainful face crossed her mind. Somehow, she knew in her gut that neither time nor the email was going to be enough with that woman.

*But what the heck* will *be?*

# CHAPTER 19

# A Blessing or a Curse?

Keisha looked at her boss with outright panic in her dark brown eyes.

"You're kidding me, right?" she asked in a shaky voice. "Please tell me you're kidding."

Sheryl shook her head gently, reaching out to grasp the younger woman's hand. "Unfortunately, no, I'm not kidding."

Keisha's slim form fell back against the burgundy leather chair, her breathing shallow and fast. Sheryl was afraid she might pass out. At least they were seated in the comfortable chairs arranged in a grouping in one corner of Sheryl's oversized office. She'd only once seen Keisha this panicked, but she figured as long as she kept Keisha's head away from the sharp edge of the mahogany coffee table, she'd be okay.

"Breathe, please breathe," she encouraged her protégé.

"I'm trying to," Keisha gasped, her café-au-lait skin paling further. "But . . ." She inhaled sharply. "But you know this is crazy, right? This promotion?"

Releasing a long breath, Sheryl shook her head. "No, not crazy," she assured Keisha. "Unorthodox? Maybe. But it's not like we have a lot of options."

"What about one of your other directors? Carlos? He's smart and picks things up quickly, and he has loads of experience," the younger woman suggested, her tone urgent.

Sheryl gave her a thoughtful look. "I considered Carlos," she confirmed. "But he has a lot of other important things on his plate—"

"More important than the Portal Project?"

"No, but—"

"Then have Carlos do it!" Keisha insisted. "Look, Sheryl. I appreciate your confidence in me, but I'm already drowning. Between the SEC investigation, the design work, and overseeing my team of programmers, it's already more than I can handle."

"Patrick told me that you're already doing a lot of the project management."

"Huh," Keisha smirked, calming a bit. "Well, ain't that the truth."

"So, if you're doing the job—"

"No, ma'am. Helping Patrick out with the project management software is one thing. Running the whole team? The whole project? That's entirely different," Keisha was quick to point out. "Plus, if someone else can actually *do* Patrick's job, I'll have more time to get my *real* work done."

Sheryl leaned forward, putting her elbows on the desk and cupping her chin in one hand. *Keisha's making some good points.* She considered how she could move Carlos's workload around.

"You don't think Carlos would be too heavy-handed with you?" Sheryl asked. Carlos had a bit of a temper and too often thought he was right about everything. Two things Sheryl had been mentoring him on, with some success, but those tendencies were still there.

Keisha shrugged, her face regaining some color. "He might try," she quipped. "But I can handle *him*."

Laughing outright, Sheryl dropped in her hands in mock defeat. "Are you sure you don't want the director role, Keisha?" she said grinning. Then paused, her face more serious. "It would be a big step forward for you."

"Oh, I do want it." The younger woman sat up straighter, her superior height now apparent. Sometimes it amazed Sheryl that Keisha wasn't a fashion model instead of a serious, very talented programmer. She not only looked like a model, but she dressed like one too, even today, as she added, "But not now. And not with this project. Honestly, I feel like you'd be setting me up for failure!"

"Keisha!" Sheryl's hazel eyes widened in shock. "I would never do that to you!"

Head tilting, Keisha eyed her mentor. "No, not intentionally. I know that, Sheryl. But seriously, thanks but no thanks . . . this time."

Her heart sank, but Sheryl knew that Keisha was probably right. Not for the first time, she marveled at the young woman's instincts and sense of integrity. *She could surely teach a few people in much higher positions a few lessons.*

"Okay then," she finally said, accepting Keisha's decision. "We at least need to talk about the project. I didn't like the report from Patrick this morning. Shall I call him in or would you like to go over it without him?"

Delicate lines formed on Keisha's broad forehead as she frowned. "You better get him. He knows more about the rest of the team than I do."

While Keisha was the lead programmer on the project and had the bulk of the interface team under her direction, Patrick had some of the database and infrastructure team members reporting to him. In total, the team was a mere fourteen people, much too small to be handling a project the size of the Portal Project.

Rising, Sheryl crossed to her desk to call Patrick. She reached him immediately, and he agreed to join them.

"So, how much are the AI tools helping the project?" Sheryl asked Keisha as she walked back and sat down again.

Keisha groaned. "Some days a lot. Other days, they just seem to make things worse."

"Worse how?"

"Well, for the normal stuff, the tools are great, and they've really sped up some of the backend programming that can be tedious. But with the interface?" Keisha grimaced. "Because our design is so new and innovative—if I do say so myself—the AI tools don't always get it. In fact, they've messed it up a couple of times. So, we're not using them for the interface at all now."

"Nothing? Is that slowing things down?"

"Of course, but there is another reason to be cautious," Keisha explained. "This interface. It's new, innovative, and *proprietary*. We're using a third-party AI programing tool, and, well, I don't want to teach it to program our interface. You know that someone will copy it soon enough, but I don't want to give them the coding too."

"Wow. Great thinking," Sheryl replied, grateful for the younger woman's foresight.

"AI is great, but we have to be careful," Keisha warned, her forehead wrinkling again. "Copyright and proprietary information do not mean much in that world."

Sheryl nodded. "So true," she murmured, recalling Paul Haven's rash words. *Does he have any idea?*

Patrick walked in a moment later, laptop in hand, and they all turned their attention to the project. Keisha was able to provide some additional insight that should have given Sheryl some hope, but the news really wasn't good. It was going to take a lot of work to get the project back on schedule—providing the investigation didn't interfere as much as it had been in the last month.

*The investigation. How does Patrick leaving affect that?* Although Keisha had worked directly with Sheryl in uncovering the nefarious behavior of the two former directors and their apparent helper Rachel Solowitz, Patrick had been involved in a peripheral way, and so the SEC had interviewed him. He was one of their witnesses.

"You'll have to stay available for the investigation, even after you leave, Patrick," Sheryl interjected abruptly.

He blinked. "Yes, of course. I know that," he promised her. "But I can leave, right? I'm not obligated to stay here or in New Jersey, am I?" His voice rose in concern.

"No, I'm sure you can leave," Sheryl said, but she paused, doubt creeping in. "But we should tell Joaquin. Soon. Now."

"Um, okay," Patrick said, his freckles darker against his sudden pallor. "Should I—"

Not waiting for him to finish, Sheryl once again crossed to her desk and placed a call to Joaquin. At the urgency in her voice, he agreed to come right down.

"Should I leave?" asked Keisha nervously. Sheryl noticed her smoothing her black hair, which today she wore in an elegant bun.

"No, stay. This shouldn't take long, and we still need to finish up with the project plan," Sheryl advised.

"Okay," Keisha tugged her bright aqua sweater down so that it lay evenly over the top of her black pants.

Sheryl watched her curiously and was startled to catch Patrick briefly rolling his eyes. She remembered thinking that Joaquin might be interested in Keisha in December, when they were all working together to discover what was wrong in the database. *Maybe the interest isn't just one way?*

Her speculation was interrupted by Joaquin's hurried entrance. Gesturing him into the fourth and only empty chair, she quickly filled him in on Patrick's situation. But not before Joaquin courteously greeted them all with a formal handshake. Now Sheryl couldn't help paying attention. *Did he linger just a bit longer over Keisha's hand?*

In the conversation, the compliance officer was immediately concerned by Patrick's resignation and reiterated Sheryl's assumption that Patrick would have to stay available, at least by phone or video call, until the investigation was over. "I'll be happy to provide a letter for your new employers, explaining your relevance as much as I can," Joaquin offered.

Patrick, looking worried, agreed. "That would be great. I didn't even think I'd have to explain all this to them, but it makes sense. I . . . I'm sure they'll be okay with it." He looked between Sheryl and Joaquin. "I hope so. It's not like this will take a lot of my time. Not like Keisha. Right?"

"No, I'm sure it won't," Joaquin concurred. He turned to Keisha, who had been watching him attentively during the conversation.

"Are they still bothering you a lot?" he inquired, although he knew the answer. Keisha ran everything she sent to the SEC by him and Sheryl.

Blushing, Keisha shook her head. "Not as much," she answered quietly. "As you are aware."

"I wish you didn't have to be as involved, given your deadlines here," Joaquin said sympathetically. "But only you can do the database research."

"It's okay. I'm managing," Keisha demurred, surprising Sheryl with her uncharacteristic meekness.

Joaquin nodded and stood. "I'll get you that letter, Patrick, before you leave." Then he nodded to the two women and strode out of the office. Keisha's gaze followed him.

"Ahem," Patrick said loudly, drawing Keisha's attention back in a playful manner. Her tawny skin took on a deep red undertone. He turned his attention back to Sheryl.

"Is Keisha taking over for me?" he asked curiously.

"No, not right now," Sheryl answered.

"Oh." Patrick looked back and forth between the two women. "You'd do a great job, Keisha," he volunteered. Keisha looked pleadingly at Sheryl.

"We decided that Keisha needs to concentrate on the interface," Sheryl told him. "You know how tricky that is."

Patrick nodded. "Yeah. It really is. That's probably a good move, but—"

"Let's finish up here," Sheryl interrupted. "You and I can discuss your workload later. Our first and immediate objective is to get this project back on track."

"Yeah, right," he murmured.

Sheryl pointed to one of the red flags on the project plan, still visible on Patrick's laptop screen. "What's the problem here?"

Keisha made a huff of disgust but didn't answer the question.

"Oh that," Patrick said. "It's part of the backend database setup."

"I can see that," Sheryl snapped. "But what's the problem?"

"Well, um, Chang-Ho doesn't agree with part of, uh, Keisha's interface design, so he's been, um, reluctant to make the changes she needs," Patrick stammered.

"Reluctant?" Sheryl echoed in astonishment, her pleasant alto voice suddenly bordering on soprano.

"He means that Chang-Ho has flatly refused to make the changes," Keisha explained angrily, her face flushed again. "Nor will he let anyone else do them."

"Keisha," Patrick protested weakly.

"What? You know it's true, and you won't stand up to him," she accused hotly. "Even though you know he's throwing everything off schedule."

Sheryl's eyes darted between the two of them. Keisha was sometimes too emotional, but she seemed deadly serious about this. "Why is this the first time I'm hearing about this?" she demanded, turning her focus on Patrick.

"Because I thought he would come around," Patrick defended, but his words held no heat. If anything, he sounded defeated.

*Is this part of the reason he's leaving?* Sheryl wondered. *Or why Keisha won't take the promotion?*

"Patrick, you know damn well he wasn't going to," Keisha snarled. It was clear to Sheryl that they had had this argument before.

Sheryl pushed her dark bangs back from her forehead, feeling weary. "Patrick?"

"Okay, so maybe I was optimistic about Chang-Ho," he confessed. "He's extremely talented, as you know, and I was trying to see his point of view."

Keisha snorted.

"How badly is this holding you up?" Sheryl asked her.

"You can see!" the younger woman almost yelled, pointing at the screen. "The project is almost at a complete stop at this point. I've done all the workarounds I can." Her nearly black eyes shot daggers at Patrick. "He knows that."

Unable to stop herself, Sheryl groaned in dismay. "Okay, okay. Is there anything else?" she asked, her chest feeling like a band of steel was wrapping itself around her.

"Well, since you asked . . ."

# CHAPTER 20

# Seeing Ghosts

**Thursday, January 20**

Stepping out of Brittany's luxurious sedan, Alisha had a sudden, unexpected, and unpleasant tingling in her spine. Confused, she rolled her shoulders, but the feeling persisted. Moving her shoulders again, she realized that the sensation wasn't impacted by her movement. *It's foreboding,* she thought with surprise. *I've never felt anything like it before.*

Alisha watched Brittany move confidently across the icy parking lot, despite heels that were twice the height of her own. Following more slowly, Alisha was careful to place her feet on the patches of dry pavement. She still was not used to this cold and ice. But the chill that went through her again had nothing to do with the weather. *What the heck?*

Alisha had been surprised when Brittany suggested stopping for lunch together before going back to the office. No, not surprised. Shocked. She was amazed at how much her boss's attitude had changed since her apologetic email. Not that she was any less demanding. Clearly, the older woman was as driven as anyone could be. But now, her demands were tempered with helpful hints and what seemed suspiciously like kindness.

The two women had traveled together, locally, for the last two and a half days. Alisha had been impressed by how gracefully Brittany had handled Walter, without making it seem that the whole incident had been Alisha's fault. Her boss had also been gracious with the other customers, walking the tightrope of a salesperson with agility. She had equally cajoled them and been firm with pricing and deadlines.

On her part, Alisha realized that she could learn a lot from Brittany. More than she expected, and she had started treating the other woman with more respect and admiration. On the whole, it had been a very pleasant and productive couple of days.

Still, Alisha was a bit leery about the suggested luncheon. Yes, they had eaten together yesterday, but it had been a quick stop, not a full-scale meal at a restaurant. And the looks of the building in front of her indicated that this was a genuine, sit-down restaurant.

*Is that what's gnawing at me?*

"This okay?" Brittany asked, turning to check Alisha's progress, her pink cashmere scarf blowing in the stiff breeze. Her boss clearly had no hesitation about this place.

"Yeah, it's fine. It looks nice." Alisha picked up her pace, wishing she had her snow boots on. Her feet were freezing.

Brittany chuckled. "It's very nice. My favorite Italian restaurant. You do like Italian?"

"Oh, I love Italian," Alisha assured her, "although there wasn't a lot of great Italian in California. Not like here. I never knew that New Jersey had so many great Italian restaurants!"

Brittany grinned, and it was as if the world suddenly went from monochrome to color.

*What? She's grinning?* Alisha was seeing a whole new side of her boss.

"Yeah. We get spoiled here in Jersey. Best Italian in the country, in my opinion. Well, there are some good ones in New York too."

"You're not the first person to tell me that," Alisha murmured cautiously, still unsure of what to make of Brittany's new level of friendliness.

"Don't look so nervous," Brittany laughed delightedly, pulling open the right side of the large, wooden double doors. "I promise no lectures or guidance. I thought it would be nice to get to know each other better."

Alisha's eyes widened. "You do?" Then immediately wished she had kept her mouth shut.

Smiling, Brittany nodded and paused in the small foyer. She turned to face Alisha fully. "Yes, I do. Look, I'm not quite the ogre you think I am. I'll admit we got off on the wrong foot. I had heard-well, you know-and I was pissed. I like Dave, and you gave him a raw deal." She held up her hand when Alisha tried to speak. "No, let me finish. I know that it was more complicated than that, especially with some of the language and explanation in your email that Elizabeth approved. And you did take responsibility for your actions. I'm a big fan of that. So, let's put this behind us. I really don't like being a witch, you know." Her whiskey eyes twinkled. "Well, most of the time, anyway."

Alisha managed to keep her jaw from dropping on the floor, but just barely.

But the older woman was already gliding through the next set of doors into the restaurant. Alisha scrambled to follow, glowing in Brittany's approval.

*This is a really nice change*, Alisha thought as they followed the hostess through a maze of tables adorned with white tablecloths and bright red napkins. The half-full room was filled with the soft clink of silverware and muted conversation, and the rich aroma of tomatoes and garlic tantalized her nose. Her mouth watered in anticipation.

As they settled their coats on the back of the leatherette chairs, a loud laugh from the bar across the room caught Alisha's attention. It was incongruent with the atmosphere and chillingly familiar.

The unpleasant tingles in her spine came back. Stronger this time.

Afraid to look, Alisha sat down with her back to the bar and forced herself to smile at Brittany. "It smells fantastic in here," she exclaimed, her voice over-hearty, even to her own ears.

"What's wrong?" Brittany was instantly alert and concerned.

The loud laugh came from the bar again.

Brittany pursed her lips. "What an idiot. Someone has obviously had too much to drink," she said, looking over Alisha's shoulder at the offender.

Alisha shuddered, her mind flashing back to the many times Liam had "invited" her to go out for a drink after work with him and a few of the other guys. The invitations had not been optional, or so he had implied. He had been just like that guy at the bar, loud and inappropriate, in more ways than one.

"It's only a couple of guys," Brittany informed her with disgust, a delicate crease forming on her forehead. "I hope management makes them quiet down."

"I hope so too," Alisha muttered, dragging her mind back to the present.

More laughter. This time, it sounded way too familiar.

*It can't be.*

Brittany picked up her menu. "Everything here is soooo good," she told Alisha. "But let me point out a few of my favorites. Plus, we'll want to hear the special. Giovanni is a magician in the kitchen."

"Oh, you must come here a lot," Alisha said. "How wonderful." She tried to make her voice sound convincing, but she felt anything but wonderful at the moment.

"Yes, I'll confess to coming here a lot. I even let my husband bring me here occasionally too."

Alisha glanced at the large marquis-cut diamond on Brittany's left hand. She had gotten the distinct impression over the last few days that her boss had a great marriage. It seemed much greater than just a ring, and the soft smile on the older woman's face now reinforced that view.

"For special occasions or date nights?" Alisha asked, desperate to latch onto a subject and drown out everything else.. "Oh, those too," Brittany said breezily. "He knows I love to eat! Now, let's talk about—"

"Well, well, well. What have we here?" A man's voice cut in.

Every muscle in Alisha's body went into high alert. She put her hands on the edge of the table, ready to push back and flee.

A hand came down on her shoulder and she immediately flinched, even as the sneering voice added, "No need to run away. We're all friends here. Aren't we, Alisha?"

Alisha looked across the table at her boss's stunned face, which she was surprised to see mirrored her own.

"Liam Moriarity," Brittany said flatly. "What in the hell are you doing here?"

Liam laughed mockingly. "Ah, so good to see you again, Brittany. You always were my favorite colleague."

"Liam, you are not welcome at this table."

"Brittany, I'm hurt. I thought I could have a nice little catch up with my friend Alisha here—and you, of course. But I see she's told you her little lies too." To Alisha's dismay, he pulled out one of the extra chairs and sat down, a smirk on his admittedly handsome face.

"Liam, I didn't lie, and no one invited you to sit down," Alisha said stiffly. "Please just go away."

"Now why would I do that when I can have the company of two such beautiful women?"

Alisha half rose from her chair but sank back down at the arrival of a large, dark-haired man wearing a chef's jacket. His short, silvered hair was in disarray, and he had an exuberant smile on his lean face.

"Brittany, my friend!" He leaned over and kissed both her cheeks.

"Giovanni, thank you! I'd like you to meet my colleague, Alisha," she said warmly. "We came in for a special treat."

Giovanni gave Alisha a warm smile. "Welcome, my lady."

He turned back to Brittany. "And this gentleman?"

"Is no gentleman," Brittany answered quickly. "He was not invited to join us."

The sneering smile left Liam's face. Giovanni was at least six inches taller and thirty pounds heavier than his younger counterpart.

"You are the one who has been making all the noise at my bar," Giovanni accused in a thick Italian accent. "I no like troublemakers in my restaurant."

Liam quickly stood up, his hands slightly supplicating. "I know the ladies and was just saying hello."

"Well, the ladies no seem to like your hello. I think it's time for you to leave."

"Uh, sure. No problem," Liam agreed, losing his bravado, as usual, when confronted by a worthy opponent. "I'll take care of my bill and be on my way."

"You do that." Giovanni stood with his arms crossed, waiting for Liam to leave.

"You bet. Alisha. Brittany. Sorry this got . . . cut short."

Giovanni cleared his throat.

"I'll be on my way, but I hope to see you again soon," Liam finished, and nearly scurried away from the table.

Alisha felt her shoulders sag, and she let out a long breath that she hadn't realized she had been holding. Brittany sighed too.

"Thank you, Giovanni," Brittany said warmly to the chef. "That man . . ." She shuddered, and Alisha didn't miss the obvious distaste her boss had for Liam.

"I make sure he leaves," Giovanni assured her, turning to observe the bar area where Liam was settling his bill, the chef's arms still crossed in front of his robust chest.

All three waited in tense silence, and Alisha could hear Liam say a few brief words to the man with whom he had been interacting. She expected to hear the door swish open with his departure.

But it didn't. Instead, she gradually heard his footsteps approach her from behind again. Giovanni dropped his arms, his hands balling into fists at his side. Brittany gasped softly.

Liam addressed Giovanni as he approached. "I'm leaving," he offered, "but I have a message for Alisha first." He stopped right in front of Alisha's chair, looking at her intently with his eerie gray eyes. "Your father said to tell you hello . . . and that he is extremely disappointed in you."

As Alisha reeled back in shock, Liam turned on his heel and stalked out of the room like a cat who had finished toying with his prey.

Silence that hung in the air, weighty and cold.

"Alisha, are you all right?" Brittany's soft and concerned voice barely penetrated the waves of shock, fear, and disbelief that were washing over Alisha's body in violent waves. "You are white as a ghost. Here, drink some water."

Brittany picked up Alisha's water glass and handed it to her, while Giovanni alternately hovered and glared at the door where Liam had disappeared.

Her hand shaking badly, Alisha managed to take the glass and a sip of water, but she could barely taste it with the bile rising in her throat. *My father and Liam. How the hell did that happen?*

"Excuse me," she murmured, rising. She rushed toward the ladies' room, grateful it was clearly marked at the back of the room. She barely made it to the first stall before she threw up what little content was still in her stomach from breakfast. Dry heaves followed as her body convulsed again and again.

She barely heard the swish of the door as Brittany swept in.

"Alisha, my God, I'm so sorry. What can I do?" her boss asked.

Unable to speak, Alisha just shook her head. Tears streamed down her face. *Had her father really sent that message? Or was Liam making it all up?* Unfortunately, it sounded all too much like something her dad would say to completely discount it.

"Here." Brittany thrust a cool, damp paper towel in her hands.

Gratefully, she wiped her face as the older woman led her into the small seating area in the restroom. Alisha sank into one of the plump vinyl chairs and took several deep breaths. She was relieved when some of her nausea and shaking subsided.

"Mon Dieu," Brittany murmured, sitting down in the chair next to Alisha. "What a monster that man is. How could he do that?"

Alisha sighed. "That's Liam."

"I never liked that man, and I was glad when LSM fired him," Brittany stated emphatically, gently patting Alisha's hand. "But what is he doing in New Jersey? And what's this about your father? That can't be true." She paused, looking inquiringly at her younger employee. "Can it?"

"I don't know, Brittany," Alisha replied, her voice ragged. "I don't know how they can even be connected. Sadly, the words are not out of character for my father, but you never know with Liam."

"Mon Dieu, what a monster," Brittany repeated.

"Pretty much," Alisha agreed, fighting back more tears. *Is this never going to end?* She thought she had escaped Liam by moving to New Jersey. *What* is *he doing here?*

Alisha's phone, which she had stuck in her jacket pocket, started to vibrate. She pulled it out, somehow unsurprised to see the name on the caller ID.

Brittany looked at her with eyebrows raised. Alisha showed her the phone, a photo and undeniable words displayed across the screen.

"I guess Liam wasn't lying," Alisha answered the unspoken question.

The phone buzzed again.

Alisha swiped up on the green button. *Might as well get this over with.*

Her father's irate voice echoed in the small space, even without being on speaker. "Alisha! Just what have you done now?"

# CHAPTER 21

# Choosing the Road Less Traveled, or Not

By Thursday, news about Sheryl's upcoming keynote had spread like wildfire. Once Joaquin had reluctantly consented earlier in the week, the NAIT had wasted no time promoting Sheryl and the topic of her presentation. She had been receiving excited and congratulatory messages all morning.

Sheryl was delighted. Paul Haven and the Alpha VC group, however, were not.

Not that they informed her directly. Paul sent John Hargrove with the message and the charge to dissuade her.

"Paul, or rather Paul representing Alpha, has asked me to persuade you to politely disengage from the NAIT keynote," John informed her in an unscheduled in-person visit. To be fair, he had called first, but he had seemed so anxious to talk that Sheryl had moved a few meetings around to accommodate him.

"But why? Even Joaquin conceded that it would be good publicity for The Diamante," Sheryl reminded him. "And *you* encouraged me! Do you agree with this?"

John's head dropped. "Damn it," he said under his breath.

Sheryl waited.

Finally, the executive coach raised his head and looked her in the eye. "No, I can't say that I do," he admitted. "But they're pretty riled up about this. They were not happy with you before; this could make it worse."

"You mean that it *will* make it worse," Sheryl corrected.

John nodded, a piece of hair falling onto his forehead as he did. He impatiently pushed it away; his gray eyes still locked with her hazel ones.

"I'm pretty much in a no-win situation with them, aren't I?" she asked, her shoulders drooping in defeat. All the elation she had felt with the announcement and subsequent congratulations dissipated.

"No, not really," John assured her. "If you come around to their way of thinking. Promoting your philosophy about supporting employee's emotional state isn't exactly in line with that."

Sheryl looked up at the ceiling. "What? So I need to turn into a Paul Haven clone? Or worse, a Hank Turner one? Do they want me to start a Ponzi scheme too?" Her voice rose with anger and disgust. "They don't want someone to think? To challenge them? To be creative?" she ranted.

"Whoa. Slow down," John soothed. "I didn't say that or mean that. I don't think they do either. No one is asking you to do anything illegal. I promise. They just don't want you doing this."

Pushing her bangs back, Sheryl propped her elbows on her desk. This time, John sat across from her, not in the comfortable chair grouping as they had before.

"I'm not going to withdraw," she said emphatically. "I don't care what they say. I'm excited about this speech *and* this topic. More leaders need to hear it. Especially those at Alpha."

John's head bobbed in a vigorous nod. "Bravo! It's not easy to choose the road less traveled."

"Is that what I'm doing?" Sheryl asked, abruptly arrested by his words. "I don't think of myself as a rebel. But isn't that what that phrase means?" A thought occurred to her. *Dave probably doesn't see me as a rebel either.*

"Not a rebel," John quickly advised. "More like an adventurer, someone who isn't afraid to blaze a new trail when the old one isn't going anywhere." He grinned self-consciously. "And yeah, I'm a big Joseph Campbell fan."

"Joseph Campbell?"

"*The Hero's Journey*," he prompted.

"Oh yeah. I remember now. I haven't read any of his work for a long time. And not much of it at that."

"You should," he recommended. "I think you are definitely on a hero's journey. It might give you some encouragement."

"Are you going to get in trouble with Alpha if I don't back out?"

Sheryl asked, suddenly concerned about the implications for him. After all, Alpha had hired him.

His shoulders briefly rose. "Maybe, although I'm not sure how much 'trouble.' They could stop paying me or having The Diamante pay me."

"What about your other clients?"

"Oh, I'm not worried about that. Most of my clients are trying to get out from under leaders like Paul themselves. Especially my female clients. I've found that women are a lot less tolerant of bad behavior than men are—not to make too general of a statement."

"Well, I'm sorry that your mission failed, for your sake. Although I don't think they picked a very good emissary," Sheryl grinned, a twinkle in her eyes. "Your heart really wasn't in it."

John gave a short bark of laughter. "No, it was not," he agreed. "I'll just say that you couldn't be budged." Sheryl shot him a look.

"Will they do something to sabotage me?" She was instantly aware there might be other possible repercussions.

"No, it's unlikely. After all, you're a high-level executive in one of their companies. If they make you look bad, they'll look bad. Especially since you are a woman. They know they can't afford that." John paused and leaned forward in his chair. "But they will try to put pressure on you. Maybe even try to force you out, although they know they are walking a fine line there. Because you were the public hero in bringing down Hank and Anthony, they can't go too far. For now."

Sheryl sighed and rubbed the back of her neck, trying to ease the tension there. Being in a battle with the company's investors was not how she envisioned her board tenure would be like, but it started that way and had continued to be. *Hero's journey, my foot.*

"I'll keep that in mind," she said simply, knowing that he was right. "Will the speech help or hurt my position?"

"Oh, it will help. The more visible you are, the harder it will be for them to jettison you, especially if you are making a good impression. Which you will," John assured her.

Releasing her breath in a whoosh, Sheryl smiled ruefully. "This is . . . well, it's more than I bargained for," she confessed.

"I know, but you'll be fine. I'll be here to help you navigate this, and, trust me, I have a lot of experience with the Alpha VC types. A lot."

"I do trust you," Sheryl said, surprised to hear herself. But it was true. Somehow this man, with his blunt honesty and subtle support, had won her trust, despite who was paying him.

"Good." John smiled and rose. "Now, I'll get out of your hair. We'll talk next week. I'll do what I can to smooth things over with Paul, but he'll probably pop by to talk to you himself."

She groaned.

"Don't worry. You can handle him. Just don't back down. It's that simple."

"Ha! We both know it's anything but simple," Sheryl retorted.

"Road less traveled," he reminded her. "It's your path, if you choose to follow it."

With a quick wave, he let himself out.

For once ignoring protocol, Sheryl didn't escort him. Instead, she rolled the conversation around in her head. *Am I really an adventurer? And how does that change things?*

In spite of herself, Sheryl felt the spark of something inside of her ignite. And she realized she was unexpectedly excited to find out.

"I feel like a whole new world has opened up for me," Sheryl explained, when she called her friend Cindy later Thursday afternoon in Colorado. She timed the call to catch Cindy's lunch break, Mountain time, which was about 2:30 p.m. Eastern time.

"Wow! That's wonderful, Sheryl," Cindy enthused. "I couldn't be more proud of you. I'm going to be there in the front row when you give your speech. I already got approval from my boss to attend the conference." Cindy was also in IT, although she had remained a programming specialist rather than pursuing the management route as Sheryl had.

"Yeah! You can't imagine how relieved I am to hear that," Sheryl told her. "I'm going to need all the moral support I can get."

"Oh, it sounds like you will," Cindy confirmed. "I have an idea for you though. Last weekend, I took this somatic breathing course. It's online and very cheap, but it was really valuable. We've both done a fair amount of breathwork, so it's not really *new* information. But this course puts it in context and gives you tools to use the breathing techniques more effectively. You should try it!" she cajoled enthusiastically. "I'll send you the link. It will really, really help your stress management . . . and I have a feeling that you're going to need a lot of that."

"Ooh, that does sound interesting," Sheryl replied, rolling her shoulders trying to ease the ever-present tension there. "And, there's no doubt I need stress management. Because it's not only work."

"Dave too?" Cindy asked knowingly.

Sheryl pictured her friend's warm brown eyes full of sympathy, as she knew they would be. Cindy's husband had left her for another woman a few years back, which is what prompted her move to Denver.

"Yeah, I'll tell you about that another time," Sheryl stated carefully.

"Of course," Cindy said, changing the subject. "How's the Portal Project?"

Sheryl's shoulders turned as rigid as rock. "Don't ask," she moaned. "I'll be lucky to still have a job by the time I give my speech in June!"

"That bad?"

"Worse."

"Can you fix it?"

"I'm going to give it my best shot," Sheryl said boldly. "I have some ideas, but Patrick is leaving and Keisha just told me about a bunch of problems that Patrick has somehow omitted."

"Yikes! Does Keisha have solutions?" Cindy knew from previous conversations how much of a rock star Keisha was.

"Some, but not enough. She's good, but she's young. She just doesn't have the experience to handle some of this stuff, although she's learning fast."

"Who's going to take Patrick's place? Keisha?"

"I asked her, but she said no. Probably wisely," Sheryl admitted.

"Wow. It takes a lot of courage to turn that down," Cindy said, who was very experienced at turning down promotions that she didn't want. "I assume it's more 'not now' than 'no'?"

"Yes, definitely 'not now.' I'm going to move some other projects around and put Carlos in charge. He has the most relevant experience."

"I'm sure he'll be able to help," Cindy encouraged.

"Yes, he will. I know it," Sheryl answered firmly, but she wondered even as she said it if it was wishful thinking.

"I've gotta get back to work, and I'm sure you do too," Cindy interrupted her thoughts. "Let's talk over the weekend."

"Good idea! I'll call you Saturday morning."

"Not too early," Cindy warned playfully. Sheryl had forgotten about the time difference a time or two in the past and woken her.

Sheryl laughed. "No, not too early. And don't forget to send me that link."

"Will do. Talk soon!"

Ending the call, Sheryl leaned back in her chair. So many thoughts swirled through her head. The Portal Project. The NAIT keynote. Patrick. Keisha. The upcoming board meeting. Dave. She locked in on that last thought.

*Dave. How's he going to take this latest round of attacks from Alpha VC? And my response?* If his reactions last fall were any indication, he wouldn't be happy . . . or supportive.

*But he apologized for that*, she reminded herself. *And said he would listen. And he did.* But his harsh words last Saturday came back to her. "You're so busy crusading at your company."

Sheryl sighed, rubbing her neck again. *Is taking the road less traveled and crusading the same thing?*

"You're on a hero's journey," John had told her earlier. Something within those words resonated with a stark truth to her.

*But do I really want to be?*

# CHAPTER 22

# Facing Reality

Alisha closed her eyes and mentally braced for her father's onslaught over the phone. She heard the soft squeak of vinyl as Brittany settled into the adjacent chair in the women's powder room.

*Really?* she thought distractedly. *She can't give me some privacy?* Then suddenly she was almost glad she was there.

"You are a disgrace to the family name, Alisha Marie," Sam Carson ranted, and her face flushed, knowing Brittany could hear everything. "I can't believe that you tarnished the name of a good man like Liam Moriarity!" he yelled. "Your mother ought to have raised you better than that. Ellen certainly would have!"

Alisha cringed at the reference to her stepmother. That Ellen would have "raised her better" was a common, ongoing theme with her father, but he had no idea who Ellen really was. Ellen was gorgeous, big-breasted, and wily as a fox. She acted all dependent on her husband, but, in reality, she played him like a fine violin. She had done her best to keep Alisha away from Samuel and their two boys. Her father had never seen that in her. He had only bought into Ellen's lies about Alisha's supposedly bad behavior.

Her father's next words snapped Alisha's attention back to his present tirade.

"Liam would have made you a fine husband," Sam stormed. "He makes good money and would have been able to keep you in line! I think you still have a chance if only you would act more like Ellen, be more accommodating to him."

*What?* Alisha put her free hand up to her suddenly throbbing temples.

"But Dad," she started to protest when he paused for a breath.

"Don't interrupt me!" he screamed.

Alisha started to pull the phone away from her ear because his diatribe was so loud he was hurting her ears, but she didn't have a chance. Brittany leaned forward and snatched the phone out of Alisha's hand.

"Assez!" her boss spoke sharply into the phone. "I will not allow Alisha to listen to any more of this. *Vous* êtes *un salaud*! You have *no* idea what you are talking about."

With that, Brittany pressed the red "end" button and turned to look at Alisha. "*Alors*! No wonder you have troubles with men."

Alisha's mouth dropped open. "I can't believe you just did that." Her voice lowered to a whisper. "No one hangs up on him."

A single shoulder rose and fell. "Well, I did," Brittany stated matter-of-factly. "He was berating you. I could not allow it. *You* should not allow it."

"But he's my father!" Alisha protested, stung by the older woman's words. She shifted uncomfortably in the vinyl chair. "You have no idea what he will do now—"

"His parenthood does not give him a license to abuse you," Brittany said softly but firmly, her whiskey eyes full of firm compassion.

Alisha's phone started to vibrate. Brittany rejected the call.

"He'll keep calling, you know," Alisha warned her. "If he was mad before, he'll be furious now.

"So?" Brittany raised her right shoulder again. "We will turn the phone off. He should not be calling you during the workday anyway."

The phone buzzed, and Brittany calmly turned it off.

Alisha's body started shaking. "You have no idea what you're doing," she moaned. "If he already had Liam cued up on his side, God only knows what else he's done or will do. All my life, he's just tormented me. It's never going to stop. And you're just making it worse!"

She wanted to pull her hair out. *I wish everyone would just go away. I can't take this anymore.* Flopping back in her chair, heedless of her boss's presence, she was fuming. *She had no right. None!*

"Alisha, listen to me," Brittany's urgent voice broke into her thoughts. "You are a grown woman. You don't have to talk—or listen—to your father if he is treating you like that."

"Yeah, right," Alisha said scornfully. "As if he would accept that."

Sighing deeply, Brittany grasped her employee's hand. "I know what I'm talking about, I promise."

"Like your father treated you like this? Ha!"

"No, not my father," Brittany said, her voice suddenly quiet, but with an edge. "My grandfather. My mother's father. He was as evil as your father sounds."

"My father isn't evil!" Alisha sat up, indignant at the insult.

"No? Then what do you call what he was just doing?"

Alisha's eyes widened. "Trying to help me?"

"Really? And how is that helping you?"

"Well, it isn't," Alisha admitted ruefully. "But he thinks it will. He has my best interest at heart." *At least that's what everyone has said . . . all my life.*

Brittany cocked her head. "You don't sound like you believe that."

Swallowing hard, Alisha wiped her still-damp eyes. "I do," she answered weakly. "He's . . . he's my father. He wants the best for me, doesn't he?"

"Is marrying Liam what's best for you?" her boss queried gently.

"Of course not! Don't be ridiculous!"

"Yet, that's what he said he wanted for you."

"He just doesn't know Liam. That's all. You know how Liam can be, all charming and schmoozy."

Brittany nodded. "Yes, I do. But why would your father believe Liam instead of you?"

"Because he always does. Men count much more than women in his world," Alisha responded sharply, then felt immediate remorse.

*What am I doing?* she thought, suddenly horrified. *I shouldn't be saying these terrible things about my father, especially to my boss. She's going to . . . I don't know. What does she think?*

Alisha tried to reframe. "Look. He's just old-fashioned. He does mean well," she told Brittany sincerely. "He's not really as bad as he sounds."

"Saying that you don't count is not old-fashioned. It's archaic. I heard him, Alisha, with my own ears. He's not a nice man."

"But he's my father!"

Brittany squeezed her hand and gazed at her sympathetically.

*Oh my God!* Alisha thought, dropping her own gaze. *He's my father. And Brittany heard how nasty he was. Why am I trying to deny it? Brittany's just saying what Julie always says, but that's Julie. This is my BOSS!*

Feeling utterly humiliated—again—Alisha looked up. "You said your grandfather?"

"Yes, my maternal grandfather was 'old-fashioned' too," Brittany said softly, using air quotes. "He wanted all his women, including me, barefoot and pregnant in the kitchen."

Alisha couldn't imagine Brittany barefoot and pregnant in the kitchen—not like that—and she continued listening, fascinated.

"He was appalled that my parents allowed me to get an education," Brittany continued. We all heard about it. In terms very similar to what your father was saying. But he was especially controlling and nasty to me when my parents weren't around."

"What did you do?"

"At first, I tried to defend myself, but that only made things worse. Then, I started ignoring him, but that was 'disrespectful'—or so he said."

"My dad says that too," Alisha murmured.

"I'm sure," Brittany squeezed her hand again. "Then, I started avoiding him. My parents got upset at me for this at first. It was all my fault. But when he turned his attacks on them, they saw the wisdom in avoiding him too."

"You stopped talking to him completely?"

"Yes. I stopped talking to him, seeing him, going to his home, taking his calls. All of it," Brittany confirmed. "It was hard, and it broke my grandmother's heart. Especially when her daughter stopped too."

Alisha tugged on her ponytail. "What did he do?"

"He ranted and raved, especially to my grandmother," Brittany paused, and a sheen of her own tears filled her eyes. "Then, he made her stop seeing us altogether."

"That's awful! What did she do?" Alisha leaned forward, fascinated and horrified by her boss's story.

"She snuck away to see us when she could, but it was hard on her. To see the pain on her face; it was hard on all of us."

"But your parents supported you? My mom would be really upset if I stopped talking to Dad."

"They didn't at first. Trust me, I had many battles with them. But I learned that the only solution is to cut toxic people from your life—if you can. I also learned that it's not easy. My husband helped me finally and fully make peace with it. But only after working through most of it on my own. I would have never been ready for a relationship with him if I had not done the work to forgive and heal myself first."

"Wow! That's amazing. But I don't think I can be strong like you."

"Alisha, you don't have to talk to your father. Would you allow *other* people to talk to you like that? Liam, for instance?"

"Of course I wouldn't," Alisha assured her. "Well, eventually, I wouldn't," she admitted sheepishly.

"Your father is no different. Harder, yes. But he has no right to talk to you the way he did. No one does," Brittany reiterated confidently.

"I really don't have to talk to him?" Alisha asked doubtfully.

"No, you don't."

A thought occurred to Alisha. "What did you say to him? The French?"

"I told him he is a bastard."

"What?" Alisha was stunned by Brittany's audacity, whether her father would understand the words or not. "He's going to kill me."

"Will he truly?" Brittany challenged, although a few lines creased her forehead.

"Truly what? Kill me?" Alisha paused, considering. "No, not physically," she admitted. "But . . ." She shuddered. "I don't think people, especially women, ever stand up to him."

"Has he always been like this?" the older woman asked bluntly, sliding her chair closer to Alisha's.

"Pretty much. Ever since he started seeing Ellen twenty-two years ago, he's been even more harsh with me and my mother. Especially after the boys were born." Her eyes filled with tears, remembering her father's triumph at finally having sons, and his gloating satisfaction ever since, taking them on trips, golfing, and showing them off to his buddies whenever he could. "He was so happy about having sons. Like they were everything."

Brittany reached out and grasped Alisha's hand. "Tell me your story," she said, her rich whiskey eyes filled with empathy and warmth.

Sobs overtook Alisha, and as tears gushed from her eyes, she gasped for air and was shocked to feel her boss's arms encircle her. Other than Julie, no one had ever condemned her father—especially not over her and her feelings. Even her mother often defended him, despite her own resentment. Samuel Carson was larger than life. Handsome, charismatic, charming, rich. He had everything, and people, men or women, rarely confronted him or stood in his way. But especially not women.

"He's so . . . perfect," Alisha sobbed. "And all he wanted was sons. You heard him. He thinks women are here to . . . wait on him. And Liam? Liam is just like him. Except my dad is more polished. He thinks Ellen is perfect because she's so submissive. But she isn't. Not really."

She felt Brittany's hands rubbing her back. It felt nurturing.

"I never do anything right, even though I'm better than my brothers at golf and tennis, and all the sports my dad likes," Alisha continued, her sobs starting to abate.

"Ahh, so that's why Dave Simmons was so attractive," Brittany murmured.

"He is so *nice*! And *kind*," the younger woman agreed. "He made me feel special."

Brittany released her embrace and took Alisha by the shoulders. Her gaze was so sympathetic that Alisha felt tears form again. She blinked them away.

After waiting patiently for Alisha to regain control, Brittany's eyes turned fierce. "There's another thing I learned from that situation with my grandfather. The answer is not a man—any man," her boss advised. "The answer is you. Dave may have seemed like a savior, I can see that now. I had men I thought would be saviors too." She paused. "Only you can save yourself."

Alisha sat motionless. Stunned by her boss's words. *I've heard them before,* she thought. *Sheryl. And Julie. But it seems different coming from Brittany. So much more* real.

Releasing her grasp on Alisha's hand, Brittany rose and gracefully walked over to the bathroom counter. She grabbed a handful of tissues, saving a few for herself and handing the rest to Alisha.

"Is everything okay in there?" Giovanni's deep accented voice penetrated Alisha's stupor.

"*Oui*, Giovanni, we are fine," Brittany answered quickly.

"That man, he is gone. Took his car and drove away. He no bother you again."

"That's a relief," her boss called. "Thank you."

"Now, come eat!" he urged them. "I have some beautiful food ready for you."

Brittany shot a questioning look at Alisha, who nodded.

"We'll be right there," the older woman assured her friend.

After a few seconds, Brittany turned back to a still sniffling Alisha. "Are you okay? I didn't mean to be so rough on you, but . . ." She shrugged her right shoulder again.

*I wish I could do that*, Alisha thought, admiring once again the luxurious style of her boss. "It's okay," she assured Brittany. "Give me a minute to clean up the mascara."

"Don't turn your phone on when I leave," her boss warned her, handing the offending object back.

Alisha laughed gruffly. "Trust me. I won't." She cleared her throat. "Thank you, Brittany. You've given me a lot to think about. I really appreciate you sharing your story. It, well, helps to know that you've gone through something like this. Other people . . ."

"Yes, they don't understand. They tell you that you have to tolerate your family. I get it. But you really don't. It's time to face the reality of who your father is and deal with him accordingly."

Swallowing hard, Alisha nodded. "It's hard."

"Yes, it is. We all want our parents to be perfect. But none of them are. And a few are downright evil."

"And my father is one of those," Alisha murmured in a small voice.

Brittany put her hand on Alisha's shoulder. "Unfortunately for you, yes," she said gently.

They both started as Brittany's phone began to ring.

"*Mon Dieu!*"

"Who is it?" Alisha asked.

Brittany held up her phone. There was no name associated with the number, but Alisha recognized it immediately.

"Oh no!"

"Oh yes," Brittany said grimly. "Oh yes."

# CHAPTER 23

# Intersections and Connections

Gemma was astonished at how much publicity her new position at Atrium had generated—before she even started! Of course, the announcement made the trade press. But she had been taken aback that it also appeared in several prominent business publications, including *The Wall Street Journal*. She had felt a thrill go through her when her son had proudly pointed it out after seeing it while doing research for his Current Affairs class.

By Thursday afternoon, she had made a lot of progress getting through the material that Kushma had continued to send throughout the week. She had used AI to summarize many of the documents, speeding up the process enormously. Even so, there was a lot of confidential material that Gemma felt she should wade through herself, knowing that AI leaks were a rising threat to sensitive marketing campaigns.

Rolling her shoulders, she looked up from yet another tedious document and stretched. *I need a break*, she thought. Looking around at her still unfinished office, she groaned softly. *So much still to be done, and it's already Thursday. Only four days left of my freedom.* She frowned at the thought.

The chime of her email claimed her attention. Expecting yet another missive from Kushma, she was relieved to see that it was just another alumni update from her alma mater. She had attended Tufts in Boston and loved the city. Ironically, she would have gladly stayed there had it not been for Kevin. *Ugh!*

Idly, she opened the email as a distraction and was surprised to see her name in the top paragraph. *I have to give the Atrium public relations team credit. They have covered all the bases with this announcement.* She smiled to herself. *It's kind of nice to be this celebrated.*

She was about to close the email when another familiar name caught her eye. *Sheryl Simmons. Wow. There's a name from the past.*

Sheryl and another woman had shared an apartment during her sophomore year at Tufts. It had only been the one year, as Sheryl was two years ahead of her, but it had been a fun one. Gemma had been so impressed with Sheryl's dedication and smarts. It hadn't been easy for Sheryl, being in the CompSci department, which was still heavily male, but Sheryl had not only persevered, she had shined! *I wonder why we haven't stayed in touch.*

Skimming the paragraph, she was thrilled to see that Sheryl would be making the keynote speech at this year's national technology conference. What an honor! *I'll bet she'll be great.* However, she was startled to see the topic. "Corporate Grief: A Leader's Responsibility."

*Grief? What does that have to do with corporate life?*

Intrigued, she pulled up her browser and googled Sheryl's name. She was shocked to see all of the articles about the scandal at The Diamante and Sheryl's prominent role in bringing the perpetrators to justice. *Good for her!* Gemma pumped her fist. *I knew she was destined for great things.*

Clicking on a video of Sheryl at a press conference, Gemma was even more impressed by her former friend. Calm, professional, and still very attractive, Sheryl had developed a presence that was captivating. *No wonder they want her to be a keynote speaker.* Sheryl had always been a ball of energy, but there was a new confidence and, *hmmm,* power in her demeanor now.

Gemma's phone dinging with an incoming text distracted her from her thoughts. Expecting another text from Kushma, she was pleased to see it was from Anna.

**Meet cancelled today.**
**We have practice instead.**

*That buys me a good three hours of work time,* Gemma thought immediately, her shoulders relaxing in relief. Between the office renovation, the kids' activities, and Kushma's prep material, her week had evaporated. Now, she'd have a chance to finish painting today. *Yay!*

She turned her attention back to her screen. *Sheryl Simmons*. On impulse, Gemma pulled up The Diamante website and looked for the contact information. After jotting it down, she hesitated. *Should I reach out after all this time? It seems like she's such a big deal now.* She put her phone down. *Later. Maybe.*

Just then, another email notification from Kushma arrived, cementing her decision. *Five documents! Five. What does the woman think I am doing?* Glancing through them, she was relieved to see that none were marked confidential. She fed them into ChatGPT and asked for a summary. *Thank goodness I don't have to actually read most of these. I'd be doing nothing else.*

A niggle of doubt reasserted itself. *If there is this much work before I even start . . .* She shook her head. *No. It will be fine.* The little voice shot back. *Will it? Will you?*

Her phone rang. She was shocked to see that it was the number she had just written down.

"Hello?"

"Gemma? Is that you?" came the once familiar voice.

"Sheryl! I was just about to call you. I saw—"

"Your name in the alumni newsletter," Sheryl finished, laughing. "What are the odds we would both be mentioned in the same email?"

"Almost none," Gemma replied grinning. "So, you're a big shot now. I'm really happy for you."

"I don't think so," Sheryl said matter-of-factly. "And Atrium. Wow. That's a big deal."

"I Googled you. You *are* a big shot. That press conference was so impressive. How did you get so, uh, confident?"

"As if you're not?" her former friend replied. "I hope we don't get to this age without gaining some confidence. Although, it's not easy in the business world, is it?"

"Probably easier for me than you," Gemma asserted. "I've been in a pretty female-dominated world. You're still playing with all the guys."

"Yeah, but working with all women, or mostly women, must have its own set of issues. Unfortunately, we can be brutal on each other,"

Sheryl reminded her. They'd both experienced issues with the other woman who had roomed with them.

"Oh wow. You're right. Catherine. I haven't thought about her in years, frankly."

"She was a piece of work. So competitive. I've run into other women like her in the workplace, but fortunately not too often. Have you?"

"Of course, I have," Gemma agreed. "I was lucky to have a great boss though, at Viva! He was good to me."

Gemma realized that it was true. Charles had been good to her. Tough, but not unreasonable.

"So, what else are you up to? Married? Kids?" Sheryl was asking.

Filling Sheryl in on her life, Gemma glazed over her concerns about Atrium, presenting the opportunity as the blessing she hoped it would be. But, as she always had, she did tell her old friend about Kevin's cheating and his new wife. In return, she was surprised that Sheryl hadn't had children, when she'd remembered such a mothering side to her in college.

"It just worked out that way," Sheryl explained wistfully. "We would have liked to, but . . ."

"Yeah, life doesn't always work out the way we expect, does it?" asked Gemma, thinking of her failed marriage.

"It doesn't. So, where are you living? You've been commuting to New York. Are you in that area?" Sheryl inquired.

"I'm in New Jersey actually. Summit, actually."

Sheryl gasped. "You're kidding. I work just down the road from there and live out in Hunterdon County. We're practically neighbors!"

"We are! We'll have to get together and really catch up. I, uh, I could use a good friend," Gemma admitted. "I kind of lost a lot of women friends in the divorce."

"Oh Gemma, I'm sorry. I know that happens, but it makes no sense. Especially when he cheated. Damn, women should stick together more."

"But we don't," Gemma replied sadly. "Look at us. We haven't been in touch for decades, and we were really close."

"I know. We let life get in the way."

"More like work getting in the way," Gemma observed.

Sheryl chuckled. Gemma imagined her pushing back her bangs like she always had in college. *Does she still do that?*

"Too true," Sheryl answered. "Too true."

Gemma heard another voice in the background.

"Sorry Gemma. I've gotta go," her friend said. "Something has come up here."

"No problem, Sheryl. It was great catching up."

"I'll text you my cell number. This is your cell? I got it from the alumni directory."

"Yup, it is. And that would be great. Talk soon!"

"Bye, Gemma!"

Lowering her phone back to the desk, Gemma leaned back in her new comfortable ergonomic chair and smiled. *Wow. That was great, and she lives so close.* It had been a while since she had had a close female friend. Talking to Sheryl had reminded her how important that was—or used to be.

*And should be again*, she told herself.

The sharp chirp of her phone interrupted her reverie. She wasn't surprised to see that it was Kushma.

"Hello, Kushma," she greeted her new boss, infusing as much warmth as she could muster into her tone.

"Gemma. Only a few more days. Are you excited to start?" Kushma enthused.

"I am, although I feel like I've started already with all the stuff you've been sending."

Kushma cackled. There was no other word for it. "That's nothing! Just a little teaser. Have you read it all?"

"I have," Gemma replied, not quite truthfully. There was no way she was admitting to using AI.

"Good. Good," Kushma said. "But make sure you don't put the confidential stuff into AI. I forgot to tell you that."

*Of course, she assumed I would use AI.* "I didn't," Gemma assured her boss. "I know better than that."

"Ha! Excellent. I'll let you go. We'll talk again Monday."

Kushma hung up, and Gemma was left with the impression that she had just passed another little test. Shrugging ruefully, she closed her laptop and looked around the room. *Time to get back to my decorating.*

But before she could, the door to the garage crashed open. A moment later, her son appeared in the doorway. His face was red and his blond hair disheveled.

"KJ? What are you—"

"Mom, I need your help!"

# CHAPTER 24

# Is Strength of Will Enough?

**Friday, January 21**

Alisha still couldn't believe that her father had obtained Brittany's phone number and had called her. He had called her boss! She and Brittany could only guess that Liam had given him her boss' number. But Alisha wondered nervously if it could have been her mother. Denise also had Brittany's number, in case of emergency.

But by 6:00 p.m. Friday evening, that shock had been superseded by the absolute barrage of phone calls that had followed. Since lunchtime yesterday, her father had been calling incessantly. Calling her. Calling Brittany. Calling her mother. He had even become desperate enough to call Julie, who had promptly hung up on him. In fact, everyone had, except Denise. Her mother never could refuse her father anything, despite what he had done to her.

Until late morning today. The calls had abruptly stopped. A reprieve. *Or was it?*

Alisha sighed. Flopping onto the sofa, she picked up her phone. Cautiously, as if it were a snake ready to strike. *Still no new calls. Phew!*

Not that she thought her father was finished. He was nothing if not persistent. More likely, he was regrouping, trying to find another way to get through to her. In the last thirty hours, he had also had his oldest son and her stepmother try to call. With Brittany's encouragement—and Julie's—she had not answered any of them.

The only inkling of support she had received from anyone in her family was a terse text from her youngest brother:

**Hang tough.**

Not much to go on, but at least it was something. She knew that Trey struggled with playing second fiddle to the heir apparent, Samuel,

Jr. But befriending Alisha was more than his little rebellious streak allowed. He was usually just as disdainful as the rest of them. That the eighteen-year-old had texted at all was something of a miracle. And the fact that he hadn't called to bitch her out like the others. *Wow! He must be on his dad's sh*t list again.*

When the phone rang, she flinched. But it wasn't him, only her mother—again.

Deciding she couldn't take another session of listening to her mother defend Samuel Carson, she didn't answer. *Maybe I should just turn the phone off.* But this was her work phone. Customers could call, although that was unlikely on a Friday night.

*Friday night. Here I am in my half-furnished condo, dreading phone calls, and no place to go. Why did I move to New Jersey again?* She wasn't hungry. In fact, she hadn't eaten much since yesterday, when she had forced down a copious amount of amazing Italian food under the watchful eye of Brittany and Giovanni. Her stomach roiled at the thought of it.

*Maybe the gym?* She sat up. There was a nice workout space in the clubhouse that was part of the condominium community. It had been part of the draw in purchasing here. *Maybe I could meet a cute guy there*, she thought, before remembering Brittany's assertion that the answer wasn't another man.

Deep down, Alisha knew her boss was right. She might need a workout or some other distraction from the stress, but she didn't need a man.

Alisha stood up and paced across the empty dining room. The conversation with Brittany yesterday along with numerous follow-ups from the older woman and her friend Julie had triggered a bout of deep introspection that was unusual. But she couldn't avoid the facts. She was here, alone, on a Friday night. She had at least one known enemy at work because of her own misguided actions. Her father had completely turned against her, going so far as to team up with the man who had harassed her at work. And her mother was on *their* side!

She couldn't deny that her life was screwed up, but Alisha had no clue how to rescue herself. *I've always looked to the outside*, she thought honestly, turning and tromping back toward the living room area. *To people like Julie and Dave to rescue me. Even Sheryl, for goodness' sake. Am I making Brittany another crutch?*

But no, her boss, while being incredibly supportive, was not allowing Alisha to depend on her. "You are stronger than you think," Brittany had told her. "Look at all you've done in spite of the headwinds your father had created. And that email you wrote? Only a strong woman would do that. Trust yourself, Alisha. Don't rely on me. Trust yourself. And get back to work!" she had teased.

The problem was that Alisha had no idea how to do that—the trusting herself part. Her father had always pushed her, maybe not in the right direction, but he pushed her. Then Liam. Her striking out for New Jersey had been driven by her desire for Dave, a married man. And there had been boyfriends. None she wanted to think about, but they hadn't exactly been prince charming, not once she'd gotten to know them. *Ugh!*

When her phone rang again, she welcomed the distraction from her depressing thoughts.

"Julie!" she said enthusiastically. "I'm so glad you called. I've been sitting here thinking about how messed up my life is. I need a distraction."

"Maybe it's good that you think about that," Julie said wisely. "You distract yourself too much."

Alisha moaned, flopping back down on the sofa. "Stop. The last two days have been bad enough."

"I know," her friend said, her tone more sympathetic now. "But this was bound to happen. You can't keep running away, Alisha."

"I'm not running away! I just don't want to think about this stuff. Why can't things just be easy?"

She heard Julie sigh. "You know it doesn't work like that."

Alisha wrapped her ponytail around her finger. "Yeah, I know, but this is so hard."

"I wish I was there to give you a hug. You sound like you need one."

"Oh Julie, I wish that too," Alisha replied, tears filling her eyes. *Damn, I'm tired of spewing tears like a damn fountain.* She missed her friend. She even missed her old beat-up apartment in Lexington Hills, California. "Why did I ever move here?"

"You really want me to answer that?" Julie quipped. "But seriously, as much as I miss you, I think it's good that you're far away from your dad. Despite what happened with Liam, it's harder for him to get to you there. Not impossible obviously but being away will give you a chance to get some much-needed perspective on your family."

"You sound like Brittany."

"Good. I like her. You lucked out, having her as a boss."

"She sure is different than I thought she was. Between the email and my humiliating breakdown in the ladies' room, she has shown me a whole new side of her." Alisha paused, thinking back on the way Brittany had become her champion. "It's pretty incredible, really."

"There are people in the world who will support you, Alisha. Rally by your side and really support you, in a positive and healthy way. Your dad always made everything a competition between you and your brothers. It wasn't right. It still isn't. Especially since he made it clear you could never, ever win."

"But what do I do now? Cut myself off from my whole family?" Alisha wailed, the tears coming down again.

"You might have to," Julie said soberly. "Brittany is right about that too. They're toxic. Even your mother."

"Mom still thinks that Dad will get over Ellen and come back to her—after more than fifteen years!"

"Yeah, Denise is really good at delusion. No secret where you get that from."

Alisha pushed herself upright. "Hey! I'm not delusional."

"No. What about Dave? What about your father? I could go on. You don't see reality sometimes, Alisha, particularly where men are involved."

"Hmph." Thick tension filled the air for a moment.

"I'm not trying to be mean; you know I love you. I just want you to stop chasing people who you will never please and learn to please yourself."

"Isn't that selfish? That's what Mom says," Alisha countered.

"If you take it too far, yes," Julie clarified. "But Alisha, you've got a long way to go before you take it too far. Setting boundaries is *healthy*, not selfish."

"Did you and Brittany rehearse this?"

Julie's musical laughter came through the phone. "No, did she say that?"

"Yes, and something about trusting myself."

"Oh good. I like her. I hope I get to meet her sometime."

Alisha stopped pulling on her ponytail and jumped up. "That's a great idea. Why don't you come for a visit?"

"In January? To New Jersey?"

"Okay, not a great time, but I'd love to see you." Alisha swallowed hard, blinking back more tears. She resumed her restless pacing. "Please, Julie? I . . . n-n-need you."

Alisha heard a big whoosh of air.

"You've never said that before," Julie said, sounding a bit surprised.

Alisha stopped abruptly. "I haven't?"

"No, you haven't." Julie paused.

Alisha pictured her friend's delicately boned face frowning. Julie was a worrier.

"Please?"

"Let me see," Julie finally said. "I'll have to check my schedule—"

"I'll send you tickets," Alisha offered.

"Alisha, I can pay my way. I'll let you know tomorrow, okay?"

"Okay," Alisha agreed reluctantly. "But try?"

After reassuring Alisha she'd try, Julie hung up. Buoyed by the prospect of her friend's visit, Alisha wandered into the kitchen and opened the refrigerator. *I really should eat something.* She was rummaging through the sparse offerings, wishing she could afford take-out when the doorbell rang.

Startled, she spun around, leaving the refrigerator open.

The doorbell rang again. She started forward and then froze as whoever was out there started pounding on the door.

"Alisha! Open this door!"

Her heart stopped. Her father. He was here.

"Open this door or I'm going to break it down!" he threatened, in a voice loud enough that she was sure all her neighbors could hear.

She took a step forward and stopped again. Her heart was pounding so hard she could feel it vibrate against her ribs. She recalled Brittany's words. *"You don't have to take his abuse."*

But what now? He was standing outside her door, and she had no doubt he would try to break in.

Her phone rang and she ran to grab it. *Brittany. Thank God!*

"My dad's here. He's threatening to break down my door!" she cried. "What—"

"Call the police."

"What? I can't do that!"

"Do you want him there?" Brittany asked.

"No, I don't. He's scaring me."

"Alisha, call the police before you or someone else gets hurt," her boss urged. "You have to protect yourself."

"Oh my God," Alisha wailed. "I can't do that."

"Then let him in. It's your decision," Brittany said calmly. "But listen to your gut. Trust yourself. Is letting him in really the right thing to do?"

"Yes. No. God, I don't know."

The pounding got louder. "Alisha! Open up, right now."

"I'm afraid," Alisha whimpered. She had never heard her father this angry. And to fly all the way to New Jersey? A sense of certainty settled in her gut. *Nothing good is going to happen if I open that door.* The thought surprised her. "But I can't open the door," she said out loud.

"Then don't," Brittany said matter-of-factly. "You know the right thing to do—for you. I'm going to hang up so you can do it. Call me if you need me. I've got your back."

Alisha looked at the phone in dismay. The pounding and yelling continued.

*You know the right thing to do.*

She dialed 9-1-1.

# CHAPTER 25

# Why Am I Changing?

Sheryl watched her husband's face darken with some mix of emotions she couldn't quite identify. A frown? A scowl?

"Dave? What's that look?"

The furrows on his forehead deepened. "Disbelief? Disgust? I really can't believe you, Sheryl. Last fall was bad enough, but a hero? A hero's journey? What is wrong with this guy? I thought he was supposed to be helping you, not encouraging you to continue this, this crusade!"

It was Sheryl's turn to frown, delicate vertical lines appearing between her eyebrows. She twirled her wineglass, buying time. She and Dave sat in their family room, ensconced in their usual seats: Dave in his recliner, herself in a corner of the large leather sofa. A bottle of their favorite pinot noir sat on the coffee table.

"I thought we had gotten past this," she murmured.

"Past what? Your insanity?" Dave snapped.

"Past you thinking I am insane," Sheryl shot back. "You had started to be a lot more supportive after . . ."

"Don't say her name again," Dave barked. "She had nothing to do with this."

"I didn't," she snapped. "I started to say after the board meeting and press conference. You said you were proud of me. Did you mean it?"

Dave took a gulp of wine. The rich voice of Josh Groban filled the silence.

"I did mean it. I was proud of you." He paused for a beat. "I am," he added grudgingly.

"You don't sound like it," Sheryl retorted. She took a sip of her own wine.

"Look, I'm concerned," Dave said, his tone more conciliatory. "You can't keep fighting Alpha VC like this. You're going to lose. I don't know why this John Hargrove doesn't see that. He knows the players better than you do. That's why Alpha hired him."

"I don't know why you always think I'm going to lose!" Sheryl shifted uncomfortably in her seat. Pushing her bangs back, she was aware that there was more than a thread of truth in her husband's statements.

"Because I know these guys, Sheryl. They don't give up."

"I don't give up either."

Dave nodded. "No, you don't, but maybe a strategic retreat is in order. You've already taken on a lot. The memorial meetings. Layla Arch vs. Blake Jones. The investigation. Yes, you've won all those battles, but how long can you keep fighting?"

"As long as it takes?" Doubt filled Sheryl's voice. She suddenly bit her lip. *Am I taking on too much?*

"Until you don't have a job? Until you're a pariah in the investment community? That's where this is going."

Sheryl threw her free hand up. "Since when have you become such a doomsday person? Why are you always so negative?"

"Because I'm watching my wife tank her career and our marriage at the same time, and I feel helpless to stop it!" Dave growled, pushing himself out of the recliner and stalking into the adjacent kitchen. "Who wouldn't be negative in those circumstances?"

She watched Dave fling open the refrigerator door.

"I'm hungry. What are we doing for dinner? There's nothing in here."

Closing her eyes, Sheryl silently counted her breath, employing one of the somatic breathing techniques she'd recently learned. *In: two-three-four. Hold: two-three-four. Out: two-three-four. Hold: two-three-four. Repeat. Again. Reduce adrenaline. Stay alert. In: two-three-four.*

"What are you doing?" Dave snarled from the kitchen.

"Breathing."

"Sher-yl." Dave's voice took on a warning note.

"I'm doing 'box breathing' to calm down and improve my focus. Mostly so that I don't throw this wine at you."

She heard her husband groan. "Seriously?" he asked incredulously. *In: two-three-four. Hold: two-three-four.*

"Sheryl, dinner?"

Her eyes snapped open. "Let's just order take-out."

"That will take too long."

"There's chili in the freezer. You can heat that up," she offered.

"Fine." He rummaged in the freezer, finally finding the right container. Snapping off the lid, he put it in the microwave and then pulled salad fixings out of the refrigerator.

Sheryl didn't move. *I know I should get up and help, but . . .* A wave of sadness washed over her. She sipped her wine. The sounds of chopping mingled with the soft music playing. Deepening her breathing again, she inhaled the aroma of the warming chili. *Why did I even bring this conversation up with Dave? I knew how he would react. Hero's journey, indeed. He still sees me as the . . . what?*

"How do you see me?" she asked Dave abruptly.

He stopped chopping, the knife poised above the peppers on the bamboo cutting board, and turned to look at her. "What? What do you mean? I see you as Sheryl. The smart, successful, amiable woman you've always been. Until recently."

"Amiable?" Sheryl focused on that word. "What do you mean by that?"

"Sheryl, do you have to dissect everything I say? Amiable means that you get along with people. That you're pleasant to be around. You're generally positive and, well, nice." He went back to chopping. "It's a *good* thing," he added defensively.

"Hmmm . . . Is it?" Sheryl murmured more to herself than him.

"Yes!" he replied emphatically, waving the knife. "It is a good thing. People *like* people who are amiable."

"And people don't like me now? I'm no longer amiable?" Sheryl asked, sitting up straighter and twisting to look over the sofa back to see him more directly.

Dave put the knife down. "I didn't say that! Stop putting words in my mouth." He opened the lettuce crisper and doled generous servings of the greens onto two salad plates.

"Sorry," Sheryl said reluctantly. *I'm not sure I am sorry, but, well,*

*I guess that's what he means by being* amiable. *Ugh! Do I want to be amiable?* Is *it a good thing?* She twirled her wine glass again while she considered that.

The microwave dinged. She watched Dave divide the chili into two bowls, a bigger portion for himself, and spread grated cheese over the top.

"Dinner's ready. You can get your own salad dressing," her husband muttered.

Sheryl rose and went into the kitchen as he carried their plates to the table. *Do I want to be amiable?*

"Being amiable sounds like being a doormat to me," she said, once they were seated at the table.

"A doormat?" Dave rolled his eyes. "Where do you come up with this stuff?"

"I'm serious, Dave. It does. It's not that I don't want to be nice and get along with people, but I can't do that at the expense of myself, my conscience."

Her husband put his spoon on the table. "What do you mean? What has changed? You are so different in the last year or so. I hardly know you anymore." This time, he sounded more frustrated than angry.

"I don't know," she said slowly, searching her mind for answers. "It's just that I have this . . . drive in me. No, that's not the right word. I've always had drive, but it's different now. Less about succeeding than . . ." She let out a puff of air as she sought the right words to describe what seemed indescribable.

"Less succeeding? Sheryl, you're at the brink of breaking through to the pinnacle of your career! You should be totally focused on succeeding!"

"I am focused on succeeding, but it's different. I don't know how to describe it. I need to be *me*. To succeed on *my* terms, I guess."

Dave looked incredulous, his eyes wide, eyebrows raised. "Is this because you're going through menopause?" he finally blurted.

"Dave!"

"Well, it's a legitimate question," he defended himself.

Sheryl sighed. "Really? If there's a problem with a woman, it has to be hormones? Like when you blamed everything on PMS?"

He waved his spoon. "I didn't do that, but hormones play a role. They do. For men too."

"Yes, they play a role. I can't deny that," Sheryl admitted. "But . . ." *Is this because of menopause? Not that I'm quite there yet. But he's right that something is different now. I feel different. Less inclined to go along, to be, well,* amiable.

"What?" he asked when the silence had stretched out for a few minutes.

"I'm thinking about your question," she replied. "I'm wondering if there might be something to it. I remember that Mom changed around fifty. So did Aunt Bea. They started standing up for themselves more, being less . . ."

"Amiable?" he suggested, and they both laughed.

"Yeah. That," she agreed. "I'm going to do some research on this. I hate to blame things on hormones, but I feel like there's something important here. My gut—"

"No, not your gut!" Dave protested. "That gut causes nothing but trouble." But there was laughter in his voice, and she saw warmth back in his dark brown eyes.

*He really is a handsome man when he smiles,* Sheryl thought. *I wish, what do I wish? That he was more supportive? That I* trusted *him more?*

"Dave, I need to trust you again," she blurted, flushing with dismay. *I didn't have to say it like that.* She knew it to her core when the warmth left his eyes, replaced by a cold, anger.

"We're not going down that road again. Not now." He pushed back his chair, took his unfinished bowl, and stomped out of the kitchen.

Her eyes followed as he disappeared in the hallway, heading for his office, she surmised. That's where he always retreated when he was angry or "had enough."

*You shouldn't have said that,* she scolded herself. *We were starting to bond, to find common ground.* She pushed her food away, her appetite gone. *I need to apologize for that one.*

Taking a deep breath, she rose, threw away the rest of the chili, and put her plates and utensils in the dishwasher. *In: two-three-four. Hold: two-three-four.* By the time she completed the tasks, she was calmer.

She headed down the hall to Dave's office. The door was closed. She lifted her hand to knock, but at that moment, his loud, angry voice rang out.

She held her breath as she heard the words: "I don't know if I can take this anymore!"

CHAPTER 26

# **Boundaries and Fences**

**Sunday, January 23**

Alisha rushed toward Julie the minute she stepped through security at Newark Airport. Julie dropped her bags and wrapped her friend in a tight hug.

"I'm so, so glad you are here," Alisha whispered brokenly. "And that you would come so quick. It's been such a nightmare."

"I know, but I'm very, very proud of you," Julie said softly into Alisha's ear.

A tall woman, pulling a roller bag, pushed past them, nearly knocking them over. She offered no apology, only an irritated glare as she rushed forward.

"We need to move," Alisha said, disengaging from Julie and picking up her friend's bags. "This way."

Alisha weaved skillfully through the throng waiting for their luggage with Julie in tow.

"It's so crowded," Julie said in an awestruck voice. Her curly brown hair swung around her shoulders as she looked around the huge baggage claim area.

"Yup," Alisha confirmed. "Airport. I know you're not used to it, but we'll be out of here in a jiff."

Julie's job, unlike Alisha's, did not require travel. At least it was a Sunday.

True to her word, the two women were out of the terminal and in Alisha's small SUV in less than ten minutes. The traffic this Sunday morning was light, and Alisha heard Julie lean back and yawn as she eased onto the highway.

"Tired?"

"I hardly slept on the plane," Julie told her. "I'm not sure I like red-eye flights."

Alisha snorted. "That's why they call them red-eyes. I'll have you back to my condo and napping in no time. Do you want to eat first?"

Julie glanced at her smartwatch. "Probably. I don't know if I'm more tired or hungry."

"Food first," Alisha said decisively. "I know just where to stop. A Jersey diner. You'll love it."

"If you say so," Julie said doubtfully.

"I do."

"I hate to ask, but what's happening with your dad? The last you told me was that the police had taken him away because he was pounding on your door and making a ruckus because you wouldn't let him in. Do they still have him? Are they charging him?"

Alisha cringed, even as she confidently swung around a semi. "No, he's on his way back to California, I think."

"You think?"

"The police let him go under the condition that he leave the state immediately," Alisha informed her. "They told me they followed him to the airport but didn't go in."

"Really? Do you think he went?"

"I hope so. I think what happened Friday night freaked him out. He can't afford to have a police record. It would look bad for his business," Alisha explained, her face flushing. She still felt a little guilty. "As an insurance agent, people have to trust him."

"That's for sure. So, they didn't charge him?" Julie's eyes crinkled with worry.

"No. I didn't want to press charges—at least not this time. Although one of my neighbors was really upset about that."

Alisha was grateful that at least three of her neighbors had called the police before she had. They had arrived moments after she had placed her own call, handcuffing her irate father and taking him down to the station.

"Wow. I wish I had seen the great Samuel Carson in handcuffs! He must have been beside himself."

"Oh, that's putting it mildly. I've never seen him that angry," Alisha replied, shuddering with the memory. Her voice grew quiet. "I was really, really scared."

"I'm sure you were, but you didn't back down," Julie breathed. "I'm so proud of you. He got what he deserved. Well, maybe."

"He was smart enough to calm down and apologize once he got to the police station."

"Your dad has an incredible instinct for self-preservation."

"That he does. According to the female officer who followed up with me today, he really turned on the charm with the police chief." Alisha shook her head. "She was quite disgusted. Thank goodness they didn't make me go to the station to witness that."

"I can only imagine. How were your neighbors with you, Alisha?"

"They were actually amazing. One of the ladies offered her spare bedroom to me so that I wouldn't have to stay at my condo in case he came back. So sweet. Since he was at the station, I didn't take her up on it."

"Wow! And they say people aren't very neighborly in the New York area." Julie stifled a yawn.

"I saw that!" Alisha teased as she guided her Hyundai Tucson off the exit ramp and into the parking lot of a brightly lit diner. "We're here. I need food in my stomach before I continue this conversation."

"I'm surprised you can eat," Julie said, sliding out of the vehicle and shivering in the sudden cold. "Oh my. It's freezing!"

"Ha! Let's get you inside. A hot cup of coffee will help." Alisha tugged her friend's hand. "Did I tell you how happy I am that you're here?"

Julie laughed as they pushed into the warm, steamy diner. "Ahh. And yes, you did. I'm glad too. I want to support you, as much as I can. I know what you're doing is incredibly hard and incredibly brave."

Alisha flushed. "Thanks, Julie. I appreciate that. Honestly, I feel a lot lighter now."

Julie glanced at her curiously as they followed the hostess to a booth and slid in on opposite sides. "You do?" she asked after the woman walked away.

"Yeah, I really do," Alisha confirmed. "It's weird, because I'm still scared. I know my dad won't give up, but well, I feel like I've withstood the worst. I mean, him coming to my house and pounding on the door." Alisha grimaced. "It was really bad. Scary and embarrassing. But it did open my eyes to see just how bad he can get—how bad he is, controlling, expecting his way. The verbal and emotional, uh, abuse, if you want to call it that, is bad enough, but that? That was just crazy."

"Alisha, it was *abuse*. I know you don't like to label it as that, but it is. Just like Liam."

"I know," Alisha hung her head. "But it still hurts to say that about my father." Tears glinted in Alisha's eyes as they met Julie's. "Your parents aren't supposed to hurt you like that, you know?"

Julie reached across the table and took Alisha's hand. "No, they're not, but it happens. You heard Brittany's story. You're not alone. My aunt went through something like this with her ex-husband too." Julie shuddered.

Alisha squeezed her friend's hand and looked at her gratefully. "No, I'm not alone. Thanks to you and Brittany. The police even recommended a counselor from the local women's center." Alisha tugged her ponytail. "I have an appointment next week. With Brittany's blessing."

"Oh, Alisha! I'm so proud of you. That's great! It's so awesome to see you setting boundaries with your family. Finally." Despite her weariness, Julie was beaming at her.

"It still feels like fences or even brick walls to me sometimes. Like I'm doing something wrong, but . . ." Alisha cleared her throat. "It also feels good, right? Like I'm standing up for myself in a good way. You know?"

"I do know," Julie said, sliding her hand back and picking up the oversized menu. "But it's great to see you starting to trust yourself. It's a journey, but you've taken the first, big, important steps. And you have some great people on your side." She grinned. "Like me!"

Alisha laughed. "Yes, like you. Now, let's eat! And I want to tell you about this guy . . ."

# CHAPTER 27

# Can This Bridge Be Built?

Dave and Sheryl hadn't talked, not in any real way, since the incident on Friday evening. Sheryl was worried. And tired. She felt like she hadn't slept a wink. The gap between them that had narrowed in the immediate aftermath of Alisha's confession, had widened again. *And I don't know if it's bridgeable*, Sheryl thought.

She mentally shook herself. *Wait. That isn't like me. I need to be more positive.*

By Sunday morning, she was feeling restless. She had used her precious weekend to prepare for this week's board meeting presentation, specifically the report on AI that Paul Haven wanted. But her concentration wavered between her work and the dark cloud hanging over her marriage.

She shifted through AI reports aimlessly, although she'd already thoroughly researched them and taken vital notes. She sighed. The AI research was depressing in itself, which only added to her angst. Opinions ranged from catastrophic to rosy optimism with everything in between. She was particularly disturbed by some of the communication from company CEOs that were highly publicized. One CEO had gone as far as declaring that company loyalty was dead, and that employees were there on a purely transactional level. *Kind of like treating people like robots*, Sheryl thought with disgust. *I bet they have highly productive employees there.*

Blowing out a puff of air, she pushed her bangs back and moved onto a new article. Deeply engrossed for several minutes, she literally jumped in her chair when Dave knocked on the doorframe of her office.

"Sorry, I didn't mean to startle you," he said when she yelped.

Sheryl spun around. "It's okay," she said, catching her breath. "I was reading."

"We need to talk," he stated abruptly.

"Now?"

"Please?"

"Okay, give me a minute to bookmark this article, and I'll meet you in the family room," she replied. *I don't want to have this conversation in my personal space.* She felt a pang of guilt at that thought, but she had purposely created her office to also be her sanctuary.

"Thanks," he offered before turning and walking heavily down the hall. She heard his footsteps on the stairs.

After carefully saving the article she had been reading—a somewhat hopeful one—she followed him.

Dave was seated on the tan leather sofa instead of in his recliner when she got downstairs. Two glasses of water sat on coasters on the coffee table. She gratefully picked one up as she sank onto the sofa next to him.

"Thanks for the water."

"You're welcome." He turned so that he was facing her. "Look, I'm sorry I overreacted Friday night. I'm having a hard time with this trust thing that you keep talking about. Part of me feels like you're not being fair." He held up a hand as she started to protest. "Please just listen. I said *part* of me. The other part of me gets it. I know I screwed up with Alisha. I did. And I haven't been supportive about what you want to accomplish with your career.

"It's just that, well, I feel like you're so different," he continued earnestly. "You've been changing, and I, uh, guess I haven't been keeping up. I do want to try to understand. I do want to rebuild the trust between us. I know I haven't been handling things well, but this is kind of new territory for us, isn't it? We usually don't disagree much."

Sheryl reached out and grasped his hand. "Thank you," she said simply. "That means a lot to me."

"You're welcome," he replied his voice husky. He wrapped his hand around hers. "This is . . . hard for me."

Smiling gently, Sheryl nodded. "Yeah, it's not easy. You're right that we haven't had many disagreements, and none this serious. I probably haven't handled this whole thing as well as I could have either," she admitted. "I'm so used to your support that it's really rocked me that I haven't had it recently."

He dipped his head in acknowledgement.

"It's not that I don't want to support you, Sheryl, but you're scaring me."

"Scaring you how?"

"You seem to be taking so many risks with your career. Ones you never would have taken in the past. You were always so focused on pleasing Carl, on doing what you needed to do to move forward. Now, you seem to want to throw it all away."

Taken aback by his observations, Sheryl leaned back, releasing his hand.

"Don't be offended," he urged.

"I'm not," she assured him quickly. "I'm just thinking. You've mentioned something similar in the past, but the way you just summarized it kind of took me by surprise. You're right, although I want to clarify: I don't want to throw my career away. Not at all. What's different now is that I feel like my integrity is being challenged. I've never felt the internal conflict that I've had recently. Not with Carl. Not with the way The Diamante used to be."

Dave's eyebrows drew together. "Internal conflict?"

"It started with the layoffs, if you remember."

He groaned. "Oh, I remember!"

"I told you then how I felt. The conflict."

"You did. I guess I didn't get it then. I started to, but . . ."

"Alisha."

"Yeah, Alisha kind of pushed me the other direction. To feeling like I was right and you were wrong." He smiled sheepishly. "I like being right."

Sheryl chuckled. "Don't we all. But the internal conflict has intensified again. I felt it was somewhat resolved after the memorial meetings and my confrontation with Hank Turner over Layla, but I realize now that Alpha VC is only continuing to turn up the heat. I feel like I won those two battles, but the war is just getting started. Frankly, it's exhausting to me. And having to fight you too? It's impossible."

"I don't want you to have to fight me too," he broke in, his dark brown eyes full of hurt and regret. He picked up his glass and took a big gulp of water. "I really don't."

"Thank you," Sheryl replied, grabbing his hand again. "I need you on my side. And that doesn't mean I expect you to agree with everything I do, or not challenge me. But there's a difference between asking me questions and pointing out possible flaws in my reasoning and telling me I'm crazy."

He hung his head. "I know. That's an area of improvement," he confessed.

"Have you been talking to Robert?" she asked suddenly.

Dave let out a bark of laughter. "How did you know?"

"Because that sounds just like him," she quipped, smirking.

They shared a smile. *That feels so good. It's been a while.*

"So, tell me more about this 'hero's journey' thing," he said, taking them back to the source of Friday's argument.

*The source of everything*, Sheryl understood in that instant. She felt a sudden sharp pain rip through her and winced at the flashes that came, unbidden. His near betrayal with Alisha. His condemnation of her choices at work. His sudden anger. She closed her eyes. *Can I do this?* A fragment of words slipped into her consciousness.

*"Trust is ultimately a leap of faith."* She recognized the voice was not her own, and breathed it in.

"Sheryl?"

She opened her eyes, looking into the familiar face that she had loved for over twenty-five years. There were laugh lines now around his eyes. Wisps of gray in his light brown hair. Creases on his forehead. *But it's still Dave. And I have to decide. Now.*

She thought about all the years he had supported her, all the good times they had experienced together. She thought about their shared dreams and realized many of them were still alive. The possibilities for them were there . . . *if only I can trust.*

Taking a deep breath, she nodded decisively. *Yes, I can do it. He deserves a second chance. We deserve a second chance.*

"Are you okay?" he asked, the creases on his forehead deepening.

"Yes, I am," she told him. "I want this to work, Dave. But I know I have to take a leap of faith and trust that you will catch me. I guess that's what love is, taking that leap of faith over and over again, even after that faith has been betrayed."

Dave looked at her somberly. "Isn't there a limit to that?"

"Of course there is," she replied. "After all, the definition of insanity is doing the same thing over and over again and expecting different results." She paused, eyeing him thoughtfully. "But that doesn't apply here, does it? We're not going to continue to do the same thing we've been doing?"

"No, we're not," he replied adamantly. "At least, I'm not."

"Me either," Sheryl murmured, then continued more strongly. "I know I need to be less defensive with you," she announced with sudden clarity. "I can be more understanding when you get confused or disoriented by my seemingly irrational behavior." She beamed at him.

Suddenly, they were both laughing, and he reached across and gave her a hug. "Ahh. I love your laugh."

"I think we both need more laughter," she said, wiping her eyes. "We also need to be more patient with the other," Sheryl observed, pulling gently out of his arms. "Not either of our strong suits."

"You can say that again," he grinned.

They sat there smiling at each other for a long moment. Dave sobered first.

"Now, seriously, tell me about this hero's journey thing and how you're feeling about it," he requested. "I really want to know."

"Well, the hero's journey was chronicled by Joseph Campbell through his study of many cultures around the world and their myths." Sheryl recounted what John had told her. "At different points in our lives, we are called? Driven? To venture out into the unknown in search of answers that we need. And those that others need too. We often have guides, a mentor or a spiritual guide at least, who help us, but it's ultimately a journey we have to take on our own. When we discover what we need to learn, we bring our wisdom back and share it for the good of everyone."

"That sounds . . . difficult," Dave commented.

"Yeah, I guess it can be. Whatever I'm going through now feels difficult. John said that's the nature of the journey."

Dave fidgeted in his seat, then stilled.

"Can't you just say no?" her husband asked, but without the usual bite of cynicism.

"Probably," Sheryl admitted. "But that's hard too. Maybe harder. In my case, I feel propelled forward, sometimes almost against my will. More often though, I want to. I *want* to change things. I want to make them better—not just for me but for others."

Dave looked at her and cocked his head. "I'm almost afraid to ask, but what does that have to do with the hormone thing we were talking about?" he queried gingerly.

"You know, it's interesting that you brought that up," Sheryl responded, not the least bit offended. "I did a little digging on that. There's not much out there, but I feel like the change of life for women triggers a need for independence and self-expression that wasn't so strong before in their lives. I've seen it in other women, like my mom. That's kind of what I'm feeling. I think we become less willing to keep the peace as we are when our estrogen is at full strength, if that makes sense."

Dave looked a little bewildered. Instead of answering immediately, he took another drink of water. "So, where does that leave me?"

"It doesn't mean independent of you, Dave, although I'll admit that it might, well, has shaken our relationship up a bit."

"A bit?" Dave raised his eyebrows.

"Okay, more than a bit," Sheryl conceded. "I do feel less inclined to defer to you or anyone else, where I think in the past I did."

"I'm not sure you ever 'deferred' to me," Dave said dryly.

"Maybe that's not the right word, but it covers the gist of it. I always looked to you for validation, whether consciously or unconsciously. I'm discovering a new voice, a stronger voice, and I want to use it. Like I've been doing at work."

"And the new voice is part of the hero's journey?" Dave guessed.

"I guess so. That's what John implied."

"Hmmm. I suppose that makes sense. I might need some time to wrap my head around all this. I'm still not sure what it means for us."

"It means we're having growing pains." Sheryl smiled impishly. "And you're going to have to grow too."

"Yeah, I figured that part out."

"With Robert's help, of course," she teased.

Dave rolled his eyes, imitating Robert's favorite expression. "Of course," he conceded, his voice two octaves lower. They grinned again.

"And I know it's going to take time, Dave. For both of us. I thought earlier that I needed to take a leap of faith in trusting you again. But you do, too, don't you?"

"Thank you for recognizing that. Yes. I do."

"So, we're taking a leap of faith together?" Sheryl stated more than asked. Her hazel eyes met his squarely.

"Yes," Dave replied definitively. "Together."

He reached over and pulled her into an embrace, holding her tightly. Sheryl relaxed into it. The trepidation might still be there, although she acknowledged, greatly diminished.

*But I've made a decision. I've taken the leap. All I can do is trust now. Trust Dave. Trust myself.*

She sighed, snuggling deeper into his embrace.

"But what about work?" Dave asked. "What are you going to do there?"

She pulled back, looking deeply into his eyes. "I'm going to continue to try to be the hero," she answered. "A crusader, to use your words."

He visibly cringed but nodded. "Okay."

A chill went through her. "And I'm definitely going to need you on my side," she said, knowing that the upcoming showdown at the board meeting was going to be even rougher than the last round.

"I will be. I promise," Dave assured her. And suddenly her husband squared his shoulders. He stared equally intensely back into her eyes, commitment evident on his face.

"I'm going to hold you to that," she warned, the corner of her mouth curling. "Now, I need to get back to work. We good?"

He nodded, and she gave him another hug. Then she headed upstairs again.

The email that was awaiting her confirmed her worse fears.

CHAPTER 28

# Where Does the Past Belong in the Future?

"Wow, Mom! This place sure looks different. It's like you totally erased Dad."

Gemma spun around at the sound of the deep male voice. Her son lounged in the doorway, still wearing his blue and white varsity jacket. He had recovered quickly from the panic of a minor fender-bender that had sent him flying to her for help on Friday. *Thank goodness some things are easily rectified.*

Grinning, she spread her arms to encompass the small office. "It's great, isn't it?"

Her room—as she now thought of it—had been transformed in the last few days. In the place of the dark gray walls, the mirrors, the stark glass and steel desk with black leather chair were her new white desk and tan leather chair. The walls were now a light blue, the cabinet doors white, and a soft blue rug covered just the right amount of the beautiful polished, hardwood floor.

KJ raised his eyebrows. "Well, it's different. Definitely more you than Dad. There's no trace of him left, is there?"

Creases formed between Gemma's brows. "Should there be? It's my office now. I wanted to make it my own."

"You've certainly done that," her son agreed, straightening to his full six-foot, two-inch height.

*When did he start towering over me?* Gemma felt slightly intimidated. His father had used that tactic, pitting his height against Gemma's five-foot, five-inches.

She put her hands on her hips. "KJ, is there a problem?" she asked bluntly, puzzled by the bleak look in his gray eyes.

"Are you going to erase me when I go off to college next year too?" he asked bitterly.

Gemma gasped, her hand flying to her heart. "KJ, NO!" she exclaimed. "What are you talking about? Of course not! I would never change anything in your room without asking you first. Nor would I get rid of anything of yours. Why would you think that?"

He shrugged a bit too nonchalantly. "You're erasing Dad, like you want to pretend he doesn't exist anymore."

"KJ, come sit down," Gemma said gently, motioning to the light blue armchair she had placed by the window.

"Not in here," he replied, backing away. "I don't—"

"Then in the family room, or your room," she suggested firmly.

"Mom, just let it go. I didn't mean it. I've got homework."

"No, KJ. We're going to talk. Now."

Groaning, he slung his navy backpack over his shoulder and headed toward the kitchen. "I'm getting a snack then. I can't talk on an empty stomach," he grumbled.

Stunned by her son's reaction, Gemma watched him for a moment before hurrying after him. Her sneakers made little sound in the tiled hallway.

He was already pulling a bag of chips out of the pantry when she hurried in. She started to object to his choice, then caught herself. *Let him eat what he wants right now*, she thought. *Talking is more important.*

She sat down at the head of the kitchen table, leaning back against the nubby fabric of the chair. Thankfully, the blue paint on her gray sweats was dry, so it wouldn't stain.

KJ slung himself into the chair at the other end of the table, shoving chips in his mouth.

"What's going on, KJ?"

"Nothing, Mom. I was just surprised to see such a big change. You already changed your bedroom completely—and the master bathroom. It's not a big deal. It's your space. It's your house," he said sullenly.

"No, KJ. It's our house. Have I changed any of the shared spaces in the house?" she asked reasonably.

"Not yet," he shot back, cocking one eyebrow. "I figure it's just a matter of time. You're angry with Dad. I get it, but he's still our father."

Shocked, Gemma ran her hands through her dark hair. "Wow. I didn't know that you felt like this. Yes, I'm angry with your father. He hurt me badly, but I also know that it takes two to make a relationship. But I absolutely respect that he *is* your father. I will always care for him because of that. I want him to be part of your lives, and I realize that means he will always be part of mine. And that's okay."

KJ grunted. Gemma cringed. *Every time I think we've all moved on from the divorce, it comes back again. I thought I had my anger and bitterness under control—or at least under wraps when it comes to the kids.* She watched her son devour the chips. *I guess I haven't. I'll have to do better.*

"Have I taken down any of the family pictures? Or put away mementos of our family trips?" she countered, determined to help put things in perspective.

"No," he said quickly, "but you put your wedding picture away. Plus, some of the pics with just you and Dad in them," he muttered.

"Do you blame me for that? After all, your dad has moved in with another woman." She silently cursed herself for being so defensive.

"I guess not."

"What else?" Gemma pressed, feeling simultaneously guilty and thinking that KJ's assessment was unfair. "Let's get it on the table."

"How about getting dinner on the table instead," KJ quipped, a twinkle back in his eyes.

She laughed as the tension was broken. "I'm okay with that as long as we're good?"

He stood. "Yeah, we're good. I'm gonna get a shower." Still, he ruffled her hair when he walked by. "You're such a girl sometimes, Mom."

Rolling her eyes, Gemma also rose. Glancing at her grubby clothes, she considered taking a shower as well, but she knew better. As nice as the house was, two showers at the same time just didn't work. Walking to the refrigerator, she opened the double doors and started pulling out ingredients for dinner, her thoughts far away.

By the time Monday morning arrived, Gemma was ready to dive into her new job. Her first meeting, a Zoom call, was an orientation with

HR. This was followed by a meeting with her new team of eight people, each of whom had their own teams. In total, she had sixty-seven people reporting into her worldwide, many more than she'd had at Viva! She loved the energy and enthusiasm in the group. Giving each team member a chance to bring her up-to-date on their projects helped her get a better sense of their capabilities and the group dynamics.

It was a long meeting but a good one. By the end of it, Gemma felt a renewed sense of making the right decision.

Her first official meeting with her new boss came after lunch. Kushma Panjari, who Gemma guessed to be around thirty-five, lived in Seattle and had been with Atrium for nearly five years. She appeared on the video screen in a T-shirt and hooded sweatshirt. Gemma, in what was casual for her, wore an off-white sweater and colorful scarf. Seeing Kushma, she felt overdressed and perhaps even stuffy. She brushed it aside and dove in.

Gemma's extensive crash course in Atrium's product offerings and current positioning in the cosmetics space in the last week paid off, as she was sure Kushma had intended. She was prepared for this meeting—or so she thought. In addition to what her boss had sent, she had also done a fair amount of research into competitive offerings, like Sephora and Ulta. Both retailers had brick and mortar outlets as well as strong, online presences. Mainstream cosmetics was a much more crowded field than the luxury brand she had been used to representing. However, Kushma quickly made it known she didn't want to talk about mainstream cosmetics.

"It's not what we brought you on for," she told Gemma with a dismissive wave of her hand. "I want to talk luxury cosmetics. That's your forte."

"But Atrium doesn't sell luxury cosmetics," Gemma replied, drawing her brows together in confusion.

"Not yet," Kushma replied. "That's why you're here. There's real money in luxury cosmetics, as you know, and Atrium wants a piece of that pie too."

"Oh. That wasn't clear in the interview process," Gemma murmured.

"But I can see why Atrium would want to go there." She strove to remain calm, but her thoughts were running wild.

"Yeah, well, confidentially," her boss admitted breezily, her dark brown eyes looking guilelessly into the camera. "We didn't want to give our strategy away before you came on board."

"That makes sense," Gemma nodded, but she felt her shoulders tighten with tension. *What else didn't they tell me?* It felt a little like misrepresentation, and she hoped she was wrong.

"So, what I need from you first is a profile, or series of profiles, on the high-end cosmetics consumer. What she's looking for, what kind of experience she expects, demographics, all that stuff. You know the drill."

"Sure, I do, but online shopping is not the *first* place these women go for cosmetics," Gemma warned.

"Oh, I know that," Kushma dismissed her statement with another hand wave. "You have to figure out how to change that. Surely, Viva! sold some products through online channels. What's been working for them? What hasn't? You have all the information, don't you?"

"Not all of that is publicly available," Gemma warned.

"So? You have the knowledge. That's why you're here," she stated again.

"But I had a confidentially agreement with Viva! I can't break that." Gemma's stomach churned, and nausea filled her.

Yet another hand wave. "Oh my goodness, we're not asking you to share state secrets!" Kushma laughed a little derisively. A moment later, however, her face turned very serious. "But we do want your insight."

Swallowing hard, Gemma nodded. "Of course. I can provide you with the broad strokes of the online strategy."

Kushma leaned in toward the camera, her face suddenly large and intense on Gemma's screen. Gemma had to keep herself from shrinking back instinctively, even as she could see the very straight part in the younger woman's dark, dark hair, which was pulled back from her face. Her full lips thinned as she told Gemma, "Broad strokes will do to start with."

"I'll do what I can," Gemma said soothingly. "I know you have high expectations." She hadn't been in marketing all these years without knowing how to create a win.

Her boss nodded curtly. "Good. I'm glad we understand each other. Let's meet again on Wednesday afternoon to go over what you prepare."

"Wednesday? Uh, that's not much time for all the data you've requested."

"We'll go over what you have then," Kushma replied, her eyes darting around. Gemma guessed she was no longer paying attention to the conversation.

"Okay then. I'll put together as much as I can by Wednesday."

"Good. Same time work for you?"

"Yes, that will be—"

The screen went blank and then the Zoom application interface appeared. Kushma had ended the call.

*So much for pleasantries*, Gemma thought with a frown. She took a deep breath and looked around the office, her gaze alighting on a small sand garden on the corner of her desk. Grabbing the tiny rake, she drew the tines through the sand, making wavy lines and then straight ones until her breathing came easier.

*It's not that what she is asking is unreasonable*, she argued with herself. But her sense of unease persisted. *But I didn't think I'd be in direct competition with Viva!* As she thought about it, she shifted in her chair. *No wonder they wanted me out of the office immediately.*

Feeling her chest constricting still, she picked up the little rake again. She noticed that her hand trembled slightly. Any warmth she felt after the meeting with her team had vanished.

The image of Charles's face on that last day at Viva! appeared before her eyes. His concern, but more importantly, his *distrust*. Something she had never experienced with him before.

*Did he know something I didn't? I wonder what else I have missed about this new job?*

# CHAPTER 29

# When Is Enough . . . Enough?

**Tuesday, January 25**

The reckoning came sooner than Gemma thought. She sent Kushma a detailed outline of the information she was preparing on the luxury cosmetics customer. Carefully culling any information she felt was confidential to Viva!, Gemma felt that her report was honestly quite robust and compelling. She just wanted to make sure she was on track before the Wednesday meeting.

Kushma had other ideas. "I could have gotten this information myself!" she ranted, her call coming mere minutes after Gemma's email had landed. "We hired you for your expertise, not to give me something I could have had an intern prepare—or AI."

"Kushma! There's a lot of information in there that would have taken a long time to find or track down. My expertise *is* in there."

"Well, maybe some," her new boss conceded gruffly. "But not enough. Not nearly enough."

"Anything more would be violating my confidentiality agreement with Viva!" Gemma protested. Again.

"So what?"

"What do you mean 'so what'?"

"So, who cares if you violate it? No one's going to know, and they'll never sue you. It's impossible to prove, not to mention expensive. I'm sure they expected you would." She gave Gemma an unmistakable look. "That's why they made you leave so quickly."

Gemma gripped the arms of her chair, stunned by the nonchalance in Kushma's voice.

"I'm quite sure they didn't," Gemma responded indignantly, ruffling her short hair so that it stood on end. "I've always operated with integrity. Why would I stop now?"

"Because your job depends on it," Kushma threatened. "And I expect to see a lot more depth by tomorrow's meeting. A lot more."

"What? Seriously? What if I left and violated Atrium's agreement?" But she was speaking into thin air. Her boss had already hung up.

Feeling a rising nausea, Gemma clutched her head. *What do I do now?* she asked herself. *Is she serious about my job depending on it? Would she really fire me?*

She looked over the outline she had sent. *What else can I add that wouldn't compromise Viva! Anything?*

Her hands shaking, she added a few things that were, in her opinion, on the edge. Her stomach roiled again. *Can I really do this?*

Her phone dinged with an incoming text.

**Just so you know, Atrium doesn't have an issue suing people who violate our agreements. You signed one with us too.**

A chill slithered down Gemma's spine.

"So, she heard what I said before she hung up," Gemma muttered. *It's only day two, and the honeymoon is clearly over. If there ever was one.* She thought of the mounds of documents she had read last week. The ones she thought she shouldn't feed into the AI tool. *And I tried to protect their confidentiality at every step. Argh.*

What made her most uncomfortable was the sudden clarity. *Charles had a reason for the distrust on his face—and his behavior at the restaurant the night I quit. He must have known that I'd be expected to betray my former employer.* But this fast? Gemma shivered, even though it was far from cold in her office.

*I need help. A lot of it.*

She knew she couldn't call Charles or anyone at Viva! Yet again she regretted the fact that the few girlfriends she'd had in the area had drifted away after the divorce.

Unable to work, or even sit still, Gemma pulled herself out of her chair and headed to the kitchen. But nothing there appealed to her. She spied her bright blue down jacket in the adjacent mudroom. *A walk.*

*I can take a walk.* She had even done that occasionally in downtown New York when she needed to clear her head or find some inspiration.

Bundling up against the cold, she stepped out into the bleak, January day. The gray clouds were low and dark. The wind had a biting quality that often preceded snow. Gemma lowered her head and walked into the wind.

Forty-five minutes later, she was cold and breathless but not feeling any more relaxed. Instead of inspiring or invigorating her, the walk— along with her spinning thoughts—had merely exhausted her. She had racked her brain for someone to call—and come up empty.

Gemma checked her phone, which had been left behind. There were four missed calls from Kushma, but no others. *Odd that no one from my team reached out*, she thought. She had found her team leads to be engaged and communicative so far.

The phone rang. Expecting it to be her boss again, she prepared to hang up. She was surprised to see that the caller was Sheryl Simmons.

"Sheryl!" she exclaimed, attempting to be enthusiastic and upbeat. "What a nice surprise."

"What's wrong?" her erstwhile friend asked. "Your voice still gets all high and tight when you're stressed."

"How did you remember that?" Gemma cried, astonished.

"No idea, but it all came back as if it were yesterday," Sheryl said wryly. "Now, what is wrong?"

"Well, first, can I ask, why did you call?"

"To set a date for lunch," Sheryl answered. "But it seems like you need more than that. I have a little time. Spill."

Gemma glanced at the clock. *11:45 a.m. I could claim an early lunch.*

"Gemma?"

"It's my new job," she blurted, spilling as she always had with Sheryl.

"What about it?"

"They're, um, my boss is, well, um, asking me to provide them information," Gemma ground out.

"What kind of information?" Sheryl asked. "Let me guess. Confidential stuff from your old company?"

"Yes!" Gemma gasped. "How did you know?"

"Sadly, it's not that unusual. And I seem to remember reading something about Atrium doing that."

"How did I not know that?"

"It was something obscure, not really in the mainstream press, if I remember correctly," Sheryl soothed her. "I doubt you would have seen it. I'm not even sure why I did, but every once in a while, these types of things pop up in my newsfeed."

"Because you talk about ethics a lot," Gemma surmised. "I read that."

"Yeah, I do," Sheryl confirmed. "And it sounds like you've got quite the ethical dilemma on your hands. I'm surprised they're pushing you this early though. Didn't you just start?"

"Technically, yesterday."

"Hmm, that's fast."

"That's what I thought! And, well, my new boss is rather like a bull in a china shop," Gemma told her. "Not much finesse."

"That's too bad, but again, not unusual anymore. She's probably under a lot of pressure."

"I'm sure she is. She's a little young to have all the responsibility she has. She's very aggressive, which is probably why she's there," Gemma elaborated.

"Aggressive or assertive?" Sheryl quipped. "We all know those are usually seen as the same thing in women."

Gemma chuckled, sliding into a chair at the kitchen table. She ran her hand across her head, smoothing the hair that was undoubtedly mussed by her hat. Sheryl's voice was calming her as much as the walk hadn't.

"Oh, definitely aggressive," Gemma replied. "And very blunt. You're assertive. She's over-the-top aggressive. So much so, she threatened my job if I don't cooperate."

"Really? Wow," Sheryl said, her voice low in bafflement.

"Yes, really." Gemma paused, her stomach roiling again. "What do I do, Sheryl? I'm literally sick to my stomach. If I don't cooperate, I could lose my job. And then what? I can't go back to Viva! And I'll probably be done in the cosmetics industry. I need to work. The divorce, well, it wasn't great financially."

"Divorce rarely is," her friend said knowingly. "I feel for you. You *are* in a tough spot."

Gemma choked back the sobs that were threatening. The enormity of her situation washed over her. "What am I going to do?" she asked Sheryl, her voice rising with impending hysteria.

"I don't know," Sheryl admitted. "What are your options?"

Swallowing hard, Gemma struggled to speak through the lump in her throat. "Give them what they want? Quit? But then what? I don't see many choices, and those that I do see are bad—really bad." She balled her fist on the table so hard that her short nails dug into her palm.

"There have to be more options," Sheryl encouraged her. "Although I understand why you haven't seen them. Let's brainstorm. There has to be a way."

For the next ten minutes, Sheryl threw out different and increasingly wild options that almost had Gemma laughing. Except that none of them were very feasible.

"Let's face it," she finally said. "If I leave, I'll have to change industries, which pretty much means starting over. And with AI taking so many marketing jobs already! What are my chances? And I'm old. Almost fifty."

"Yeah, over the hill," Sheryl broke in dryly.

"You know what I mean," Gemma shot back.

"Sadly, I do. IT is almost as bad as marketing. Everyone needs to be young and hip. How up-to-date are you with AI?"

"Very," Gemma assured her. "I have to be." She had worked very hard to stay on top of her profession, yet another reason she had been an attractive candidate for Atrium.

"Surely they won't really fire you," Sheryl suggested. "I mean, how would that look for them? Is Kushma bluffing?"

"She might be," Gemma admitted. "I get the impression she does like to play games, but I don't know her that well."

"You might just have to test it," Sheryl told her grimly. "I don't see that you have many other options. Not at this point."

Gemma dipped her head and rubbed her neck. *Damn. I think Sheryl is right.*

"Look, it might be a test, to see if she can trust you," Sheryl continued. "And if it's not, do you really want to work for someone who is that untrustworthy? After all, how can you trust her to not betray you or anyone else if she's so willing to require you to betray your former employer?"

"Argh. You haven't lost your ability to get right to the heart of things, have you, Sheryl?"

Her friend laughed. "I guess not," she replied.

"But I think you're right, as much as it scares me to death. I have to see what she does." Gemma was tired of her stomach clenching, but the thought of confronting Kushma was terrifying. *Which in and of itself is wrong. As gruff as Charles could be, I was never afraid of him.*

"I've been thinking and talking a lot about trust recently," Sheryl said. "It's not easy. As I told Dave on Sunday, it's a leap of faith. The question is, who do you have faith in? Do you have faith in Kushma? More importantly, do you have faith in yourself?"

"I have faith in the truth," Gemma muttered. "But I don't always know what that is."

"So true," Sheryl agreed.

It seemed to Gemma there was a lot more underneath her words. She would have to ask her, at least once she had dug herself out of the situation she was in.

Several moments passed in silence as Gemma considered Sheryl's deeper meaning. She knew Sheryl had always tried to live by her code of ethics, as had Gemma herself. *But it's not always easy . . . and the gray areas? Sometimes really gray. But is this really gray?* She shivered again. It wasn't really gray, and she knew it.

"You okay, Gemma?"

"Yeah, just thinking. Thank you for listening to all this. I know it's not why you called. I'm really grateful because I honestly didn't know who I could talk to. Your timing was perfect," she answered, her heart warming further toward her old friend.

"It's always good to be in the right place at the right time. I'm glad I could help. If I did," Sheryl added doubtfully.

"Oh, you did. I needed to audibly process. Now I just have to come to terms with it all," Gemma assured her.

"Good. Just trust yourself, Gemma," Sheryl advised. "I do."

Gemma sighed. "Thank you. I'll try."

"Great. Now, let's set a date for lunch!"

The two women agreed on a day the following week and hung up.

Gemma lowered the phone slowly, ignoring the ringing that started up again immediately. She remembered suddenly the very words she had told Anna about misjudging people. *Am I judging Kushma too harshly? Maybe this is the only way she knows? Maybe she's just trying to push me, to see how far I'll go?*

She let out a long breath. *I'll have to give her the benefit of the doubt. I guess.*

*But what if I'm wrong?*

She got up slowly and walked toward her office. Her conversation with Sheryl had confirmed one thing:

*At the end of the day, I did what I thought was right for me and my children when I took this job. I have to trust my judgment and continue to do what I think is right.*

She ran her hand through her short, red hair. *Even if it isn't easy.*

# CHAPTER 30
## Integrity or Survival?

**Wednesday, January 26**

"I don't see that you added the information I asked for." Kushma's response to Gemma's presentation via Zoom late Wednesday morning was cold and blunt.

Despite the soothing atmosphere in her new home office, Gemma's shoulders tensed. After her conversation with Sheryl, she had gone back and taken a hard look at the material she had put together for her boss. A lot of the information that had seemed questionable to Gemma had been removed. She knew it was not what Kushma wanted, but it was the best she could do—without compromising her integrity.

*I have to trust that Kushma will respect that,* Gemma had told herself. *Maybe this really* is *another one of her little tests.*

Groaning inwardly, Gemma paused before responding. "I added some." She purposely breathed in the soothing lavender aroma that emanated from the diffuser on her desk.

"Not enough. Not nearly enough." Kushma's dark eyes shot daggers through the webcam. "I'm very disappointed."

"I'm sorry," Gemma said, but the only thing she was really sorry for was disappointing her boss. It was something she had rarely experienced at Viva!, and she still felt lost in this situation with her.

"Well? If you're sorry, why didn't you give me what I asked for?" Kushma countered harshly.

"Because anything more would have been violating my confidentiality agreement with Viva!," Gemma stated firmly.

"I told you I didn't care about that."

Forcing herself not to reel back in shock, Gemma fought to keep her face impassive. "You don't really mean that," she said as calmly as she could.

"I always mean what I say," her boss retorted, her face stony. "You need to learn that about me now. When I ask for something, I expect to get it. Period. Otherwise, I wouldn't bother to ask."

This time, Gemma did recoil, abruptly leaning back against the back of her chair. Her green eyes widened with surprise as a frisson of fear raced down her spine.

"Good, I see that you understand," Kushma said, nodding in apparent satisfaction at Gemma's visible reaction. "Now, when can I get an update on this presentation?" She paused and her eyes slid away. "I have time at 5:00 p.m. this afternoon, my time," she continued.

"Uh, oh wait, that's eight o'clock for me," Gemma gasped.

"That's right," Kushma confirmed. "I'll send you an invite. And don't disappoint me this time."

The screen went blank, and the Zoom interface popped up.

*What just happened?* Gemma thought, stunned by her boss's behavior. *She can't be serious. Eight at night is one thing, but she doesn't really expect me to throw Viva! under the bus, does she?*

Her stomach roiled, and she clasped her hands over her belly. *No. It's just another test. Like the AI and the confidentiality thing,* she thought, grasping for another possibility. Any other possibility.

*"Yeah?"* another inner voice taunted her. *"You really think so?"*

Glancing at the corner of the computer screen, Gemma realized that it was nearly twelve o'clock. She groaned. Her afternoon was already full of meetings with her five US-based teams. *I'll never have time to add the information she wants,* she thought frantically. *Even if I wanted to.*

Her phone rang, startling her. She was surprised to see that it was KJ, who rarely called during the school day. In fact, it was against school rules, except under specific circumstances. Her heart skipped a beat, and she quickly answered.

"KJ? What's wrong?"

"Nothing, Mom. Sorry to scare you. Our game just got pushed back to tonight instead of this afternoon because of the snow."

"What snow?"

"Mom, it's snowing! Not a lot, and it's supposed to stop soon. But you know how freaked out everyone gets when there's a flake of snow." Gemma could visualize him rolling his eyes by his disgusted tone. She couldn't help but look out the window of her office, and sure enough, she saw a few tufts of snow blowing across the yard.

"Oh, okay . . ." she said, unsure why this news required a phone call.

"But I'm starting tonight, Mom! Coach just told me during gym," KJ answered the unspoken question. Although he was an excellent player, there was a senior point guard who usually got the starting nod.

"Wow! That's great!" Gemma enthused.

"And since it's a night game now, you can come! The game starts at 7:00 p.m. You'll be here, right?"

Gemma heard her breath release like a deflating balloon.

"Mom? What was that?"

"Oh, KJ . . . My boss wants to meet with me at 8:00 p.m.," she said, swallowing hard and massaging her jaw with her right hand. *I really want to scream now.*

"That's ridiculous. I really want you here," her son replied, his voice now quiet and a bit steely. "I don't get to start every day."

"I know, KJ, and I want to be there. Let me see what I can do," she told him, biting her lip. But all she could think was, *Oh my God, Kushma will kill me if I don't meet with her*!

"Great," KJ said, clearly interpreting her answer as a yes. "Gotta go. See ya later."

Gemma knew from the sudden silence that he was gone. She groaned out loud, ruffling her hair. Anger shot through her again, and she felt the sudden urge to throw her phone across the room. Instead, she grabbed the wooden rake from her sand garden and dragged it rapidly back and forth. The rake made deep grooves in the sand but didn't calm her—not one bit. A moment later, she heard a snap and looked down to see the rake in two pieces in her hand.

"Damn. Damn. Damn!" she cried out loud, dropping the broken rake on her desk.

Taking a deep breath, she looked around her office. The soothing colors and patterns didn't soothe. *If I was still working for Viva!, I could have gotten home in time for a seven o'clock game*, she thought. *Was I really missing that much of my kids' lives?* But she knew the truth: that her commute from New York frequently got her home closer to eight than seven.

*I have to make a decision.* The thought was swift and definitive.

She thought about her conversation with Sheryl the day before. Having been able to process aloud, she had immediately decided to honor her confidentiality agreement with Viva! And she had done so. *To what avail? Now, I still have to break that agreement and miss my son's basketball game.*

Determinedly, she turned to her personal computer. *Can I make it if I'm out of work for a while?* she wondered for the first time. She opened Quicken. She and Kevin had split their assets evenly, but she'd had the expense of buying him out of the house. Now, she had to pay the taxes and utilities without his help. The child support he provided was minimal. *And I won't get more if I quit my job. But if Kushma fires me?*

Shaking her head, she pulled up her budget. *No! I don't want to be more dependent on Kevin.*

Going through her Quicken reports, she breathed a little easier. The numbers weren't as bleak as she had imagined. She had made good money at Viva!, and unlike Kevin, she wasn't extravagant with her money. Making some quick calculations, she realized there was enough to tide her over for a little while. *Although KJ goes to college in a year and a half*, she reminded herself.

Bile rose in her throat. *Am I really thinking about quitting? Already? I haven't even gotten my signing bonus yet. It's only been three days! Not even.* Her hand covered her mouth. A sense of utter defeat washed over her as her earlier rage dissolved. *How did I get things so wrong? How?*

Gemma looked at the budget report again. Blinking back the telltale moisture from her eyes, she scrutinized it carefully. And she kept breathing. *I could do this*, she thought. *Not easily. But I could do this.*

Sheryl's words echoed in her head as she opened a report on her assets. *"Who do you have faith in?"*

Something suddenly clicked. Her stomach settled for the first time in three days. She felt her spine straighten with the steely determination that had served her so well, especially in the days following Kevin's betrayal.

*I didn't let him break me . . . and I'm not going to let Kushma either.*

Snapping the lid of her personal laptop shut, she turned back to her work computer. She opened a new email and started to type. When she was finished, she read it through, made a few small adjustments, and hit send.

Then, she sat back and waited for the fireworks to start.

It didn't take long.

Not five minutes after the email had been sent, her phone rang. Expecting to see Kushma's name, she was surprised to see an unknown number.

"Hello?" she queried cautiously.

"Ms. Morrison, this is Toni Barelli from Human Resources at Atrium. I'm afraid we haven't yet interacted," a woman's voice said calmly.

A knot formed in Gemma's stomach. "Hello, Ms. Barelli," she managed to reply.

"I regret to inform you that your employment with Atrium is terminated, effective immediately. Ms. Panjari informed me that you have already proven to be uncooperative and defiant. I'm afraid that's not a good fit for Atrium," Ms. Barelli's voice was grave. "We expect our employees to comply with requests from their managers. Apparently, you are unable to do that."

Gemma sat up straighter in her chair. Her free hand formed a tight fist. "The request that Ms. Panjari made would have required me to violate my confidentiality agreement with my former employer," she told the woman bluntly. "I simply could not do that in good conscience."

"I see." There was a brief pause. "Well, it's unfortunate that you and Ms. Panjari had a difference of opinion about that, but it doesn't change the company's position," she continued defensively. "Unless you are willing to cooperate with your boss, we are going to have to let you go." There was a bit of a hopeful note in the woman's voice as she offered Gemma one more chance.

"I *am* willing to cooperate with my boss," Gemma responded, a thread of steel in her voice now. "But I am not willing to do something that is, in my opinion, completely unethical. If Atrium expects that, then I agree it's not a good fit."

"Well, of course, we don't expect that," Ms. Barelli blustered. "I'm quite sure you've misinterpreted Ms. Panjari's request."

"Ms. Barelli, I am quite sure I haven't," Gemma stated boldly. *What in the world did Kushma tell this woman?*

"Well, to be frank, Ms. Panjari is an employee with an outstanding reputation in the company, and you are a *new* and *unknown*. I have never, ever had anyone malign Ms. Panjari, so there is no reason for me to believe you," the other woman said with a huff.

Gemma was silent, mostly because she was biting her tongue to avoid laughing. *Oh boy!*

"If you have nothing else to add, your network connection will be terminated immediately," Toni Barelli finally snapped. "You will ship the laptop and any other equipment you were sent back to the company. I will send a label to your personal email address. You will be paid for the entirety of this week, mostly because Ms. Panjari said that you did a bit of work last week before you were officially on the payroll."

"Very well," was Gemma's only comment.

"Well, I never!" The line went dead.

Gemma started laughing. A minute later she was laughing so hard, tears were streaming down her face. *That was hilarious! And, I feel so relieved!*

She shut down the Atrium laptop and pushed it away from her as if it were contaminated with some deadly disease. The only thing she regretted was letting down her new teams. Their faces flashed briefly before her. *But maybe they aren't who I thought they were either, if they're willing to work in such an environment.* Maybe they didn't know better. She wondered, in all of Kushma's five years with the company, if anyone had dared defy her.

Shrugging, Gemma unplugged the laptop, the portable printer, and the cell phone charger that she had received from Atrium. Turning off the phone, she put them all in a pile. *I'll box them up later*, she thought, her appetite suddenly returning with a vengeance. *Right now, I'm going to get lunch! Then I'll think about what's next.*

*Because after all, I do trust myself. I made a mistake with this one, a big one,* she silently acknowledged. *But I know I'll figure it out.*

# CHAPTER 31

# Searching for Hope

Sheryl felt ready to throw in the towel on her career—almost. *Why am I staying in this job if I'm just discouraged and exhausted all the time?* she asked herself. Again.

The spiral had started with the email from Paul Haven on Sunday pushing for even more staff reductions. As expected, he had used AI as an excuse. As a result, she had spent even more time researching the pros and cons of AI, the implications, the downsides, and the benefits, including late into the evenings. Now, the afternoon before the board meeting, she was still at it.

Even working in the soothing comfort of her home office today didn't help. She reached up and stretched, feeling the resistance of the tight muscles in every part of shoulders and back. The feeling was all too familiar. *I sound like a broken record*, she scolded herself, realizing that she had said almost the exact same words last fall when the initial layoffs had happened.

*Because what's changed? Every time I take a step forward, there's some other obstacle or something else to push me back.* She eyed the article on the screen. It reported on yet another threatening email from the CEO of a major company, using AI as a whip to get employees "under control." She felt the muscles in her scalp tighten in a near headache. *It's disgusting.*

Her research had continued with the same trend as it had over the weekend. More doom and gloom. More threatening CEOs. A few people with small rays of hope, but more people with attitudes like Paul Haven. That disturbed her.

Rolling her head and neck around in a vain attempt to release some tension, Sheryl pushed back from her desk and looked out the window. A light snow was falling, creating a snow globe effect on the bare trees and distant buildings that she could see from her home office window.

It made her doubly glad that she had worked from home today.

"Although I'm not sure it's helping," she muttered. Her primary reason was to finalize her AI presentation for tomorrow's board meeting. "And I'm getting exactly nowhere."

Picking up her mug, she realized that her tea had long since gone cold. Letting out a huff of irritation, Sheryl stood up and took a step towards the door when her phone rang.

"Keisha," she read out loud. She smiled, but the smile quickly faded as the worrisome thoughts overtook her again. *What kind of future is this young woman facing—inside our company and outside of it*, she wondered, a lump forming in her throat.

"Hey there," Sheryl spoke into the phone, forcing positivity into her tone.

"Hey Sheryl. How are you?" came Keisha's enthusiastic voice.

Sheryl brightened in response. "I'm better, just hearing your voice. I was just about to go get another cup of tea."

"Can you talk for a minute? I have some of the information you asked me for. I emailed it after I went over it with Patrick this morning . . . and Carlos."

"Oh good," Sheryl said. "How did it go with Carlos?" Sheryl was slightly concerned how the younger woman would respond to her new boss. Carlos had a lot stronger personality than Patrick.

"Fine," Keisha said quickly. "Carlos is okay. He's pushy, but he does listen."

Feeling her shoulders relax at that news, Sheryl sat back down in her office chair and put the mug back on a coaster. "That's good. He's smart—and you're right, he listens. I think you can learn a lot from him," she encouraged her protégé. "And he from you."

"Ha! Don't let him hear you say that," Keisha laughed.

Chuckling, Sheryl agreed. "So, what do you have for me?"

"I'm sending a bunch of stuff via email, but I wanted to point out a couple of things verbally," Keisha explained. "You know about the security and confidentiality concerns with using AI, but even with that, the new AI tool has improved our productivity. I'd estimate we're working about 20 percent faster using the new tool, and that will only get better once everyone is up to speed on it. But . . . and this is a big but . . . we're also learning where it works and where it doesn't."

"That's impressive," Sheryl murmured, painfully aware of how Paul Haven would interpret that information. "So, where are the sticking points?"

"It doesn't always get what we're trying to do. A lot of the code is very generic, and we have to spend time tailoring it. Plus, sometimes, it's hard to figure out what it's really doing. Understanding the code and making sure that it's correct can take a lot of time," Keisha said, a note of frustration in her voice. Sheryl pictured her fingering whatever statement piece of jewelry she was wearing, a habit that gave away Keisha's emotions every time.

"That makes sense," Sheryl replied. "That's one of the drawbacks, right? That the programming only does what it knows?"

"Yeah. And, I *still* don't want it to learn what we're doing here," Keisha shot back strongly. She was rightfully proud of what she had designed.

"I know, and I don't want it to either," Sheryl assured her. "We've been over that. But what I'm hearing is that it speeds some things up and slows other things down. Is that right?"

"Yeah, pretty much. It makes coding faster in some areas but reviewing it and debugging it still takes time. Sometimes more time because it doesn't always use our protocols."

"That makes sense. There are always tradeoffs."

"You understand that, but does everyone else?" Keisha asked with her usual bluntness.

Sheryl flinched. "Why do you say that?"

"Well, I've heard rumors that *some people* want to replace the programmers with AI."

"Keisha," Sheryl chided gently, but she felt her chest constrict. "Rumors. They're just rumors." *What is on the company grapevine? And how accurate is it? More than I know?*

"Well, after everything that's in the news, the rumors make sense," Keisha retorted spiritedly. "Too many CEOs are talking about how many jobs they can replace with AI bots. Especially programmers. And after what happened here last year with the layoffs, I'm sure that *those people* are talking about it too."

Nodding grimly to herself, Sheryl realized that she wasn't the only one that was discouraged by the media or management. "Those people being Alpha VC?"

"Yeah, and who knows who else on the board. I hope you're not?"

"Keisha! Of course, I'm not. I know the pitfalls too. And you know I believe in people."

Sheryl heard herself speak as if from a distance. *Yes, I do believe in people, but how am I going to win this fight if no one else fights for people too?* The enormity of all the research she had just done hit her again, causing her heart to thump more rapidly.

"I hope so," her protégé responded doubtfully. "You are our best hope. We all think that."

Barely stopping herself from groaning, Sheryl answered in a moderated voice. "Look. There are other leaders in the company who are responsible too." She paused, realizing that she wasn't 100 percent sure of that. "Everyone is tossing big ideas out there, but we still don't know how all this is going to play out. For example, you just pointed out some of the real problems with AI."

"Yeah, yeah," Keisha said with a hint of sarcasm. "That's why you need all this stuff for the board meeting tomorrow."

"The board needs to look at the facts," Sheryl stated strongly. "That's what I'm going to provide. Facts. Not speculation or crazy theories."

"I know you are," Keisha replied, sounding calmer. "It's just scary. You know that."

Sheryl sighed, pushing her bangs back from her face. "It is," she acknowledged. "It is for everyone. It's a time of uncertainty, and we're all unsettled. The only thing we can do is trust."

"Trust what?" the younger woman challenged.

Taken aback, Sheryl hesitated, staring out the window and watching a bright red cardinal swoop through the gently falling snow. *Good question*, she thought. *I wish I knew.* She suddenly felt as if she had a heavy weight on her shoulders. *I'm so overwhelmed myself. How do I help Keisha or the others who are looking to me for hope? That's what I need to do, right? As a leader? Provide hope. Direction and hope.* An ache formed behind her eyes. *But what if I don't have it?*

*Breathe.* Sheryl continued the patterned breathing. Allowing the anxiety to lessen and her heart rate to return to a pace closer to normal. *Breathe.* A sense of peace started to penetrate.

The silence, however, stretched so long that Keisha interrupted her. "Sheryl, are you still there?"

"Yeah, I'm here," she replied, realizing that she had somehow managed to connect with her higher self even in just those brief moments of breathing. "Just gathering my thoughts."

"Hmmm. It's not easy, is it?" the younger woman said wisely.

"No, it's not," Sheryl admitted, pausing to do another round of breathing.

"So, what do we trust?" Keisha asked again. "I trust you, but not the rest of the executives. And I don't know how much one woman, one person can do. You've already done a lot, but . . ."

*Oh God,* Sheryl thought closing her eyes, her heart rate ticking up. *How do I answer her? She's saying everything that I've been thinking. Breathe in: 2-3-4. Hold: 2-3-4.*

Suddenly, her eyelids snapped open. *Of course!*

"Trust ourselves," she answered Keisha decisively. "We need to trust ourselves, and trust that everything will work out. It usually does—even though we can't always see it in the midst of change."

"That's not much to go on," Keisha replied cautiously, fear still tinging her voice.

*She's afraid!* Sheryl realized anew. *I'm afraid. I'd guess everyone is, with all this uncertainty.* A surprising thought occurred to her. *I'll bet even Paul Haven is afraid.*

"No, it's actually a lot to go on," she countered firmly. "We are all a lot stronger and more resilient than we give ourselves credit for. Especially someone as bright and talented as you are. You have every reason to trust in yourself and in the possibilities for your future."

Sheryl realized as she said it that her words applied equally to herself. *Why haven't I been trusting myself instead of all the naysayers and doom mongers out there? Why aren't I trusting what I believe in? Why have I let fear rule me? Again?*

Sheryl gentled her voice. "Look. It's going to be okay. We might go through some rough patches along the way, but it will work out."

"How do you know that?"

"I've learned it really does work out—although, as I said before, not always in the way we expect it to. But I believe in possibilities. As long as we are looking for *possibilities* instead of dead ends, we can find solutions," she said, astonishing herself. "Look at what we've been able to find, discover, and solve on the Portal Project! Look at all the amazing new coding and discoveries you have made!"

*It's true*, Sheryl realized. *I do believe in possibilities. That is precisely what has given me hope in the past.*

"Yeah . . ."

"Keisha, I'm serious," Sheryl said with a sudden rush of energy. "We are part of something bigger. Bigger than ourselves. And certainly, bigger than AI." It was true, she understood, thinking back on everything that had unfolded in the last six months or so. Everything that had seemed hopeless. *When I had faith, I could do things that I didn't expect.*

"Okay, boss," Keisha was saying. "I trust you. And you're right, about trusting myself." She made a self-deprecating sound. "My parents always tell me that too."

"Ah, the wisdom of parents," Sheryl teased, feeling lighter than she had in days.

"Yeah, you would say that."

"Listen, is there anything else?" Sheryl asked, wanting to get back to the presentation with her new perspective. "I'll call you if I have questions about what you sent over."

"No, that's it," the younger woman confirmed. "And thanks, Sheryl. You helped. More than Carlos or Patrick did." Keisha took an audible breath. "You know, they might need to hear this too."

"Oh, they will," she assured her, suddenly filled with inspiration. "You can count on that. Everyone will."

Sheryl had a sudden vision of another set of meetings. Ones that would probably send Paul Haven into orbit. She grinned. *But he's going to hear it too.*

Her email dinged with an incoming message just as she hung up with Keisha. The headline caught her eye immediately.

## "HUMAN INTELLIGENCE HAS BEEN DETHRONED"

Her heart sank, until she saw the sender. Arianna Huffington. Curiosity piqued, she opened the email, scanning the content quickly, then clicked the link to read the rest.

What she first read summarized the fears that had been plaguing her. Then her eyes landed on one particular paragraph, and her body settled as something inside her recognized the truth:

"Now that our intellect has been dethroned, we can find meaning in what really defines us: our infinite and never-dying soul."

*Yes!* Sheryl thought, the idea resonating deep in her heart. *Yes!*

She turned back to her presentation with renewed vigor, pleased with the ideas that this article had triggered. *Now, I finally have something hopeful to present.*

Yet, despite her optimism, a big question loomed in her mind: *Does Paul Haven—or anyone else on the board—believe that he has a soul?*

# CHAPTER 32

# Coincidences and Opportunities

Gemma laughed out loud as she and Anna hurried across the high school parking lot. Her breath formed a billowy white cloud in the cold, night air, and Anna looked at her curiously.

"You okay, Mom?" she asked, clearly puzzled by her mother's ebullience.

"I'm great!" Gemma answered, pulling open the glass door to the gym entrance. "I'm excited to see KJ play."

"I've never seen you this excited about that before," Anna muttered.

Gemma, shrugging out of her long down coat, merely grinned. Despite the fact that she was technically unemployed, she was content, even happy. The sense of freedom and, yes, pride that had erupted after her call with Ms. Barelli had surprised—and pleased her. *But it makes sense*, she realized. *I'd already been feeling so much pressure and inner conflict. There's no way I would have ever been happy working for Kushma. Ever.*

One of Anna's teammates raced up to her as they entered the large atrium and whisked her off to join a group of giggling girls. Gemma smiled as she watched her daughter animatedly join the conversation, happy that the girl was developing a good social network at the high school.

Looking around to see who she knew and could sit with, Gemma saw a group of mothers from Anna's swim team huddled in the middle of the lobby. One of them, a blond that Gemma had seen before, looked up and met Gemma's eyes, briefly. She quickly turned back to the group. A little of the euphoria dissipated. *I'm still a working mom and divorced to boot.*

Continuing her scan, she noticed Rhonda and Emily Conroy standing off to the side of the high-ceilinged room. It looked like Rhonda was encouraging Emily, who was shaking her head. She remembered what Anna had said previously about Rhonda not being accepted by the other moms and walked toward them.

"Rhonda, Emily! How are you tonight?" she greeted them pleasantly.

"We're good. Excited for the game," Rhonda answered a bit too brightly. "Aren't we, Emily?" The woman was dressed in jeans and a Blake Academy sweatshirt that was at least a size too big, but her makeup was light and not smudged.

The girl shifted uncomfortable. "Yeah, Mom," she mumbled, looking down at the tiled floor.

"I'm sure it's going to be a good game," Gemma said cheerfully. "Do you have a son on—"

"Emily! Come sit with us," Anna's voice came from behind Gemma. She turned to see her daughter beckoning her teammate to join her.

Emily flew past her a second later, not even pausing to say good-bye to her mother. Gemma's heart swelled with pride as she watched Anna guide Emily toward the larger group. She noticed a couple of the other girls smirk, but they all moved off as a group toward the gymnasium doors. Clearly, her daughter already had some influence, even as a freshman, Gemma realized happily.

Turning back to Emily's mother, Gemma smiled. "Shall we go find seats?" she asked. "My son KJ is starting tonight, and I don't want to miss any of it."

Rhonda stiffened with apparent surprise. "Yes, thanks. Let's do that. Thank you."

"Do you have a son on the team?" Gemma asked.

"No, Emily wanted to come to the game, and, well, she wasn't sure who she could sit with," Rhonda explained. "It was really nice of Anna to include her. I was afraid she'd end up sitting with me."

"Ah yes, a fate worse than death to a teenage girl."

Chuckling, the two women made their way through the throngs of teenagers who appeared more interested in each other than the pending game. Gemma looked around, taking it all in. *I'm so thankful to be here*, she thought, her giddiness bubbling up again. *And with no dire threats hanging over my head.*

"You seem happy tonight," Rhonda observed as they settled on the bleachers near center court. "Did you start your new job? Do you like it?"

"Uh, well, that's a long story," Gemma deflected. "But it's not the job that I'm happy about."

KJ, warming up with the rest of the team, caught sight of her at that moment and gave her a big grin. She smiled back, waving subtly so as to not embarrass him in front of his teammates. After all, it wasn't cool for a high school junior to acknowledge his mother at the game. KJ flashed a quick thumbs up before he caught the ball and went back to warmups.

"Handsome boy," Rhonda noted.

"He is," Gemma beamed. "And a nice guy too. I'm proud of him."

The whistle sounded, signaling the end of warmups and the teams went back to the benches. Gemma whooped when KJ's name was announced as the starting point guard, but the sound was drowned out by loud cheering from a group of girls sitting nearby. She was close enough to notice KJ flush, although he didn't look toward the stands.

"I wonder which of the girls he likes," Gemma said softly to her new friend.

"Let's see if we can figure it out," Rhonda answered conspiratorially. "I can spy for you."

"Ha! Good idea."

The game started. Gemma held her breath when KJ got the ball and cheered when he made a great pass to set the boy at center up for dunk. *So far, so good.*

She chatted idly with Rhonda during the game and was surprised to learn that the dowdy woman was an attorney who had worked at a well-known New York firm. "And you left that to stay home with Emily?" Gemma asked curiously.

"Yeah, I know," Rhonda acknowledged. "It sounds crazy, but the hours. The pressure. I decided I really wanted to spend more time with Emily and Leo, my youngest, when I had the chance. Fortunately, my husband is very successful, so we could afford it."

"Will you go back?" Gemma couldn't imagine how Rhonda would

manage that with her appearance. New York could be tough if you didn't fit the image, and Rhonda didn't.

"To being a lawyer, yes," Rhonda answered. "To New York and a high-powered firm? No way. I do some work on the side now, just to keep up my skills, but whatever I do, it will be more low key. Plus, I'm not the sleek, fashion plate I used to be," she added with wry self-deprecation. "Maintaining the image was as much work as the work."

"I get it about the pressure and hours," Gemma agreed emphatically.

"Do you? From what Emily said you have a pretty high-powered job. And now with Atrium? That must be a lot of pressure."

Gemma's green eyes widened.

"Sorry. Too blunt sometimes," Rhonda apologized quickly. "Feel free to ignore me."

"No, it's okay," Gemma said, realizing that she actually meant it. "You summed it up well. Too well. I've only just recognized how high-pressure my work life has been."

"And it's worse with Atrium?" Rhonda guessed. "But you seem so happy tonight."

"Can you keep a secret?" Gemma asked. "I actually got fired from Atrium today."

Rhonda's brown eyes grew round. "Really? Whoa. After what? A week?"

A roar from the crowd interrupted them, and Gemma looked up to see KJ streaking down the floor with the ball. He made an easy layup at the other end. Gemma jumped up and whooped again. KJ grinned in her direction.

Settling back down, Gemma adjusted her lightweight sweater, which nearly matched the royal blue of the school's colors.

"You have to tell me what happened," Rhonda whispered, curiosity all over her face.

Gemma glanced around and lowered her own voice. "Well, it was all about confidentiality—or lack thereof." And she proceeded to tell her new friend the whole story, while still keeping an eye on the game.

"You know you can sue them for that," Rhonda informed her when she had finished.

"I can? I hadn't thought of that," Gemma said. "I'm just too happy to be free. I feel like I should be upset, but I just feel like a huge burden has been lifted. I mean, I couldn't even have been here tonight if . . ." She shuddered.

"Well, you could," Rhonda assured her. "Although it's not without risks. What are you going to do for work? Can you get your old job back?"

"I doubt it," Gemma replied. "They weren't too happy with me when I left."

"Yeah, that's always tough," Rhonda agreed.

Gemma jumped up again as she saw KJ steal the ball from an opposing player. "Go, KJ!" she yelled as she watched him make another layup.

"He's having a great game," her new friend said. "I'm guessing he'll be starting again."

Grinning, Gemma fist pumped. "I hope so!"

After that, conversation dwindled as they both got absorbed by the exciting game. KJ was pulled to the bench a few times, but never for long. Gemma was hoarse from cheering by the end of the first half.

"I'm going to get some water or something," she said to Rhonda as the teams headed to the locker room for the break. "Want anything?"

"Sure, water would be great. Thanks."

Gemma hurried away, anxious to beat the lines. When she returned, Rhonda was nowhere to be seen. Puzzled, Gemma settled in to watch the game as the teams took the floor again.

Rhonda appeared about ten minutes into the second half. "What did I miss?" she asked. "We're still ahead?"

"Yes, still ahead, although KJ hasn't played yet this half. I guess the coach is giving the other guy a chance," Gemma told her. "He's a senior."

"That's always rough on a coach," Rhonda murmured.

At the next break in the action, Rhonda turned to Gemma. "So, would you consider a job outside the cosmetics industry?" she asked abruptly.

Startled, Gemma blinked. "What? Um. I guess so," she answered. "In fact, I might have to after the Atrium debacle."

"Would it be hard to learn another industry?"

Gemma paused, considering. "Hard? Probably not. I'm a pretty quick study, although it would require extra effort and research. Still, with AI these days, it's a lot easier."

"Are you familiar with AI?" Rhonda cut in.

"Of course. I have to be. It's all the rage in marketing these days. Maybe too much so," Gemma said a bit flippantly. "But in all seriousness, yes. I've taken a number of courses on AI and use it regularly." She shot Rhonda a quick grin. "As long as confidentiality isn't at risk."

"Oh, I didn't think about that," Rhonda said. "I have to admit I'm a bit behind on AI, although I'll have to get up to speed if I decide to go back to lawyering."

"Yeah, it's affecting every industry these days," Gemma agreed.

"So, you're comfortable with technology, and you would be okay learning a new industry," Rhonda stated.

"Yes and yes. It might be fun," Gemma confirmed. "But why all the questions."

"Well, I talked to my husband during half time. He and his partner are looking for a new marketing executive," the other woman explained. "They had to let the last one go because of issues with confidentiality, if you believe that."

"What? That's a pretty wild coincidence!"

"You could say that. Anyway, I told Owen, my husband, about your situation," she paused, putting her hand over her mouth. "Uh oh, I hope that's okay?"

"Sure, it's fine," Gemma said. "I assume that he'll keep it to himself, yes?"

"Yes, I told him that it was a secret, so to speak," Rhonda assured her. "But here's the thing. He'd like to talk to you about the position at his firm. He was impressed by your ethics, as I was. He has a technology company that's grown enormously in the last decade, but they've kind of gotten stuck recently. Roman is looking for someone with fresh ideas to help them go to the next level. But he's kind of gun shy after the last guy."

"I'll bet," Gemma muttered, her head spinning. "Wow! I didn't expect this when I came here tonight."

Rhonda laughed. "Me either. But there you have it. Will you speak with him?"

"Of course!" Gemma cried. "Why not? It sounds like an interesting situation. A new one for me, no doubt, but kind of exciting. I'd love to learn more."

"Great! Let's exchange numbers—"

The crowd erupted in a loud cheer, and both women looked up to see KJ racing down the court again.

"He must have stolen the ball again!" Gemma crowed unabashedly.

Her friend laughed. "Yes, it seems so."

KJ proceeded to net another layup and the crowd cheered again.

"You watch your son play," Rhonda directed. "We'll finish *after* the game."

"Sounds good. And thank you, Rhonda. I can't tell you how much this means to me."

"You're welcome, Gemma, but it's not a big deal. It seems like it might be a good solution for everyone." Rhonda paused, leaning closer to Gemma. "And . . . I think I see which girl KJ has his eye on," she continued in a teasing tone.

Gemma looked across the bleachers, following Rhonda's subtle pointing. *She might be right*, Gemma thought, seeing a cute blonde girl who looked like she might be beaming at her son. *Hmmm.*

The referee's whistle blew, drawing her attention back to the game. Smiling, Gemma could barely stop herself from bouncing in her seat. *I'm at the game. I have a new friend. And, I might have a lead on a job. Already.* She thought about Sheryl and their recent conversation. *I'm glad I trusted myself and did what was right. And tonight, I found out that there are people out there that value integrity.*

CHAPTER 33

# Humanity or AI?

**Thursday, January 26**

"In conclusion, rather than look at AI as a replacement for humans, we have the unique opportunity to unleash aspects of *ourselves* that we've only touched on in the past. The human spirit is what is unique and valuable, not our rational minds." Sheryl looked around at each face of the boardroom as she continued, "If we choose to cultivate and nurture the human spirit here at The Diamante, we can create value that will put us *ahead* of our competition," Sheryl finished with a flourish.

There was a moment of stunned silence. Then, Blake Jones began to applaud. Several others, including Alex and Janine, joined in wholeheartedly. Sheryl fought to keep her face calm, despite her urge to grin. Not everyone was smiling or applauding. She continued to stand tall and confident at the end of the long, black table in her tailored gray suit and pale pink blouse, waiting for the other shoe to drop.

It did. Paul Haven exploded. "Are you kidding me?" he sputtered, pointing at the final PowerPoint slide on the screen behind Sheryl. "How in the world did you get to this level of an organization with an attitude like that? Human spirit! What are we having, a revival meeting or something? Religion has no place in the boardroom."

Expecting this response, Sheryl smiled placatingly. "I never mentioned religion, Paul. Human spirit is the essence of being human—whatever that means to you. It represents the creative, resilient, visionary side of humanity. Perhaps the nonrational side?" She had deliberately used the word "spirit" instead of "soul" because of the breadth of its meaning.

"Nonrational is right," Paul mocked, his face twisting in a sneer that threatened to make her stomach plummet. He turned to the rest of the group, focusing primarily on Blake. "I can't believe anyone is buying into this!"

"I think she made some good points, Paul," Blake Jones responded quickly, his brown eyes warm as they met Sheryl's gaze. "There *is* more to humans than our so-called rational side." He paused, looking straight at Paul. "You're displaying it now, in fact."

Paul's face turned red. "What are you talking about?" his voice was so high he was nearly screeching.

"Your temper. Your anger. That's not rational," Blake pointed out calmly. "That's emotional. Yet another aspect of being human."

"It's normal to get angry at such nonsense," Paul snarled, waving to the screen. "I thought a numbers guy would have more sense."

Sheryl looked around the long, narrow room again, trying to gauge the reactions of the other seven board members. Her eyes came to rest on the newest board member. Martin Cameron. A stocky black man with salt and pepper hair. He had just been appointed as Anthony Russo's replacement representing Alpha VC, pending shareholders' elections in the spring. With Todd Fisher still on "leave," he tipped the balance of the board in favor of nonexecutive directors. It was usually even.

Martin was looking directly at her. His light eyes, she couldn't tell if they were blue or gray, were bright and alert and assessing. *I'll bet he got quite an earful about me before the meeting even began*, she thought.

"As the numbers guy," Blake was saying, "I have some alternative cost-cutting measures to review. In lieu of layoffs." Sheryl issued a silent hurrah. *He kept his word!*

"Great! The more cost-cutting, the better," Paul said enthusiastically, ignoring the last part of Blake's statement.

"Now wait a minute. Just how much cost-cutting do we need?" Duncan asked, a frown deepening the already plentiful lines on his rugged face. As the most senior nonexecutive director, he was used to commanding attention. "I thought the numbers looked quite good." He leveled a dark look at Paul. "We don't seem to have suffered any damage from the scandal Alpha VC caused."

"Alpha didn't cause the scandal," Paul snapped, but Sheryl noticed that he briefly glanced down and fidgeted with a button on his designer suit.

Duncan nodded in acknowledgement, his blue eyes watchful and assessing.

"Duncan asked a good question, Paul," another director continued probing.

Leaning forward as he addressed the group—and turning his back to Sheryl—Paul spoke condescendingly. "We need cost-cutting because you've been operating The Diamante too extravagantly in the past. We can be leaner, more efficient, and more profitable. A lot more profitable," he pontificated.

Determined not to be excluded from the conversation, Sheryl quietly returned to her seat. Still, she deliberately left her final PowerPoint slide on the screen that hung above the credenza. It simply said: "Human Spirit = Competitive Advantage" in the bold silver of The Diamante's corporate colors.

"We're already *very* profitable," Alex retorted. "What kind of return are you looking for?"

"And are you just trading long-term profit for short-term gains?" challenged Blake.

"No wonder Alpha wanted to change the board. We need to change the executives too," Paul retorted. "Why wouldn't we want to make more profit?" He looked at his colleague. "Martin, help me out here."

"I know Alpha wants a short-term gain so that they can sell their shares in a few years," Martin said bluntly, surprising Sheryl and perhaps the rest with his honesty. "We have to maximize the profit during that time."

Paul's charcoal eyes shot daggers at him.

"And what about after?" Sheryl asked, her stomach in knots with the tone of the conversation. She surreptitiously took a deep breath in a vain attempt to calm her fraught nerves.

"Who cares?" Paul answered insolently.

A stunned silence followed. Sheryl was so shocked that she struggled to breathe, much less respond. Paul's true colors had just been laid out for everyone to see.

Finally, Martin broke the silence. "I think Paul got a little carried away," he said tactfully, his voice deep and confident. "Of course, we're not trying to ruin the company. But we do see room to optimize things, especially utilizing AI. Sheryl provided us with some great information and an, um, interesting vision for the future. However, we feel strongly that a leaner staff would be better for the company."

He turned to Sheryl. "You weren't clear how much of the customer service department would be displaced by the new portal. I assume all of it?"

The head of sales and marketing sat up. "All of it? No way."

Sheryl's hazel eyes focused on Martin. "No, not all. We'll still need coverage for those questions and issues that fall outside the scope of AI."

"Why? If the AI is good enough, we shouldn't need that," Paul jumped back in.

"People like to talk to people," Blake broke in. "How do you like getting stuck in an AI loop when you call the electric company?"

"I don't get stuck. I know how to work through the prompts," Paul shot back smugly.

"Enough!" Alex held up his hands, his usual boyishness vanquished by the grim look on his face. "Paul, Martin, you've asked for another 10 percent reduction in staff. The executive team doesn't feel that's feasible. Not unless we also want to cut projects or reduce our analytical output. Or compromise the customer service that is the hallmark of our brand."

Sheryl watched as most of the board joined her in nodding.

"Blake has found other areas where we can save the equivalent of 6 percent of our payroll costs, on an ongoing basis," Alex continued. "Sheryl had just given us a very balanced presentation on the pros and cons of AI, where it's working, and where it's simply not as effective. You know the SEC continues to monitor and change their guidelines about what the financial analysts can and cannot do with AI. Yes, Sheryl—"

"Went on some kind of religious kick about humanity vs AI," Paul interrupted snidely. "Are you going to pat her on the back for that too?"

"Paul!" Martin said sharply.

Sheryl spoke up before Alex had a chance to reply. "Paul, Martin. What I was logically conveying by referencing the human spirit is that we are much more than just ones and zeros . . . and even dollar signs.

Yes, we are very good at rational thought. The Enlightenment movement, otherwise known as The Age of Reason, that began around the seventeenth century taught us that our rational thought is what made us—humans—unique and special. It was wrong. AI is and will continue to be very good at analysis and rational thinking. Perhaps even better than we are. And that's why we need to recognize and develop our *real* gifts as humans," she continued passionately. "The creative and visionary spirit is what has really allowed us to thrive. We can't just abandon humans in favor of AI. For so many, many reasons. But especially creativity, out-of-the-box thinking. That's why we're guarding the portal design from AI. Because it's special. Unique. It will continue to set The Diamante apart—"

"Until someone else copies it," Paul countered.

"Sure, but by then, we'll be able to create something else, and again, better! That's why we need talented and creative programmers—and financial analysts and customer services reps and accountants. We can't rely on AI to run our business. People do that. With AI help, certainly. But the bottom line is that we have an opportunity to nurture the kind of creativity in our people that can set us apart—especially if everyone else is relying on AI. It's not only good for the company. It's good for our staff, ourselves, and society as a whole."

"Bravo!" Blake said.

Paul's face turned red again. Sheryl was afraid he was going to explode, but he held his tongue.

Martin looked thoughtfully at Sheryl and then turned back to Alex. "So, what is the executive team proposing?"

"We're proposing that we use Blake's cuts to offset 6 percent of the proposed layoffs," reported Alex. "We'll use a considered strategy of attrition, retirement, and a few layoffs to achieve the other 4 percent in expense cuts."

Sheryl closed her eyes, heartbroken that Alex was still talking layoffs. *I thought we had agreed.*

"But we could get a 16 percent reduction if we do both," Paul crowed. "That's even better."

"I'm not sure that's necessary, Paul," Duncan told him sternly. "I've been on this board longer than anyone else here. I know this company, and we *do* have something special here, as Sheryl rightly pointed out. We always have. Although the practices of the last year have shaken us up. Now, I know Alpha wants a big return for the large stake that they took in the company. But let's not get greedy. You're already getting what you asked for, even though not one of these executives wants to do another round of staff reduction."

"But—" Paul started to argue.

"Paul, that's enough," Martin cut him off. "I think Management's proposal is fair. It *is* what Alpha wants. The fact that they were creative enough to come up with viable alternatives to layoffs speaks highly of them."

"Thank you, Martin," Alex said gravely.

"Hmph," was all Paul managed to get out.

"Shall we take a vote?" Blake asked.

A surly look on his face, Paul, as acting chairperson, requested a motion to close the discussion. Protocol followed, and a vote ensued.

One by one, everyone at the table voted for Alex's compromise solution. Even Sheryl. Her heart ached as she pondered more staff reduction, especially after the promises she had made, but she was grateful that they were much less than Alpha had wanted. She shared a commiserating look with Blake, who looked equally disturbed.

"Is there any other business?" Paul snarled, half rising out of his chair at the head of the table. "If not, let's—"

"Yes, I have a last-minute report on the investigation into The Diamante and Todd Fisher," Alex interrupted. "It was so last minute, in fact, that's why it wasn't listed on the agenda."

Paul sat back down. "Well?"

"I'm happy to report that Todd Fisher has been cleared of any involvement in the pyramid scheme that Hank and Anthony created," Alex said gravely. "Neither the FBI nor the SEC will be pressing charges."

"That's *good* news," Sheryl breathed. She almost felt as if the entire board heaved a collective sigh. The whole debacle had been heavy on everyone, no matter their position on the board.

"It is good news," Alex agreed. "Plus, they've also ruled out any involvement from anyone else at The Diamante—except of course for Rachel Soloway and the two salespeople they already identified. We're all cleared."

"Awesome!" Blake cried.

"Glad to hear it," Duncan added.

"Can we fire him now?" Paul chimed in, turning to the head of HR. "No matter what, we can't have Todd back here."

They were all quiet, realizing that the implications for the former president of the firm were still bad. Even though he hadn't done anything wrong, his leadership had been tainted. *Trust again*, Sheryl thought, feeling badly for her former boss. *It's so important and yet . . .* Her mind focused on Paul Haven and his behavior. *Some people obviously care nothing for it.*

Janine, looking chagrined, took a breath and responded. "I think the best course of action is to ask for his resignation. Give him that dignity at least. Unfortunately, his name has been tarnished, despite the fact that he didn't do anything wrong."

"Our clients won't trust him," Duncan sadly echoed Sheryl's thoughts.

"All right," Paul said shortly. "As long as he resigns." He glanced at Alex, then Martin, who subtly shook his head. "Now are we done?"

"I don't have anything else," Alex replied, his face pale.

With Todd officially gone, his time as interim president was likely at an end, Sheryl guessed. *Although I wonder, does Alex even want the presidency?* Somehow, she didn't think so.

"Then, we're adjourned," Paul snapped, almost jumping out of his chair, a sullen look on his face. He rushed out of the room without pleasantries, leaving only a trail of expensive cologne in his wake. Martin stayed long enough to shake hands with everyone and give Sheryl a murmured compliment on her presentation before he, too, departed.

Sheryl was surprised when Duncan pulled her aside. "Well, young lady," he said in his courtly way, oblivious to the inappropriateness of the phrase. "You certainly know how to shake things up. This board has become quite interesting with you on it. Guess we needed a feminine perspective and all." He chuckled. "You keep it up. You're doing good, despite what those cretins are saying."

Sheryl smiled and squeezed the older man's hand. "Thank you. I really needed to hear that."

He winked and then turned to take his leave of the others. The rest of the nonexecutive directors accompanied him out.

Alex sank back into his chair as the door closed and the EDs now had their own privacy. "Phew! That was some meeting. I was afraid of how that would go. We're outnumbered now with Todd out. Thank God for Duncan. He saved our bacon."

"He sure did," Blake agreed, sitting back down himself.

Alex turned, his boyish face earnest. "Sheryl, I agree with what Duncan said. What you said today was truly inspiring. I've never looked at AI that way. I have a whole new perspective to consider now. We all do. And I would like to add, never doubt that you are making a difference here," he continued urgently. "Even though we had to give in to more staff reductions today. You won't always win, but you are making us think. And that's a good thing. Thank you for that."

"Alex, thank you. That means a lot," Sheryl replied gratefully, a warm smile on her face.

"You knocked my socks off," Janine chimed in. "Wow! I may need you to work in HR instead of technology with that kind of thinking. Brilliant!"

Sheryl laughed. "Well, to be honest, I just came up with that last bit yesterday. Believe me, it was a struggle to find something positive to say." She sobered. "But what I said really resonated with me. The part about nurturing the human spirit in our staff. And ourselves. It's a different way of looking at leadership. And honestly, I'm excited about it. The more I've been thinking about it, the more I realize it is more of an opportunity than a death knell to humanity—if it's used well."

"I think you have us all excited about it, Sheryl," Blake told her.

"That's great to hear," she chuckled, "because I think I know now what my keynote speech is going to be about in June!" She grinned around the table at her colleagues. "And guess who's going to have to listen to me practice!"

CHAPTER 34
# Let Freedom Ring

**Friday, March 25**

Alisha watched Dave and Robert from across the crowded Mexican restaurant. She still wished, at times like now, that she could somehow be included in their close-knit friendship, but she was learning that boundaries were good and healthy. Perhaps for the very first time, she respected the limitations on their friendship, especially after all Dave's wife, Sheryl, had done to help her out.

Looking back down at the bright tablecloth and napkin in front of her, her thoughts turned inward.

*It's been over two months since my confrontation with my father*, she mused as she waited for Brittany to join her. Two months with no contact, although he certainly had tried. Her dad was nothing but persistent. With support from Brittany and Julie, as well as the counselor from the women's crisis center, she had resisted all his overtures, including blocking his numbers and changing her personal cell phone number.

Plus, she had taken her mother to task. Reluctantly giving Denise her new number, she had told her in no uncertain terms what would happen if she gave the number to her ex. Shocked by her daughter's new resolve, Denisa had complied. So far. It had been tough going with both her parents and her oldest brother, but she was proud of herself for the progress she had made.

"Alisha! I'm sorry I'm late," Brittany greeted her, breathless from hurrying in from the cold. She unwrapped a bright blue scarf from around her neck. "Brrr. It's been a cold March!"

"No worries," Alisha assured her. "I haven't been waiting long. And you're right. This California girl can't wait for a real spring!"

Robert's loud guffaw suddenly echoed through the room, and both women turned to look. His tall form was bent over in laughter, and Dave looked both embarrassed and frustrated. Alisha noticed that several other members of the LSM team were also looking towards the men. In fact, at least half the restaurant was full of LSMers.

Brittany arched an elegant eyebrow. "Ça alors! That's quite a ruckus," she observed with a sly grin.

"Looks like Robert is having some fun at Dave's expense," Alisha said, with a quick smile. "Not that *that* is anything new."

"No, those two do seem to enjoy ribbing one another."

Settling in her seat, Brittany picked up the tattered menu and scanned it with a skeptical air. "Remind me why we come here?" she asked.

Alisha laughed. "Because it's close, cheap, and good food. Plus, everyone from the office comes here."

Brittany shuddered, but Alisha could see the humorous gleam in her eyes.

"I think I'll have a margarita," her boss announced. "I know it's not usually done, but it's Friday and you've had a banner week. Let's celebrate!"

"Ooh, good idea," Alisha agreed. "And yes, I'm delighted that Walter not only renewed his contract this week but also expanded it! Can you believe it?"

"Yes, I can. You've done a great job with that account, Alisha. Especially since you've been fighting Penny all the way."

Alisha straightened, her mouth forming a round "O."

"Yes, I'm aware," Brittany chuckled at her reaction. "I do have eyes in my head. And report tracking on my computer."

"I didn't know you knew," Alisha said. "She's been driving me crazy, although she seems to have eased up in the last couple of weeks."

"That's to your credit," her boss told her. "You've acted the professional in every instance." She paused to glance at Dave and Robert. "No one can find any fault in your behavior these last few months. Even Penny sees that."

"Well, I'm glad for that!"

The bells over the door jingled and a blast of cold air swept across the restaurant as someone else hustled in. Engrossed in her menu, it took a moment for Alisha to realize that the good-natured chatter in the room had gone largely silent.

When she looked up, her heart stopped. She forgot to breathe.

"*Merde!*" Brittany said quietly. "The nerve of that man."

"Well, well, well. What have we here?" Liam's smooth voice cut across the silence.

Alisha barely registered that both Dave and Robert rose to their feet. She found her stomach instantly upset at his voice.

"Look what the cat dragged in. You are not welcome here, Liam," Brittany said in a loud, icy voice.

"Now, now, Brittany. It's a public restaurant," Liam chided her in a condescending tone. His dark hair was slicked back from his face, which was ruddy from the cold but still suntanned. Dressed in a wool coat, it made Alisha uncomfortable just how handsome and sophisticated he looked. She wished he didn't.

Dave and Robert both took a step in their direction, but Brittany motioned for them to stay.

"Liam, we all know you are only here to cause trouble, and I'm quite sure no one wants that. Especially you," her boss replied.

Alisha tugged on her ponytail, her gaze bouncing between Liam and Brittany. *I feel like I should do something, but what?*

"I'd much rather talk to the lovely Alisha than you," Liam sneered. "No offense, of course."

"I don't want to talk to you," Alisha said a little stiffly, but she sat up straighter in her chair and subtly adjusted her plaid wool jacket.

"Well, your father wants you to talk to *me*," he answered, as he edged closer to their table. "He's heartbroken that his baby girl has been ignoring him."

Alisha swallowed hard. "That's none of your business," she stated firmly, drawing on the skills she had been learning in counseling. Despite her heart pounding, she kept her head up and maintained steady eye contact with her former tormentor.

Liam now fully approached the table, putting his hands on a chair, learning over both women. "I'm afraid you're wrong there, my dear."

Brittany stood up. Even with her ridiculously high heels, she was several inches shorter than Liam, but no one watching saw that. Her presence was powerful and potent.

"Alisha said she did not want to speak with you. I do not want to speak with you," Brittany spoke resolutely, her whiskey eyes flashing fire. "I believe I can safely say that most, if not all, of the people in this room do not want to speak with you. I suggest you leave now Mr. Moriarity."

Alisha was a little surprised to see Liam take a step back. Every eye in the room, including the bartender and wait staff, had their eyes on him. Alisha glanced over to notice that Dave and Robert were not just standing at attention, their fists were clenched by their sides. Brittany, however, was magnificent to behold.

Putting a hand to his heart, Liam gave her a doleful look. "You wound me, Brittany. We were colleagues once."

Brittany didn't bother to respond. She stood there, continuing to stare daggers at him, her breathing calm but her posture straight and strong. In her wine-colored dress with a large gold necklace, she looked like a queen.

Alisha watched Liam's eyes dart around the room. *No doubt looking for support.*

"Well, I see this isn't the time or place," he conceded. "I'm sure they'll be a better, more, uh, *intimate* time for Alisha and me to talk—."

Alisha immediately cut off Liam, and whatever Brittany was about to reply. "If you approach me again, I'll file for a restraining order," she said matter-of-factly, keeping her gaze calm but unyielding. "After what happened with my father, you know I will. There will be NO intimate time to talk, or any other for that matter. Now get out of here!"

She was surprised—and pleased—to see Liam blanch under his tan. His eyes narrowed, and he opened his mouth to speak. But no words came out. Instead, he turned on his heel and left as abruptly as he had come in.

Everyone in the restaurant burst out in applause.

Brittany's olive skin flushed, but she gave a good-natured smile and wave. "Sorry about that folks, but thank you for your support," she said in a voice that carried, then sat back down next to Alisha. "Ouf! That was something," she said to Alisha.

"You're telling me!" Alisha picked up her water and noticed her hands were shaking.

Her boss reached over and covered her free hand.

"Bien joué!" she said softly. "That literally means, 'well played.' I mean it. Liam has just witnessed something in you he has never seen before. A bully hates to be bested. You cannot trust him, but he will not try this particular scheme again."

Taking a gulp of water, Alisha gave her a grateful look.

"Wow! Brittany! You were incredible," Dave Simmons said, as he and Robert finished striding over to their table. "Just incredible."

Robert's deep voice chimed in. "You were both incredible. That guy. Does he have some nerve or what? But Alisha, compared to the last time I saw you with him at that golf game, I have to give it to you. You really stood up for yourself."

"Thank you, guys, for your support," Alisha spoke up. "You being on guard made it easier, for me anyway."

"Yes, for both of us," Brittany concurred. "True gentlemen. But thank you for letting us handle it. Strong women can do that."

"You reminded me of Sheryl, my wife," Dave said quietly. Then he let out an *oof!* as Robert dug an elbow into his ribs.

"Yeah, they didn't really *need* us, did they Dave? But they *appreciated* our *support*."

Dave looked up at the ceiling and rolled his eyes. "Yes, Robert," he ground out. "Point taken. I get it."

"Private joke, gentlemen?" Brittany raised one shoulder.

Alisha giggled. After listening to Dave lament his wife's growth for months last fall, she knew precisely what Robert was needling him about. Dave had been tremendously upset and, Alisha knew now, threatened by the new power that his wife was claiming in her work and in her own life.

"You could say that," Robert said with a laugh. "My buddy Dave here is trying to wrap his head around how to *support* a strong and independent woman. You just gave him a fine example, both of you."

It was Dave's turn to elbow Robert. "Enough! They don't need to hear all that," he grumbled.

"No, indeed, we do not," Brittany agreed with a chuckle, sharing a knowing look with her protégé. "But I'm glad we could help you out."

Dave groaned. "I'm just glad you two are okay," he said, clearly trying to change the subject. "And Alisha, I've never seen you stand up to Liam like that. That was great."

"Yeah, we've both noticed a big change in you in the last few months," Robert added. "You're more, um . . ."

"Confident?" Brittany supplied. "Self-sufficient?"

Robert snapped his fingers. "Got it. Yes, confident. And more comfortable in her skin."

"That's right," Dave agreed.

Alisha blushed and twisted her ponytail around her finger. She blinked back a few tears.

"Thanks, guys. I'm a work in progress, but I have been working hard. Dealing with stuff I should have dealt with before," Alisha said, assuming that Dave would understand because of their previous conversations.

Indeed, he gave her a knowing look, but all he said was "good for you." Robert nodded.

"Well, gentlemen," Brittany interjected. "Alisha and I are about to order some margaritas to celebrate the renewal *and* expansion of one of Alisha's most challenging accounts."

Alisha gave a quick nod when her boss shot her a questioning look.

"You are welcome to join us, if you'd like," Brittany continued.

"Thanks, Britt," Robert said. "But we've already ordered. You ladies have a lot to celebrate, I think. Enjoy!"

With mock bows, they headed back to their own table.

"I hate when he calls me 'Britt'," her boss muttered.

Alisha laughed. "And that's why he does it. Robert is such a tease."

"That he is but a good guy too."

"Yeah, definitely that."

Their waiter appeared. "Ladies, may I take your drink order? My boss would like to offer the first round on the house for your magnificent performances."

"What?" Alisha gasped. "She doesn't have to do that!"

"Never turn down a free drink, girl, *when* you trust the source," Brittany overrode her. "We'll have two margaritas. On the rocks. With salt."

"Yes, ma'am," the young man replied, and hurried off to fetch their drinks.

Brittany gave Alisha a smug look. "We strong, independent women deserve some pampering too," she pronounced.

Alisha grinned. "I guess we do at that, don't we?"

A moment later, the waiter was back with the biggest margaritas Alisha had ever seen. He placed them on the table with a flourish and whisked away.

Her boss grabbed her drink and raised it in Alisha's direction. "To you, Alisha. I'm so proud of you and what you've accomplished in the last two months. I've already seen a big change in you. Here's to your continued growth and success!"

Alisha raised her glass and clinked it gingerly with Brittany's.

"Thank you, Brittany. I honestly feel a lot better. It's been tough, especially with all the crap my father continues to pull, including tonight. But I feel like I'm breaking free. And the freedom from him and all his games and manipulation. Wow! It's amazing."

They each took a long sip.

"I really appreciate your support," Alisha continued. "I wouldn't have gotten this far without it."

"Maybe not this fast," Brittany noted. "But you would have gotten there. Freedom is too valuable not to fight for. And you've done that. You have a fire in you that is not easily quenched, and I like that."

"Yeah. I never thought I'd be free of him—ever. But I'm getting there. I'm finally learning to trust *me* more than him."

"Music to my ears! Now let's order. I'm starved." Brittany waved the menu.

Alisha laughed, looking fondly at her boss. *It's all about who to trust, isn't it?*

# The Show Must Go On

## Monday, June 19

Five months after her board presentation on the human spirit, Sheryl stood on the very large stage, a big smile on her face as a wave of appreciative applause washed over her.

*I did it!* she thought with a mixture of triumph and relief. *My first 'real' keynote, and they seem to be loving it.*

Despite the ballroom turned lecture hall being filled with over a thousand tech moguls and IT professionals from around the nation, the loudest cheering came from a section near the front. Sheryl looked down at the group assembled there with love and gratitude. Dave, of course, was in the front row, on his feet. She loved that their dear friend Robert was standing very tall by his side. Both wore big grins. Alisha was also there, next to a dark-haired woman, clapping enthusiastically. All three had wrangled spots representing LSM Consulting at the company's booth in order to be there for Sheryl's talk.

Of course, her best friend Cindy, being in IT, had flown in from Denver and was right there on the other side of Dave cheering wildly. Her curly hair was already in disarray as she practically jumped up and down. Sheryl returned her grin, feeling a surge of love for the woman who had been her biggest supporter.

The representation from The Diamante was equally energetic. Keisha, dressed flamboyantly in red and black, was whooping out loud, which almost made Sheryl laugh. It had been tough to decide who to bring with her, as her whole team had wanted to come. Ultimately, Keisha and Carlos had been rewarded with the trip because of the success of the Portal Project. Carlos looked embarrassed by Keisha's antics, but he gave Sheryl a big thumbs up when he saw her looking their way.

Unexpectedly, Joaquin, The Diamante's compliance officer, had also made the trip to Atlanta, where the conference was being held.

Sheryl wasn't sure if he was there to support her or police her, but he had been adamant about coming. Seeing his attention focused on Keisha though, Sheryl suspected that the trip might have had very little to do with her. Not that either of them had said a word, but Sheryl had observed a growing closeness between the two over the last few months.

In the next row, right behind Dave and Cindy, stood Gemma Morrison, who had an arm around the shoulders of her teenage son KJ. Gemma's free hand was making a series of fist pumps in the air. *It has been so great to revive that friendship over the last few months*, Sheryl thought before turning her attention back to the wider audience.

Almost everyone was on their feet, clapping. There were a few people with stern looks and crossed arms, but not many. And almost no one had left. It seemed that her talk had resonated far more than she had expected.

Sheryl had used her January board presentation as the basis for the speech after talking to the organizers about expanding the scope of her talk beyond just the "memorial meetings." They had been thrilled, especially with the human side to the AI angle, as that was obviously a major theme for this year's National Association of Information Technology conference. Although she and her colleagues were still working through how to implement her ideas to nourish the human spirit at The Diamante, she could point to the "memorial meetings" as one possibility of many.

It was nearly fifteen minutes later before Sheryl could extract herself from the crowd of IT professionals who wanted to ask more questions and congratulate her. She had been astonished when several high-level executives had asked if she was available to come speak to their company's leadership teams and boards. *Oh my!*

Finally, she made her way over to her friends and family. Dave immediately wrapped her in a big hug, spinning her around.

"I'm so damned proud of you!" he said. "You were incredible." His eyes were sincere as he added, "This is a whole new side of you that I've never seen before. I'm so impressed, Sheryl."

He paused to clear his throat, and Sheryl thought she saw a bit of extra moisture in his eyes.

Sheryl's heart melted—again. She and Dave had come a long way since winter. There were still times when certain emotions haunted her, but she was glad that she had taken that leap of faith. Dave had worked hard to continue to prove his loyalty and love, as she had in return. As a result, their relationship was stronger than ever and deeply rewarding. They were talking more, compromising when necessary, and being incredibly supportive of each other. They were even planning a two-week trip for their anniversary, and Sheryl never needed a vacation more.

"Thank you, honey," she said into his neck. "I'm so glad you could be here. I love you."

"I love you, too, sweetheart," he replied, giving her a decorous kiss.

Robert pulled her away and into a bear hug. "Woman, you never cease to amaze me," he said in his deep gravelly voice. "I wish my wife could have been here. She would have loved that talk. Loved it."

"Ah, Robert. Thank you!" Sheryl answered. "We'll have to get together with the two of you soon! I'd love to see her."

Cindy broke in. "My turn!" she said as she too embraced her friend. "You were fabulous. Just fabulous. Can I come work for you?"

They laughed at the old joke. Cindy was happy in Denver, although Sheryl missed her terribly. It was very special to have her here in person today.

Gemma was next, along with her son. She clasped both Sheryl's hands. "Oh, my friend. The world needs you. What a powerful and important message. I'm glad KJ was here to hear it, especially as he is heading off to college in the not-too-distant future. I'm only sorry I couldn't bring Anna too."

A few happy tears spilled onto Sheryl's cheeks. "Oh, Gemma. I don't know what to say. It's wonderful to have you here."

An impish smirk crossed her friend's face. "Yeah, and for legit reasons too. What better way for me to learn about the tech industry? Owen agreed. It's so cool how this worked out."

Sheryl hugged her. "It *is* cool. I still can't believe how you landed on your feet!"

"Yes, and now I need to get to another session. You enjoy your triumph. We'll talk later," Gemma said, stepping away.

Alisha approached more tentatively, the older woman she had been sitting with in tow. "Sheryl, you were great!" she said brightly. "I can't imagine standing up in front of all those people. But you were so poised and confident. Wow!"

Sheryl gave the younger woman into a quick squeeze. "Thank you, Alisha. I'm glad you are here. I appreciate it."

"I'd like you to meet my boss, Brittany Mollier," Alisha said after Sheryl released her.

"Sheryl, I've heard a lot about you," Brittany said warmly. She shook Sheryl's hand. "Very, very impressive talk too. I can see why Alisha admires you so much."

"Thank you, Brittany. It's nice to meet you," Sheryl replied. "I've also heard good things about you from Alisha. She seems to be blossoming under your leadership."

"I'm finally learning to trust myself," Alisha said earnestly, and then blushed. "And Brittany is helping."

Sheryl laughed. "It's a process for all of us, isn't it?"

*But it's not just a one-time thing,* Sheryl realized with a sense of awe. *We have to learn to trust ourselves again and again. Like I have. And Gemma.* She glanced at her husband. *Dave too. It's a process. Two steps forward, one step back. We trust. We fail or stumble. We learn to trust again. Hopefully, the trust gets stronger with each cycle.*

"Now, we have to get to the trade show floor, Alisha," Brittany was saying. Sheryl watched with amusement as she herded Alisha *and* Robert away.

Left alone with Dave, Sheryl felt the tension she had been holding for weeks drain from her body. She leaned against him and let out a long sigh. "I'm so glad that's over!" she confessed.

Dave wrapped an arm around her shoulder. "You were so good. I don't think that's the last keynote you're going to be giving."

"No, it's not," Sheryl said breathlessly. "I've already had several people ask!"

"I'm not surprised," Dave chuckled and gave her another quick hug. "But I gotta run now. *I* still have work to do." Dave winked and walked away, following his colleagues to the exhibition hall, she assumed.

She had started gathering up her things when a familiar voice caused her to look up with a start.

"Congratulations, that was quite the speech," Todd Fisher said, a smile creasing his narrow face.

"Todd! What are you doing here?" Sheryl burst out.

"Oh, a little of this, a little of that," he said nonchalantly, but Sheryl saw the tautness in the way he stood. He still didn't have a job. Sheryl couldn't imagine what he was going through.

"I also hear congratulations are in order with the Portal Project," he continued. "It's a smash hit from what I've heard, although no one except your clients seem to be able to view it."

Sheryl smirked. "No, we're trying to keep it under wraps as long as possible, but we are getting great feedback about it. Keisha is a genius."

"No doubt. You always said that," he remarked.

"I'm grateful to have her," Sheryl said simply. And she was. Despite the two butting heads on many occasions, Carlos and Keisha had made a great team. Even without being able to replace Patrick, they had managed to deliver and release the new Portal on May first, as promised. The first few weeks had been a little rough, as they hadn't had time for the deep testing Keisha thought they needed, but all-in-all, it had been a very successful launch.

"You should be. The industry is all abuzz about her design. I'm sure you'll have everyone trying to steal her away," Todd told her.

"Oh, they already are," Sheryl told him. Keisha gleefully informed her of each new outrageous offer, but the young woman had sworn her loyalty to Sheryl. Of course, it didn't hurt that Sheryl had given her a big raise and a promotion. An Associate Director now, Keisha was pleased with the new responsibilities and felt ready to take them on.

"Well, good luck, Sheryl," Todd said, shaking her hand.

"You too, Todd. I'm sorry about what happened with you and . . ."

"Yeah, me too. I hope I'll see you around sometime time," he responded and turned to walk away.

Heart aching for him, Sheryl watched his progress for a moment before a thought struck her. "Todd, wait a sec," she called after him.

He pivoted quickly, a look of surprise in his bright blue eyes.

"I have an idea for you," she said warmly. "Let me give you the name of my coach. Paul hired him for me, but he's been great. He might be a good, um, resource for you too."

Looking wary, Todd nodded. "Yeah, okay. Couldn't hurt, I guess," he said uncomfortably.

"It's just a thought," Sheryl assured him. "Give me your cell number, and I'll text you his contact info."

Todd pulled a crisp white business card from his pocket and handed it to her. "I'm old-school, still," he said with a wink. "And thanks."

With a quick wave, he retreated, leaving Sheryl alone in the large room, except for the staffers who were quietly cleaning up and preparing for the next session.

Her phone rang. Expecting Alex to call, she was surprised to see that it was John Hargrove.

"John?"

"My spies tell me you did an outstanding job with your presentation," he teased her. "Nice job."

"Your spies?" Sheryl laughed. "Why doesn't that surprise me? But thank you. I do think it went well."

"Of course, it did. I had no doubt. You're a hell of a lady. It's been my pleasure to coach you and play a small part in your success today," he said seriously. "Even though it's not what Paul had in mind." Sheryl could hear the smile in his voice.

She pushed her bangs back. "Thank you, John. I've enjoyed working with you too. And you have helped me." She paused as a errant thought popped into her head. "You're not quitting as my coach, are you?"

John laughed out loud. "No, of course not, although with Paul gone, I have to talk Martin into paying me."

Paul had thankfully resigned from the board just before the elections in May. Martin was now officially the Alpha VC representative, along with another man that also seemed less zealous about cost-cutting than his predecessors.

"Oh, yeah, Martin."

"He's not a bad guy. Better than Paul," John reminded her.

"Oh, I know. He's a better Chairperson of the Board than Paul was, even though it is temporary. He's tough, but not unreasonable," Sheryl replied. "We get along okay. So far."

*Because I trust Martin*, Sheryl thought. *More than I trusted Paul or Hank.*

"You'll do fine with him. After all, you have a great coach," John teased, before his tone turned serious. "One more thing, I did hear that The Diamante is officially looking for a new president. Alpha VC refused to support Alex, even after all the good he's done."

"I know," Sheryl said. "Alex told me earlier. I honestly think he's relieved. He loves investments. He's happier as the Chief Investment Officer."

"That's good to hear," John said. "Well, I'll let you get back to your adoring public. I'll see you next week. Usual time."

"Thanks for the call, and all the support, John," Sheryl responded warmly. "Talk soon."

After the call ended, Sheryl looked around the now empty room and took a deep breath. She felt exhausted and exhilarated at the same time. But mostly, she felt satisfied. *I've taken some big leaps of faith in the last year*, she reminded herself, *and this is where they've brought me.* She thought about her conversations with John. *And I guess I've survived the hero's journey—this time.*

But somehow Sheryl didn't think it would be the last one. She mentally shook herself. *No, I don't need to think about that now.*

A familiar curly-haired head popped through one of the doors. Cindy.

"Hey lady, you ready to go? I know you've got to be hungry since you didn't eat breakfast."

"I am starving . . . and glad that's over," Sheryl grinned at her friend. "I can't believe you were here for my speech. I'm so happy about that."

"I'm glad too," Cindy returned her grin. "It's wonderful to be here for your moment of triumph. With all that you've been through in the last year, I'm so, so proud of you."

Sheryl's grin faded. "It had been a lot, hasn't it?" she replied seriously.

"Yes, it has. From the layoffs to your memorial meetings. Dave's ridiculousness with both your work and that *girl*." Cindy's pleasant face contorted with disgust for a moment. "I'm so relieved that's behind you, but, man, how well did you handle that? Even talking to her and bailing her out."

Sheryl laughed out loud. "I still can't believe I did that!"

"But look at what good it did," Cindy told her. "Amazing. And Alisha was even here today cheering you on. Plus, you had the board confrontations on top of that about Blake, and then the whole investigation with Rachel and that Hank guy. All the while trying to put your marriage back together. I'm getting exhausted just thinking about all of this."

"And I'm getting exhausted reliving it," Sheryl agreed, chuckling softly. "But it does put it in perspective."

"Not to mention the whole AI and more layoffs thing with the new guy from Alpha VC. Paul, right?" Cindy paused, looking proudly at Sheryl. "Yet, it all led you here, didn't it? If it wasn't for that press conference about the investigation where you totally rocked and the memorial meetings and your AI board presentation, you wouldn't be here being the amazing leader that you are." Cindy rushed over and gave Sheryl a hug. "I'm so proud to be your friend!"

Squeezing Cindy hard, Sheryl blinked back some threatening tears. "But I couldn't have done it without you, my friend, without your support. You've been there every step of the way, all the way back to college. You've given me some of the best ideas that I've used and just been a rock for me. I love you so much!"

Pulling back from the embrace, Sheryl saw tears filling Cindy's eyes, too. "Girl power," Cindy said hoarsely. "Or I guess I should say woman power."

"No, it's the power of having someone you *fully trust* on your side," Sheryl responded. "Male or female, there's nothing more powerful—or important—than that."

"Amen," her friend said. "Now, let's stop this mushiness and find some food."

Sheryl picked up her notes, purse, and laptop bag. "Yup! I'm ready. Let's go."

# About the Author

**Karen Ann Bulluck**
**DARING TO TRANSCEND**®

Karen Ann Bulluck is a powerful story-teller and risk-taker. A best-selling author, speaker, and founder of *DARING TO TRANSCEND*®, Karen elevates the stories of women leaders to inspire change in business culture as well as their personal lives. Through her books, newsletters, and speaking, she encourages women to take risks, embrace authenticity, and make an impact beyond the bottom line.

Karen was the first woman promoted to Executive Vice President at AM Best Company. Her career was marked by taking the risks to make many cross-disciplinary changes and have an impact on a wide variety of people and processes.

Karen is an engaging and inspiring speaker and the author of the **Ascending Ladders Series** of novels, ***Discovering Power, Pursuing Truth,*** and ***Embracing Trust***. She is also a contributing author to three international best-selling anthologies.

Karen can be reached at:
Email: karen@daringtotranscend.com
Website: www.daringtotranscend.com
LinkedIn: www.linkedin.com/in/karenannbulluck
Facebook: www.facebook.com/karenannbulluck
Instagram: https://www.instagram.com/karenannbulluck/

# Full Reviews

*"Rarely does a novel capture the high stakes of corporate life while keeping such a firm hand on the human heart.* **Embracing Trust** *is a visceral exploration of integrity—how easily it fractures and the immense courage required to rebuild it. I saw my own professional dilemmas reflected in these pages, finding the story equal parts cautionary tale and hopeful roadmap."*
**-Gary Fretwell**
#1 International Best-selling Author, Speaker, Consultant
https://garyfretwell.com

*"Trust. It's a funny thing. It's so important and yet so fragile at the same time."*

*"As a woman in leadership, this story by Karen Ann Bulluck, moved me deeply.* **Embracing Trust** *reveals the real-life tension leaders face when values, ambition, and integrity collide. The women in this book embody the strength, humanity, imperfections, and relatability of the women in my own circles and experiences. Their journey reminds us that trust is earned, sometimes broken, but always worth rebuilding. This is much more than a corporate novel. It is a rally cry and a call back to courage, self-trust, and heart-led leadership. I highly recommend it."*
**-Karen Gray**
President, Texas Business Women
Founder/CEO Gray Coaching
https://coachkarengray.com

*"This poignant business novel is deeply relatable, capturing the loss of trust in colleagues — and ourselves — that many face today. Its powerful women navigate difficult circumstances, offering a moving, courageous roadmap for any woman finding her own way."*
**-Brynn Ammon**
President, Credit Union Solutions, Jack Henry

*"Karen Ann Bulluck's **Embracing Trust** is a nuanced, courageous exploration of what trust truly demands of others and, most importantly, of ourselves. Through three compelling women, Karen masterfully weaves the complexity of trust across business, leadership, and private life, especially in high-stakes, male-dominated environments. This book is a quiet call to integrity, instinct, and humanity, reminding us to lead with conscience, resist premature judgment, and surround ourselves with those who genuinely root for our becoming."*
**-Dr. Brigitte Bojkowszky**
Brand Identity Strategist | Success Mindset Coach | Retreat Host |Podcast Host
BridgetBrands
https://bridgetbrands.com

*"A brilliant look at the human side of leadership roles. Sheryl's approach to management offers a revelatory exploration of trust with herself, and several others. The author is proving that humanity is the true engine of creativity and results. The character development is excellent and pulled me into the story from start to finish. This series is a must-read for aspiring leaders at any level."*
**-Suzanne Catlett**
Founder-CEO-Investor
LinkedIn: https://www.linkedin.com/in/suzanne-catlett-0948a583/

*"This third book in The Ascending Ladder Series, Embracing Trust is captivating reading from the first paragraph. The characters are vibrant. The stories and their experiences are totally relatable to real-life personal experiences. I loved how the author wove in the Hero's Journey, and showed so clearly how intricately peoples' lives are woven together through lifetimes. She asks in the story, 'Trust what?' Such a great question. No spoilers here, but in my opinion this is a brilliant piece of writing, and the reader comes away feeling hopeful and empowered."*

**-Sherry Lynn Campbell**
#1 International Bestselling novelist of *The Storyteller's Quilt: Beginnings Are Boundless*
WonderEddy.com

*"Oh, what an enjoyable read! It's honest, relatable, and speaks to the messiness of work and life in a way that feels very human. It's a reminder that trust-in ourselves and in others-still matters, especially as AI changes everything.*

*If you've been feeling worn down by the modern workplace or quietly questioning what feels 'off,' this book will make you feel seen and a little less alone. I hope it also encourages more of us to stand up for, and believe in, the power of people, and the courage it takes to truly embrace trust."*

**-Kendra C. Parker**
Director of Talent & Capability
www.withkendraparker.com
LinkedIn: Kendra C. Parker | LinkedIn

*"In business and life, we have relationships where we either respect and embrace with trust or fracture when trust is broken. The stories of how these three women each encounter different responses to their choices and how they deal with those reactions are situations many of us have experienced and many others will encounter. Valuable insight can be gained from the events shared in these pages.*

*This third book in the series has me wanting a fourth, as I'm curious to see what these women might embrace and accomplish next. Even if you missed the first two, you can enjoy these journeys of* **Embracing Trust.***"*
**-Susan K. Younger**
Relationship Architect – Engaging Humanity in the Workplace
https://skyounger.com/
LinkedIn: https://www.linkedin.com/in/susankyounger/